About the editors

Chant is Reader in Geography at the London School of Economics. Cathy McIlwaine is Lecturer in Geography at Queen Mary and Westfield College, University of London.

The Commonwealth strives towards creating a world where '... women and men have equal rights and opportunities in all stages of their lives to express their creativity in all fields of human endeavour, and in which women are respected and valued as equal and able partners in establishing the values of social justice, equity, democracy and respect for human rights.' *Commonwealth Plan of Action on Gender and Development, 1995*

THREE GENERATIONS, TWO GENDERS, ONE WORLD

Women and Men in a Changing Century

Compiled by

SYLVIA CHANT AND
CATHY McILWAINE

Commonwealth Secretariat

Zed Books Ltd
LONDON & NEW YORK

Three Generations, Two Genders, One World: Women and men in a changing century was first published by Zed Books Ltd, 7 Cynthia Street, London N1 9JF, UK and Room 400, 175 Fifth Avenue, New York, NY 10010, USA in 1998.

Distributed in the USA exclusively by St Martin's Press, Inc., 175 Fifth Avenue, New York, NY 10010, USA.

Cover designed by Andrew Corbett
Set in Monotype Garamond by Ewan Smith
Printed and bound in the United Kingdom
by Biddles Ltd, Guildford and King's Lynn

Library of Congress Cataloging-In-Publication Data

Chant, Sylvia H.
    Three generations, two genders, one world : women and men in a changing century / prepared by Sylvia Chant and Cathy McIlwaine.
          p. cm.
    Includes bibliographical references and index.
    ISBN 1-85649-603-1. —ISBN 1-85649-604-X
    1. Sex role—Commonwealth countries. 2. Generations—Commonwealth countries. 3. Social change—Commonwealth countries. I. McIlwaine, Cathy, 1965–   . II. Title.
HQ1075.5.C723C48 1998
305.3–dc21   98-19782
                                    CIP

A catalogue record for this book is available from the British Library

ISBN 1 85649 603 1 cased
ISBN 1 85649 604 x limp

CONTENTS

FOREWORD

The initial idea of *Three Generations, Two Genders, One World* originated in the Gender and Youth Affairs Division of the Commonwealth Secretariat in 1994. The aim was to develop a gender-sensitive social history project by compiling in-depth information on changing gender ideology and practice. Since that time much work has been carried out by many people across the Commonwealth to transform this concept into the present book.

One may well ask why bring out yet another book on gender issues. It is true that there is an ever-increasing plethora of literature on the subject, but much of it deals with the economic and legal aspects of gender equity. The very concept of gender remains fluid and open to change through a variety of demographic, political, social and cultural processes. These complex processes and their effect on the gender roles in society are still largely unexamined, especially at a comparative level.

This book seeks to shed some light on the differing concepts of gender and the ways in which the position of women and men has changed across generations. Using selected country case-studies of Commonwealth countries that span the range of the United Nations Development Programme's Human Development Index, each of the chapters provides a brief overview of the political economy of the country concerned and of its economic position relative to other countries. The theme of gender roles and relations is developed along three different lines: divisions of labour by gender; male–female disparities in household decision-making; and constructions of masculinity and femininity.

The initial study was set up as a project in oral history aimed at creating linkages across three generations of a household through informal interviews with representatives of each generation. These interviews provided generational as well as gendered perspectives on the experience of living through critical historical events, the evolving meaning of male and female, social interaction, and the changing notions of community and culture. Some of these oral histories are distinct national studies that have been published in their own right. This book attempts to synthesise, in somewhat broad strokes, the experience of the nine selected Commonwealth countries with regard to changing gender ideology across three generations and to develop a comparative picture of gender and generational change in these countries.

We owe a debt of gratitude to the many institutions and individuals who made this study possible. Thanks are due to the national academic institutions in both developed and developing countries of the Commonwealth who worked in partnership with us. Crucial to the success of the endeavour were the people responsible for collecting and compiling information for the original reports from the selected countries. It is not possible here to mention all the many individuals who took part, but some are particularly noteworthy: Michele Kefala (Cyprus), Dr Patricia Ellis (St Vincent and the Grenadines), Dr Christine Barrow (Barbados), Dr Nancy J. Pollock (New Zealand), Professor Fatima Daud (Malaysia), Greta Hofmann Nemiroff (Canada), Raghib Hasan Majed and Atif Hasan (Pakistan), Dr Julia Wells (Zimbabwe), Suzi Hewlett (Solomon Islands) and Augustine Meti (Commonwealth Youth Programme, South Pacific Centre).

Thanks are also due to the commendable work of Sylvia Chant from the London School of Economics and Political Science and Cathy McIlwaine from Queen Mary and Westfield College, who edited this volume and gave it its current shape. Last but not least, we would like to thank Nusrat Husain who co-ordinated this project in her capacity as senior project officer of the Commonwealth Youth Programme at the Commonwealth Secretariat.

We also acknowledge the many students, parents, grandparents, researchers and professors who are the principal agents and participants of this study. The lives of the people described in these narratives have sensitised and moved us deeply and we hope it will do the same for all the readers of this volume.

Eleni Stamiris, Director
Gender and Youth Affairs Division,
Commonwealth Secretariat

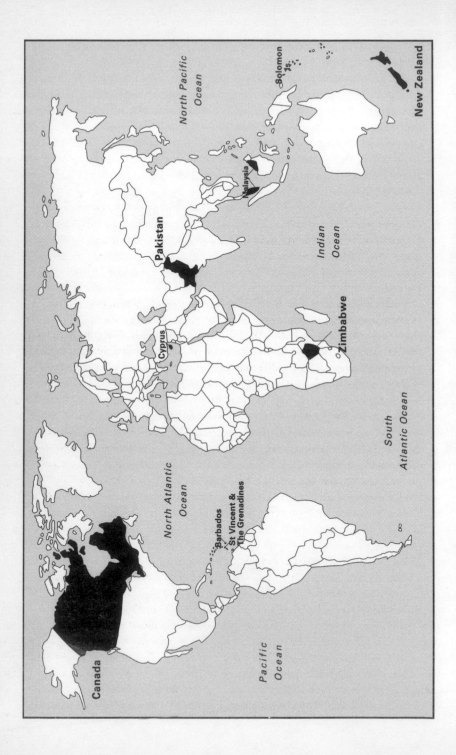

CHAPTER I

INTRODUCTION

The real wealth of a nation is its people – both women and men. And the purpose of development is to create an enabling environment for people to enjoy long, healthy and creative lives. This simple but powerful truth is too often forgotten in the pursuit of material and financial wealth (UNDP, 1995: 11).

Three Generations, Two Genders, One World is the culmination of a multi-country research project undertaken by the Commonwealth Secretariat which now forms the basis for this book. Although the constructs of 'gender' and 'generation' are vital elements of people's identities throughout the world, there are many differences in the meaning and interpretation of these terms across time and space. While age may be used as a proxy for membership of different generations, the timespan between one generation and another varies greatly among nations. Proceeding through different 'life course' stages (youth, adulthood, middle age, old age and so on) may be more accelerated in some places than in others, and involve different characteristics, meanings and implications.[1] Although studies of the life course are less numerous than those of gender, especially for developing societies, generation is a topic of growing concern within feminist research and is increasingly recognised as a variable and dynamic entity (see González de la Rocha, 1994; Katz and Monk, 1993; Kawar, 1997; Sen, 1994).

The variability of generation is partly a result of its intersection with gender. Three decades of dedicated research on the roles and relations of men and women in different parts of the world have led to a broad consensus that gender, too, is a fluid construct. Constituted by, embedded within, and impacting upon a multitude of economic, demographic, social and cultural processes, gender is inherently diverse and inherently amenable to change (see Parpart and Marchand, 1995: 14). Yet while the rejection of naturalising and transhistorical conceptualisations of gender is now accepted, we are still at a stage where our understanding of how these complex processes operate, and what they might imply for successive generations remains stubbornly elusive. This has been the case especially in the 1990s: alongside fast-changing realities of development, post-modernist scholarship and its emphasis on questions of difference, representation and identity have challenged many of the certainties formerly attached to feminist political economy thinking (González de la Rocha, 1997; Parpart, 1993). Whereas explanations for gender roles, relations and inequalities in the past were often grounded in a common (not to mention ethnocentric) set of starting points, in the late twentieth century, reductive approaches to cross-cultural complexities have all but entirely been abandoned. Despite the infinite variability of geographical settings in which gender (and generation) are constructed, however, people's inter-relations with these dynamic social formations evidently matter in everyday life. From whichever perspective one looks, there are often marked similarities in what it means to be male and female in different parts of the world.

For these latter reasons, exploring gender in a comparative geographical (and historical) context remains both illuminating and worthwhile. On one hand, notions of 'three generations' and 'two genders' may be too unwieldy to make sense of individuals' lives without recourse to several other cross-cutting criteria such as class, ethnicity and 'race' (McIlwaine, 1995). On the other hand, people occupy one world, which is fast becoming smaller through the globalising influences of changing patterns of production, exchange and resource use, through advances in information technology and communications (Massey, 1996), and through the influence exerted over policy by multilateral institutions. Awareness of difference as well as consonnance, and of how patterns of gender interweave with local constellations of economic, political, social and cultural processes, is important in illuminating the myriad ways in which gender roles and relations are constructed. It also offers scope to find ways in which movement towards greater equality between men and women might best be approached in their local environments, as well as on a world scale (Parpart, 1993).

With these considerations in mind, one of the most meaningful ways to interrogate gender is arguably to explore what men and women think and say about local constructions of masculinity and femininity and how these affect their daily lives, as well as their longer-term plans and aspirations. Aside from the intrinsic value of looking at the intersection of gender with generation, drawing on perspectives from different age groups can also tell us something about change over time, notwithstanding the fact that 'messages' about gender tend to alter as people move though their personal life trajectories (see Harris, 1995: Chapter 3).

The fieldwork for this volume is grounded in a people-centred methodology (see below). It aims to illuminate what gender means, and how it is perceived to be changing, in nine countries: St Vincent and the Grenadines, Barbados, Malaysia, the Solomon Islands, Pakistan, Cyprus, New Zealand, Canada and Zimbabwe (see map on p. viii). All these countries are member states of the Commonwealth, and the information draws primarily upon reports commissioned by the Commonwealth Youth Programme of the Commonwealth Secretariat in the early 1990s. The rationale behind the reports was to provide a basis for informing decision-makers about changes in gender roles, values, attitudes and relationships across three generations of young women and men in selected countries (see Commonwealth Secretariat, 1995b: 16). This represented one of various initiatives which, in the run-up to the Fourth Women's World Conference in Beijing in 1995, contributed to the Commonwealth's own *Plan of Action on Gender and Development*.[2] The reports, in turn, were derived from surveys (usually conducted out of university departments) in which young women (and often young men as well) interviewed their siblings, parents and grandparents on matters of crucial relevance to gender, such as gender roles and relations, socialisation, sexuality, courtship, marriage, family organisation, fertility, education and employment.

Before looking at the themes of the research and the organisation of the case-study chapters, it is important to dwell a little on the methodology used in the Commonwealth surveys studied.

Methodological considerations

The nature of the project surveys Although the methodology used to collect data from informants in each country varied, and fuller details are given in the respective chapters, as a general rule, the samples were relatively small (fewer than one hundred participants in most cases). In other words, they provide an indicative rather than a 'representative' or 'typical' series of commentaries. Beyond this, the scope of the information is compromised by the fact that, as opposed to being spread over a broad cross-section of people, most of the surveys (except in St Vincent) involved interviews with family members by university students. The students, in turn, constituted an upwardly mobile segment of the population, in comparison not only with their parents and grandparents, but with many of their peers as well. The basis of most of the surveys in single university departments also meant that the youngest generation of participants were geographically localised, even if the origins of many of their forebears lay elsewhere in their respective countries, not to mention overseas. In the Canadian survey, for example, which incorporated interviews by university students in different parts of the country, and from a range of ethnic groups, the parents and grandparents of some of the interviewers had been overseas immigrants.

Another factor affecting the comparability of information between countries was the varied ages of respondents in each generational cohort. Although most of the student interviewers (and their siblings, where relevant) were in their late teens or early twenties, most of the middle generation of informants were in their late thirties to early fifties, and in the eldest generation, sixty and over, in around half the countries (New Zealand, Canada, Cyprus, St Vincent and Barbados) a number of elderly respondents were in their nineties. Variations in age partly reflect differences in life expectancy between countries, age at marriage and/or birth of the first child, and so on. On one hand, this clearly has implications for the historical context in which groups from different places grew up, and means that we are not, strictly speaking, comparing like with like. On the other, however, we tend to view the stretching of the age spectrum as positive since it allowed us to gain insights on change over a substantial part of the twentieth century. Additionally, in cases such as Zimbabwe, where the eldest generation of women also recalled the lives of their mothers and grandmothers, this permitted us to derive glimpses of gender as far back as 1900 and beyond. Aside from the fact that the surveys constituted a fascinating exercise in oral history, it should be noted that in some of the countries, recovering the history of women through the voices of women themselves was something that had rarely, if ever, been attempted previously.

The ties of kinship made the methodology much more intimate and participatory than is common among most fieldwork-based studies of gender, with significant ramifications for those involved. In many cases the interviewing process gave young researchers an opportunity to learn much more about their family heritage than they would normally have done. Many of the young generation also felt that more detailed knowledge of their parents' and grandparents' pasts led to greater understanding and closeness, especially where contact between the generations had waned (a factor that seemed to be especially marked in Barbados, Canada and Cyprus). The value of these kinds of outcome was generally deemed to overshadow some of the problems attached to the kinship ties of interviewers and interviewees, one being that openness on topics such as sexuality and married life was often compromised by family intimacy. At the same time, the experience of having grown up with their informants gave the young a basis for observation and comment. It also provided them with a unique perspective on the veracity of their elders' accounts. For example, parents would sometimes paint a picture of their children's upbringing with which the latter did not concur. In our view, acknowledgement of such disparities enriches the research process and allows for recognition of the ways in which people create, build upon and/or feed into discourses that help them make sense of their lives and actions. It also draws attention to the ways in which interviews tend to uncover 'representations' rather than 'realities', notwithstanding the fact that the former have their own validity as a window on human experience.

These observations dovetail closely with those identified in wider debates on research methods and epistemology. Discussions of reflexivity in feminist circles, for example, have emphasised the importance as well as the difficulties of 'recovering women's knowledge and voices' (Parpart and Marchand, 1995: 18). Some of the stumbling-blocks commonly identified include the ways in which information is affected by the nature of interviews (where they take place, what is asked about, how questions are asked), relations between the researcher and the 'researched' (for example, relations of power, deference and so on), and the characteristics and standpoints of the interviewer (such as politics, research agendas, personal experiences). These impact upon what is revealed, what information is used in the research account, and how it is presented, the inevitable conclusion being that 'truths' are 'constructed' and cannot be read off dialogue as realities (see Maynard, 1994; Phoenix, 1994; Thompson, 1992). As Maynard and Purvis (1994: 6) have pinpointed: 'There is no such thing as "raw" or authentic experience which is unmediated by interpretation.' In the case of the present research, these latter observations are even more pertinent given that the bulk of the material passed through a number of hands before it emerged in this final form.

Editing the chapters Having had no direct involvement in the collection of the survey material or, for the most part, in its collation and preliminary analysis, the editors relied mainly upon reports prepared by project directors (mostly university lecturers and established freelance consultants), whose names and affiliations are given in the notes to each of the case study chapters).[3] Without their trawl of the raw information, the compilation would undoubtedly have been much more difficult.

To allow for greater comparative scope, there has been an attempt to 'standardise' the case study chapters. This was not always easy, since the reports themselves were uneven in various respects, mostly due to the differing nature of the original surveys. First, although in most cases male and female students or young people interviewed men and women in the older generations, in some countries – such as Zimbabwe and Canada – men's views were not solicited, and in others – such as Malaysia – the young respondents themselves replaced the views of older people with their own interpretations. Additionally, in Barbados, although female students conducted the interviews, their own opinions were not recorded in the final report. Second, although the Commonwealth Secretariat specified a broad outline of the themes to be discussed, some reports contained greater coverage of certain themes than others. In some cases this reflected the participatory manner in which the research at the grass-roots had evolved and what people wanted, and felt able, to talk about. In other cases, it conceivably indicated the importance attached to different aspects of gender in different places. Again, the use of complementary source material was valuable in guiding us towards a better idea of what had influenced the content of the final report, as well as allowing a broadly comprehensive coverage of themes in each chapter. The themes are discussed below.

The case study chapters: organisation, themes and comparative perspectives

As noted above, the focus on different themes varies in accordance with the original country report, but each chapter begins with an overview of the political economy of the nation concerned, and something of its colonial and contemporary development. Within these sections, we often refer to statistical indicators that provide some idea of how the country stands in relation to other countries in the world for selected criteria. These include measures such as per capita GNP, and various development indices devised by the United Nations Development Programme (UNDP).

One UNDP index we made frequent use of is the Human Development Index (HDI). The HDI was originally devised in 1990 as a means of assessing development achievements beyond economic growth and mean per capita GNP. With an emphasis on social and welfare dimensions of development, the calculation of the HDI is grounded in the premise that there are certain basic capabilities that people must possess in order to participate in and contribute to society (see UNDP, 1995: 18). At present the HDI comprises three major components: 1) life expectancy at birth; 2) educational attainment (weighted two-thirds towards adult literacy, and one-third to a combined primary, secondary and tertiary enrolment ratio); and 3) income, measured on the basis of the average global real GDP per capita in purchasing power parity (PPP) dollars.

The second UNDP index we made considerable use of is the Gender and Development Index (GDI). Making its first appearance in the UNDP's *Human Development Report* of 1995, the GDI is based on the same capabilities as the HDI but incorporates gender disparities in each measure. Where these are large (in relative terms), a penalty is imposed such that the GDI is effectively the HDI adjusted for gender inequality in the country concerned (UNDP, 1995: 73). A third index, the Gender Empowerment Measure (GEM) centres on political and economic aspects of gender, and comprises four main variables: the share of parliamentary seats occupied by women; the proportion of women in the administrative and managerial workforce, the female share of professional and technical jobs, and women's overall percentage of earned income (UNDP, 1995: 73).

While these indices are undoubtedly much more useful than standard per capita GNP figures in analysing a country's development profile, and are commendable for their sensitivity to gender, they are still relatively crude measures and cannot say much about the complex differences among societies. As such we desist from presenting them in any form of comparative overview and feel they are better contextualised (where relevant) within more detailed discussions of the development trajectories of individual countries.

The themes discussed in each chapter are introduced below, and we take this opportunity to highlight some of the similarities and disjunctures among countries that seemed salient to us in the process of writing, particularly in respect of changing patterns of gender over time. Having said this, we stress that it is extremely difficult to talk about the countries here in any profound or comprehensive manner. This is partly because 'change' occurs from different starting points in different contexts, and partly because evidence of change was so diverse among countries, whether in the minds of the survey respondents or in respect of wider, more objective, indicators. For example, it seemed to us that in the case of Pakistan, gender was marked more by continuity than change across three generations, whereas in other countries, such as Cyprus, Zimbabwe and the Solomon Islands, change appeared to have occurred only in a restricted number of spheres, such as marriage and education. Recognising the paramount importance of situating observations about 'change' within country-specific discussions, we also feel that our readers should be able to interpret the material in their own terms. Our comments in the following discussions should accordingly be regarded as subjective and tentative, and in no way as guiding pronouncements.

Gender roles and relations The theme of gender roles and relations is clearly extremely broad, so we chose under this heading to concentrate primarily on three elements that featured consistently in the country reports: 1) divisions of labour along lines of gender; 2) male–female disparities in power and household decision-making; and 3) constructions of femininity and masculinity.

One factor common to all countries was that gender divisions of labour, while showing change in a number of areas, tended to assign the bulk of unpaid, home-based reproductive activities (such as childcare and domestic labour) to women. Even if, in countries such as St Vincent and Barbados, women have long played a very important part in the economic life of households, breadwinning has usually been the normative priority of men. Yet although this seemingly ubiquitous gender division of labour seems to have been upheld during three generations of survey respondents, in virtually all countries in this century women's roles have been expanding. While motherhood and home-making remain primary, these responsibilities are now accompanied by increased participation in paid labour and/or income-generating activities. Given that in most cases (except New Zealand, Canada, St Vincent and Barbados) men's participation in domestic work and childcare does not seem to have risen substantially, it might be argued that women nowadays are shouldering a greater overall burden of labour within households than in previous decades. As Katz and Monk (1993: 275) have summarised in relation to their own multi-country volume on gender and life course, female-selective responsibility for reproductive labour has led to a situation in which there are 'extensive webs of care which absorb women's time'.

Women's expanded roles in economic activity were often identified by respondents as intersecting closely with increased urbanisation (especially in countries of the South such as Zimbabwe), and with the shift from agricultural production to an industrial and/or service economy (for example, Cyprus, Malaysia and New Zealand). While these trends may have added to women's labour loads, they also seem to be associated with rising female household decision-making. Of course, we cannot assume that increased involvement in decision-making is beneficial to women since this may refer only to certain types of decisions (perhaps mundane), and may simply represent an increment in their responsibilities without enhancing their access to resources (see Chant, 1997: Chapter 1; Chant and McIlwaine, 1995a: Chapters 3 and 7). However, in many of the case study countries it seems that women's rising access to employment and increased decision-making have contributed to 'empowering' women in a variety of ways, especially in enlarging their personal autonomy, and conferring greater power in their relations with men.

In most cases, women have welcomed these changes more than men, and in many countries (especially Canada, New Zealand and Zimbabwe) it seems as if young women are much less likely than their forebears to conform to traditional gender roles. Having said this, gender equality is not unilaterally welcomed, and resistance to the expansion of women's spheres of activity and influence often varies generationally, as well as between genders and among countries. Not all the surveys included men and women of all age groups, but in Barbados, for example, most resistance to shifts in women's roles was expressed by elderly men, whereas this applied most to young men in St Vincent and Malaysia.

Concepts of masculinity and femininity were also marked by competing claims and opinions. For example, among respondents in countries such as Pakistan, Malaysia, the Solomon Islands, St Vincent and Barbados, being male or female was seen to be a natural and relatively fixed attribute, dependent on physiology and/or divinely ordained. This was often associated with psychological and intellectual traits. For example, men's physical strength was often associated with an assumed superiority in respect of strength of character. People also recognised that inflexible concepts of 'male' and 'female' could imprison men and women, with regret being expressed in both St Vincent and Barbados that men were unable to show their feelings. However, in the bulk of countries it also seemed to be increasingly acknowledged that childhood socialisation and what people learn from their parents, teachers and religious figures plays a critically important role in shaping identities, and that gendered characteristics are thus amenable to change.

Socialisation and childhood   Accepting the notion of socialisation as 'the inculcation of gendered values into children from birth' (Humm, 1995: 270), this theme in the survey emphasised early life and growing up. In most contexts, children's attitudes and behaviour were strongly influenced not only by what their parents told them, but by the roles expected of them in different economic contexts. For example, in countries such as Barbados, Cyprus and New Zealand, where many of the eldest generation had grown up in rural areas, boys used to help in the fields and girls in the home. Important factors accounting for shifts in these patterns were the decline of family production and rural–urban drift, with evidence indicating that the participation of children in economic aspects of household life has declined. Although in many countries daughters are still expected to play more of a role in domestic responsibilities, in some countries, such as New Zealand, Barbados, St Vincent and the Solomon Islands, boys are increasingly encouraged to do housework. This is partly an imitative process, as their fathers have become more involved in childcare and domestic duties, and partly the result of a move on the part of women to encourage their sons to help them now, and/or to assist their partners in later life.

Yet even if gender divisions of labour among children might be blurring in some instances, it was widely identified that boys and girls continued to be treated differently by their parents. One of the main axes of differentiation was that boys, in many places, continue to be granted considerably more freedom than their sisters. In countries such as New

Zealand and St Vincent, restrictions are placed on daughters because of considerations about their safety, and in the latter, fears of unwanted pregnancy. In Pakistan, the crucial factors limiting young women's autonomy seemed to be guarding their morality and safeguarding the reputation of their families. In Malaysia, Barbados and the Solomon Islands, it was noted that girls are increasingly given the same freedom as their brothers, including equal access to schooling and higher education. One factor in this shift is the expansion and reform of education systems. Another is that women are much more likely to enter the labour force once their education is complete, as well as to view employment as an integral part of their adult life (see below).

Parenthood and parenting   Despite the above tendencies, motherhood remains a vital component of adult women's identities in most countries in the volume, and mothers were usually perceived by their offspring, throughout the generations, to have played a more prominent role in their lives than fathers. In some countries, such as St Vincent and Canada, this was sometimes due to father absence; in others, such as Pakistan and New Zealand, it often derived from the fact that men played little role in everyday aspects of parenting.

Maternal images in many countries centred on the altruism of mothers, who were often described as self-sacrificial and caring. Fathers were frequently deemed to be more concerned with the material well-being of their offspring, and to be the ultimate holders of authority in household units. In many respects this reflected the broad division of adult roles, and the privileges accruing to men in their normative position as providers. In countries such as Zimbabwe, however, where mothers tended to attach more importance than fathers to furthering their daughters' careers, women managed to exercise power and influence in effective, if covert, ways.

Recognising that in some countries – such as St Vincent, Malaysia, Pakistan and the Solomon Islands – parenting duties were also performed by relatives such as aunts, uncles and grandparents, the strictness of parents and guardians was noted to be diminishing over time. This is accompanied by waning discipline in schools, in particular the declining use of corporal punishment, and lower levels of religious observance (for example, Barbados and Cyprus). By the same token, in countries such as New Zealand parents felt their roles had narrowed over the generations with the devolution of various functions to schools, churches and welfare agencies. Beyond this, sanctions on the use of physical force against children in the home as well as at school had increased in New Zealand following legislation introduced to protect children's rights.

In the wake of a discernibly 'softer' approach to disciplining offspring, concern was expressed in some countries that parents nowadays were not doing their duties as they should. In Barbados, for example, the rise in female labour force participation was seen by older men as being respons- ible for a lower quality of parenting and inadequate control of children. In New Zealand, men's apparent increasing irresponsibility as fathers was attributed a major part in diminished levels of parental care. Inadequate parenting was seen not only to cause unruliness in children and adolescents, and problems of truancy, violence and drug use (for example, in St Vincent, Barbados, the Solomon Islands and New Zealand), but to lead to a situation in which children would themselves grow into inadequate parents.

Sex and sexuality Sex and sexuality constituted one of the most difficult subjects on the interviewers' agendas, yet was one of the most illuminating in respect of understanding barriers to changes in patterns of gender. In particular, discussions tended to indicate reluctance to embrace dimensions of masculinity and femininity that lay outside the norm of matrimonial heterosexuality. Homosexuality, for example, was rarely mentioned in the reports, but where it did feature, as in the accounts of Barbados, Zimbabwe and the Solomon Islands, it referred to male homosexuality and met with negative attitudes. Canada stood out as the only country in the survey in which lesbianism was discussed. This was regarded in a broadly positive vein because of its association with greater tolerance of social diversity.

Resistance to non-heterosexual/conjugal sexualities possibly stemmed partly from the fact that older people had much less access to information about sex than the young generation. Today, information is more widely available following the introduction of sex education in schools (such as in Barbados, St Vincent and the Solomon Islands), and, in Pakistan and Malaysia, because of increased exposure to Western films and media as well. The latter was by no means regarded as necessarily desirable, however, with respondents in countries such as St Vincent and the Solomon Islands being acutely aware of the way in which greater freedom of behaviour was associated with 'modern epidemics' such as HIV/AIDS.

Although heterosexual marriage remains in many countries the most acceptable context for sexual relations, in St Vincent, Cyprus, New Zealand and Canada premarital sex has attained gradual acceptance over time (albeit not among the eldest generation). Along with this, there has been less importance attached to the ideal of female virginity on marriage. Never- theless, double standards still prevail in many places: while men are given a fairly wide licence to have casual relationships, promiscuous behaviour among women continues to be regarded as a 'bad thing', if not the heinous deed it was formerly constructed as in Zimbabwe, Cyprus and Malaysia.

Courtship and marriage   A persistent feature of male–female relationships in many countries is that men tend to instigate relationships with women rather than the other way round. In certain contexts this might be seen as having placed greater pressure on men, in that in the past, contact with the opposite sex (generally with a view to marriage) was usually articulated via the use of go-betweens (for example, in St Vincent, Cyprus and the Solomon Islands). By the same token, the declining use of intermediaries (and chaperoning) has also led to greater autonomy among young men and women alike, who, in countries such as Malaysia, Zimbabwe, Cyprus and the Solomon Islands, were forced in previous generations into arranged marriages, often accompanied by dowry or bride-price arrangements. Even today, however, particularly in Pakistan, parents play a major part in choosing or vetting their offspring's marriage partners.

While people have always taken a range of elements into consideration in evaluating marriage partners, it seems that in many countries women are now less likely to assess their husbands on an economic basis as on their personal qualities. In Canada, most women were concerned that their men would be good companions. There has also perhaps been greater acceptance of the fact that people may have a number of partners prior to wedlock. In St Vincent and Cyprus, women may well have more than one boyfriend before marriage. In fact, in St Vincent, where marriage has usually been the end stage rather than the beginning of a long-term co-resident union, marriage rates are actually increasing rather than falling.

Although courtships in previous generations could be protracted, in all countries but the Solomon Islands, age at marriage has risen in the last 20 years (UNDP, 1995: Table A2.6). In many countries, including Cyprus, Zimbabwe and Pakistan, the gender gap in age at marriage has narrowed as women spend more time in education, and/or assert themselves for greater equality in their relationships. Beyond this, in Cyprus and Zimbabwe, marriage is no longer necessarily a goal in women's lives, and in countries such as Canada and New Zealand it is increasingly being eschewed in favour of cohabitation. Part of the reason is that in the wake of rising divorce rates, marriage is viewed as an inherently unstable institution.

The rising incidence of divorce in these latter two countries is interpreted as a product of influences such as increased life expectancy, the greater social and economic freedom and power of women, and in New Zealand specifically, the revival of ancestral Maori ideals. Moreover, whereas female divorcées were regarded as social outcasts in earlier times, as divorces become more prevalent the stigma is observed to be diminishing.

Fertility and family organisation   While mounting levels of divorce conceivably play an important role in contributing to declining fertility in some contexts, pronounced reductions in birth rates (which apply to all countries in the volume except Cyprus and the Solomon Islands) seem to be caused by a combination of factors such as reduced infant mortality, later age at marriage, increased access to family planning services, and mounting living costs. In addition, the rising demands on women's time as they have taken on greater shares of labour have probably made it difficult to cope with as many offspring as in the past. In most countries, however, motherhood remains a crucial marker of female identity.

Declining fertility in most countries has also been accompanied by falling numbers of extended family households. Recognising that concepts of 'household' and 'family' vary both between and within countries, the fragmentation of kin groups and the nuclearisation of household units seem to be fairly ubiquitous phenomena. This is attributed in many countries (for example, Barbados, Pakistan, Cyprus and New Zealand) not only to people's lack of time to invest in family relationships as their societies become more complex, pressurised and competitive, but also to labour migration, often overseas.

Another indicator of family/household change, and one especially marked in Canada and New Zealand, is the rising number of lone-parent households, predominantly headed by women. In other countries, such as Zimbabwe and Barbados, female-headed households constituted a substantial proportion of households in previous generations too, although routes into female household headship seem to be changing. In the past, female-headed households often arose through male labour migration, whereas critical factors now appear to be rising divorce rates and greater social and economic power among women to survive alone. Even where female-headed households do not seem to be growing substantially, there seems to be some evidence of a decline in male dominance within male-headed households, especially in Malaysia and Cyprus.

As 'traditional' household structures increasingly encompass a re-negotiation of intra-household gender dynamics and/or find themselves juxtaposed with alternative domestic arrangements, it is also important to note that alternatives such as lesbian households are on the increase in places such as Canada. Moreover, here and in New Zealand in particular, the waning importance of family ties means that friends and neighbours are assuming a more important role than in the past.

Education In all countries, general rates of educational attainment improved over the course of the twentieth century. While in most countries the young generation were all university students or graduates, many in the older generations had no education at all or had not gone beyond primary school, except in Canada and New Zealand. Positive trends have much to do with expanded state educational provision and legislation on compulsory education until a certain age or grade. In the past educational provision was mainly private, and there were only residual services for poorer people (especially in rural areas). In these contexts, the costs of materials such as pens and notebooks, coupled with the forfeit of young workers from family farms or enterprises, made educational expenditure prohibitive for many (for example, in St Vincent and Barbados). Moreover, in some countries, such as Cyprus, higher education was not available until the late 1980s, and in the Solomon Islands, it remains restricted to an Institute of Higher Education and to an extension of the University of the South Pacific (based in Fiji).

Despite variations, the above developments have contributed to narrowing the gender gap in educational attainment. Whereas in many countries such as Pakistan, Cyprus and Zimbabwe, elderly and middle-aged women had not been allowed to go to school, young women are now proceeding to secondary, further and higher education. In fact, in St Vincent and Barbados, women's educational attainment is now surpassing men's. Yet this is not to suggest that women in the past did not value education. Huge importance has been attached to education by women from all generations in all the case study countries for a range of reasons. In Zimbabwe and Pakistan, for example, these are related to empowerment and reduced dependence on men. Indeed, as educational provision has expanded, women from older generations in Canada and Zimbabwe have often gone to night school and/or taken university degrees as mature students. However, continued gender asymmetry is apparent in subject choice. The reports from St Vincent, Barbados, Malaysia and Cyprus show a continued tendency for men to dominate in science subjects, and for women to be more involved in the social sciences, arts and humanities, especially at higher levels.

Employment   For all countries in the volume, the twentieth century has seen an increasingly greater share of employment located in urban areas and an expansion in services and industry at the expense of agriculture. People have tended to move away from family-based enterprises such as peasant farms and into wage labour in cities, often entering professional jobs in the public and private sector.

Whether or not the rising presence of women in the labour force results primarily from changes in the structure of labour demand, or mainly from changes at the level of supply (rising education, declining fertility, changing family organisation and so on), there is little doubt that women are now more fully incorporated in the formal economic sector of most societies than in the past. Moreover, whereas in countries such as Barbados and Canada respondents noted that in earlier generations women tended to work out of economic necessity, with the exception of the Solomon Islands, employment is now seen as a central feature of women's identity. In most societies, however, women still tend to earn less than men and to be concentrated in a narrower range of occupations, even if there is evidence of some movement of women into traditionally 'male jobs', such as bus-driving (Barbados), and mining (Zimbabwe). Moreover, at a world scale, the United Nations Development Programme points out that in many ways the increase in female labour force participation is extremely modest when set against their educational achievements in recent decades: whereas there was a two-thirds increase in adult female literacy and school enrolment between 1970 and 1990, women's economic activity rates rose only slightly (from 36 per cent to 40 per cent) (UNDP, 1995: 4).

Although women may have increased their participation in the labour force, they also tend to have higher levels of unemployment than men. Bearing in mind that recorded levels would conceivably be higher still were it not for the fact that some women are registered in national censuses as housewives instead of economically active, male unemployment has also been rising in countries such as Zimbabwe, Pakistan, St Vincent and Barbados in recent years. In some cases, such as Zimbabwe, this is due to cost-cutting on the part of employers who find women cheaper; in others, such as Barbados, it is because educated men perceive themselves as over-qualified for the lower-skilled menial jobs. It is thus no surprise that overseas labour migration in many countries such as St Vincent and Pakistan, as well as Barbados, continues to be male- rather than female-selective.

Conclusion and implications for policy

It is clear that although progress towards gender equality has been made in a wide range of spheres and places, inequalities remain. It is important to ask ourselves where we, and the individual countries represented in the volume, might go from here. While this is something we address specifically in each case study analysis, it is important to consider in more general terms whether policy interventions are needed to speed up progress, or whether it might be more appropriate for individual societies to negotiate their own changes. Moreover, if policy interventions are desirable in any way, what are the potential roles for national and international involvement?

It is important to identify that gender-aware policies have already been instituted in a number of countries in the volume, whether billed as gender legislation or as part of wider programmes. Most countries in the text have introduced initiatives to protect women's constitutional equality with men, to enhance women's property rights, to promote women's representation in public sector employment, to assist women in matters of reproductive rights, and to give them protection from domestic violence. Moreover, in some countries such as Zimbabwe, New Zealand, St Vincent, Barbados, Canada and the Solomon Islands, there are specific 'women's affairs machineries' at ministerial or at sub-ministerial levels. While there does not seem to be any systematic connection between the implementation of gender-aware policies and gender-fair outcomes, there is little doubt that frameworks for gender equality are probably a 'good thing'. Indeed, even if policies can rarely initiate or direct change, they usually build upon pressure for change and reflect an attempt to renegotiate 'gender contracts' (see Duncan, 1995). The latter point reinforces the idea that policy needs both to build on aspirations and rhetoric and to be grounded in firm foundations (Parpart, 1993). For this reason, the end of each chapter comprises a statement on policy recommendations that were gleaned from people's observations and attitudes. Although there are few policy recommendations that might be 'standardised' across the countries, a number of problems for women came up with remarkable regularity, and tentative suggestions for how these might be alleviated are detailed below.

Common policy recommendations One of the most important findings for policy was that despite their increasingly multiple roles as partners, parents, domestic workers and waged workers, women tend to get little help from men in the home, whether with housework or childcare. One possible policy recommendation is therefore the need to stimulate increased cooperation between men and women in household life. Specific strategies could encompass instruction for men on shared parenting and sensitisation to the need for collaboration in housework. Encouragement of men's involvement in these spheres is vital since male unemployment may well go on increasing, denying them the opportunity of fulfilling 'traditional' masculine roles. Since shifts towards greater equality of responsibility in household and family life may take quite a long time to emerge, however, a positive short- to medium-term strategy might be to foster the development of subsidised childcare facilities so that mothers can accommodate their multiple roles with greater ease.

Another important area for policy lies in the sphere of education, with effort needed to diminish the degree of gender stereotyping in academic and vocational subjects. This would have knock-on effects in the labour market, another arena in which intervention is urgently needed. Here, critical imperatives might include greater affirmative action in public employment and the encouragement of private sector employers to adopt gender-neutral recruitment practices and to pay male and female employees equal wages. Bearing in mind the UNDP's pronouncement that: 'While doors to education and health opportunities have opened rapidly for women, the doors to economic and political opportunities are barely ajar' (UNDP, 1995: 4), greater political representation of women is also a matter requiring prompt attention. In nowhere but New Zealand (which was a pioneer in recognising female citizenship through voting rights in the late nineteenth century) do women hold more than one-fifth of seats in parliament, and in many countries (Pakistan, Cyprus, Solomon Islands), the female share of parliamentary seats is less than one-tenth of the total (UNDP, 1995: Table 3.5).

Another important potential intervention lies in trying to increase acceptance of multiple forms of sexuality and family organisation, possibly via consciousness-raising at both community and national levels, and the conferring of equal legal/civil status on 'alternative' households. This might be achieved through grassroots community development programmes or through national media initiatives, for example.

With the exception of this last issue, all the other recommendations are covered in one form or another by the Commonwealth's 1995 *Plan of Action on Gender and Development* (see Commonwealth Secretariat, 1995a: 18–20). In conjunction with the more effective gender management and monitoring advocated and supported by the Commonwealth Secretariat it is therefore possible that, by the end of plan's period in the year 2000, important changes may be under way.

The role of global initiatives Beyond this, the role of global initiatives in the above-mentioned interventions is arguably significant. Although the United Nations Decade for Women (1975–85) and subsequent UN conferences such as Beijing in 1995 (not to mention the parallel international NGO conference) may not have found as much common ground between women worldwide as anticipated, there is little doubt that these have raised global awareness of gender issues. They have also put pressure on governments to move beyond lukewarm espousal of gender concerns and at least show willingness to devise institutional measures to put moves towards gender equality into practice (for discussions see Brydon and Chant, 1993: Chapter 9; Jahan, 1995; Moghadam, 1995; Pietilä and Vickers, 1994; UNDP, 1995). More specifically, the UN Decade has been associated with the formation of 'national machineries' oriented to the 'integration of women' in development in around one hundred and forty countries, the spawning of regional-level initiatives such as the establishment of the Women's Desk of the Secretariat of the Commonwealth Caribbean Governments (CARICOM) in 1981, and the creation of women's bureaux/

units, representatives and programmes in a wide range of donor organisations. The latter, among others, include the United States Agency for International Development, the Canadian International Development Agency, the World Bank, the United Nations and the European Union, and numerous non-governmental organisations (NGOs) such as Oxfam, Christian Aid and Voluntary Service Overseas (see Jahan, 1995: 62–4; MacDonald, 1994; Moser, 1993; Pietilä and Vickers, 1994; Rathgeber, 1995; Rosario, 1995).

One of the most significant global initiatives to date – at least in principle – is the United Nations 'Convention of the Elimination of all forms of Discrimination Against Women' (CEDAW). This originated about halfway through the UN Decade for Women (in 1979), and is described by the UNDP (1995: 103) as a 'unique and path-breaking global charter of the human rights of women', upholding as it does the rights to equality in the 'private' domain of marriage, family and care of children, as well as in the 'public' domain of civil, political, social and economic rights (ibid.). CEDAW has now been ratified by 139 member states, leaving about ninety countries that have not yet done so – around half retain reservations, and around half have not signed at all. Two of these latter countries – Pakistan and the Solomon Islands – are represented in this volume. On the one hand, it is only with monitoring that CEDAW will become a truly effective tool for eliminating gender discrimination, besides which there is often a huge gap between formal rhetoric (and legislation) and popular practice (Moser, 1993: 144). On the other hand, a campaign to force unconditional ratification of CEDAW by non-signatory states is identified as part of the UNDP's current 'Five point strategy' for accelerating progress towards gender equality (UNDP, 1995: 8).

The five points of the UNDP's strategy are worth itemising here since in many respects they touch upon the more specific needs we identified from the findings of the individual country reports and which are found in the *Commonwealth Plan of Action on Gender and Development*. The CEDAW campaign falls under the first point of the UNDP strategy, which aims to guarantee legal equality of women and men within the next decade. The second point is to expand women's options in the workplace. The third is to ensure a minimum threshold of 30 per cent of women in national-level decision-making positions (for example, parliamentary or cabinet posts). The fourth point refers to the implementation of programmes aimed at improving women's education, reproductive health and access to credit. Relating to these aims, the fifth and final objective is to ensure that women have greater access to economic and political opportunities (UNDP, 1995: 8–10). These recommendations closely parallel those of the Vienna Declaration on Human Rights of 1993, which reaffirmed the principle of equality between men and women, and was adopted by 171 countries at the World Conference on Human Rights in June that year. Among the principles pertaining to gender were equal access to basic social services (including education and health), equal opportunities for participation in political and economic decision-making, equal pay for equal work, equal protection under the law, the elimination of gender discrimination and violence against women, and equal rights of all citizens in public and private areas of life (ibid.: 1).

Beyond acknowledging the difficulties of wedding principles to practice, however, it is important to recognise that many of the above recommendations fall into areas in which it is difficult to detail agreements even at a rhetorical level. For example, the Beijing experience showed that obtaining global consensus on certain matters is considerably harder than others, notably 'reproductive rights', sexual orientation, marriage, the family and employment (Moghadam, 1995; UNDP, 1995: 104). Aside from the importance of adopting a flexible stance towards diverse national perspectives, sensitivity to intra-national diversity is also paramount. This involves recognition of difference on grounds of culture, class, ethnicity, migrant status and so on, which are central to new initiatives in the sphere of gender-aware policy, and in strategies to diminish the many different types of subordination to which women everywhere in the world continue to be exposed (Chant, 1995: 115).

In view of the range of difficulties identified, it seems that the 'best way forward' is for the struggle for gender equality to be channelled at various levels, at various paces, and through a variety of institutions ranging from local women's groups, up through governments, through NGOs at local, regional and international scales, to multilateral institutions. On balance, perhaps, the really critical factor is getting both women and men involved in the 'gender agenda', when to date one of the major stumbling-blocks to equality has been that 'gender concerns' are still narrowly equated with 'women's concerns' (Levy, 1992: 135–6; see also IDS, 1995; Kabeer, 1994; MacDonald, 1994; Moser, 1993).[4]

Notes

1. We prefer to use the term 'life course' rather than 'life cycle' for the reasons specified by Janice Monk and Cindi Katz (1993) in the introduction to their edited book on geographies of women. Whereas the term 'life cycle' is imbued with implications of 'multiple turns' and links life experience with a 'relatively fixed or inevitable series of biological stages and ages', 'life course' is more open to the multiplicity of paths that individuals and households may take through life in the context of changing historical conditions (ibid.: 19; see also Tacoli, 1996). We also use the term 'stages' in a flexible way that does not presuppose an inevitability that all people in all places will pass through determined life events, at the same pace.

2. The Commonwealth Secretariat's *Plan of Action on Gender and Development* of 1995 aims to foster gender awareness and responsiveness in all aspects of the Secretariat's undertakings in member countries across the world. The main focus of the plan is 'gender integration'. This is viewed as consisting primarily of strengthening national women's machineries, building institutional capacity and mainstreaming gender analysis into all national and sectoral policies. Through these strategies, it is hoped to achieve equality and equity of outcomes for women. For full details see Commonwealth Secretariat (1995a).

3. We give only the names of the project directors in the notes, but it is important to recognise that some worked in teams and/or in extremely close conjunction with their student interviewers (for example, basing their reports on extended student essays). Student names are omitted partly because we do not have these for all the countries, and partly for reasons of confidentiality. For the same motive of confidentiality, the names of informants used in most chapters are pseudonyms.

4. This approach can be broadly aligned with the GAD (Gender and Development) approach, which is the basis of the *Commonwealth Plan of Action on Gender and Development* and is increasingly being adopted by other major agencies and NGOs. Unlike the WID (Women in Development) approach, which tends to view women in isolation, and to regard women's development as 'a logistical problem, rather than something requiring a fundamental reassessment of gender relations and ideology' (Parpart and Marchand, 1995: 13), GAD stresses the importance of considering the socially constructed nature of gender relations (Moser, 1993: 3). Accordingly it recognises that planning for change in women's situations entails transformations for men, and *ipso facto* means that the relationships between women and men need to problematised and renegotiated.

CHAPTER 2

ST VINCENT AND THE GRENADINES[1]

This chapter focuses on a community located in St Vincent, the main island of the Caribbean country of St Vincent and the Grenadines. In many ways the study of St Vincent acts as an interesting comparison with Barbados, where the research was conducted with university students in an urban setting (see Chapter 3). In contrast, the St Vincent study was carried out in the small, close-knit rural community of Rose Hall, whose population depends almost entirely on agriculture. Given the divergence between the two studies in terms of context, many of the themes to emerge from both countries were surprisingly similar, reflecting the continuities between Caribbean nations particularly in terms of gender roles and relations.

Within the broad themes identified in Chapter 1, the study from St Vincent highlights the contradictions inherent in changes in the economy, culture and ideology over time. Within a context of improved socioeconomic conditions in the community, coupled with a perceived erosion of various cultural traditions and social mores, there was both resistance to and enthusiasm for change. This is particularly apparent in the changes in gender roles and relations over time. While the Rose Hall community was broadly characterised by relatively fluid relations between the sexes, there was also evidence of adherence to traditional gender stereotypes, which, in turn, were differentiated by generation.

Country profile

Located in the Eastern Caribbean, St Vincent and the Grenadines is a multi-island nation comprising the main island of St Vincent itself and the smaller Grenadine islands of Bequai, Carriacou, Union Island, Mustique, Myreau, Tobago Cays and Petit St Vincent. According to the 1991 census, the population stood at 107,598, of which more than half was under 25 years old, and 48.8 per cent female. Ethnically dominant are people of African descent and mixed European and African origins, with a small proportion of Amerindians, Asians and Middle Easterns. The nation became a British colony in the late eighteenth century, remaining under colonial tutelage until independence in 1979 (Gearing, 1995: 189). Indeed, Queen Elizabeth II remains the head of state, represented by a governor, although the prime minister, Sir James Mitchell, runs the country via a two-party system based on the Westminster model (EIU, 1996a: 47).

The most impoverished country in the Eastern Caribbean, St Vincent and the Grenadines had a GNP per capita of US$2,040 in 1992, although there was a steady growth from 0.2 per cent between 1960 and 1980 to 5 per cent between 1980 and 1992 (UNDP, 1995: Tables 2 and 20). Moreover, social indicators reflect relatively high levels: for example, life expectancy at birth is high (at 71 years), and there is an adult literacy rate of 98 per cent (ibid.: Table 1). This is borne out by the fact that St Vincent is ranked 79th out of 174 in the HDI (ibid.: Table 1). A prosperous sugar colony in the nineteenth century, the country has continued to depend on agriculture, with banana cultivation dominating the economy for the last 80 years. While banana production is still the most important agricultural activity and foreign exchange earner (exporting primarily to Europe), the introduction of European Union regulations and tariffs on imports and recent wranglings with the USA and the World Trade Organization have meant a decline in income from banana exports by 40 per cent since 1990. Although the plantation system has been the most prevalent type of landholding, independent farming is also important, with significant numbers of the population engaged in subsistence agriculture and in the production of food crops for both export and domestic use.

Turning to gender issues, and particularly the formal status of women in St Vincent, important policy interventions have been made in recent years. During the 1980s a fairly wide range of legal reforms were implemented, coordinated through a government Women's Desk (established in 1984), which became the Department of Women's Affairs in 1987. These include the Domestic Violence and Matrimonial Act Proceedings Act of 1984, the Minimum Wage Act, the Equal Pay and National Insurance Act, and the Domicile Act of 1989. The latter was particularly important and was prompted by the fact that prior to 1980 women in common-law relationships had no automatic legal claim to property acquired in the union, and unmarried female public sector workers had no right to maternity leave and were often dismissed if they became pregnant. This is particularly poignant given that female-headed households represent 42.4 per cent in St Vincent (ibid.: Table A2.5). The Domicile Act overturned this, giving women legal rights regardless of marital or employment status. These legal reforms were complemented by a range of programmes and projects implemented through the government and NGOs, of which Rose Hall itself was the subject in 1981 (see below).

Despite this legislation, gender inequalities remain in many aspects of social and economic life. In terms of political participation, women hold only two seats in parliament (13 per cent of the total) and only 11 per cent of ministerial posts (ibid.: Table A2.4). Economically, women have always played an important role in agriculture as labourers as well as a minority of agronomists and technicians. While some women are employed in the banana industry, mainly in packaging plants, a high proportion are involved in the small-scale farming of vegetables and fruit for domestic production and export. Indeed, 87 per cent of traders in agricultural produce between Barbados and Trinidad are women. Despite their importance, however, women still earn less than men, with agricultural labourers being paid a daily wage of EC$7.4 (US$2.7) and men EC$10.4 (US$3.85). A similar pattern obtains in other sectors where women are employed: in public and civil service (often as nurses and teachers), in manufacturing, and in the informal sector, where twice as many women work as men. Overall, women tend to be paid less and to predominate in low-status jobs requiring few formally acquired skills.

Community profile of Rose Hall

Rose Hall is a small village located 27 miles north-west of Kingstown, the capital of St Vincent and the Grenadines. Situated on the North Leeward side of the island of St Vincent, 1,200 feet above sea level in the foothills of Soufrière, an active volcano, Rose Hall was established in the late nineteenth century after a hurricane devastated the neighbouring villages of Jack Hill and Louie. In the aftermath, plantation agriculture was abandoned and replaced by smallholdings and cash cropping centred around the newly created village of Rose Hall. By 1991, the village had a population of 968, comprising 236 households, although this represented a decline between 1981 and 1991 of around a hundred people, mainly accounted for by death and overseas migration (to other Caribbean islands, the United Kingdom, North America and the Middle East). The main economic activity in the village and its environs is the production of food crops for subsistence, domestic sale and export to other islands. In fact, Rose Hall is the main producer of carrots in St Vincent and the Grenadines. In addition to agriculture, there are also several public sector workers, artisans and some self-employed people. Unemployment, however, is a problem, especially among the young. The economic infrastructure of the community has improved quite considerably since the 1980s, with the majority of residents now having access to electricity, piped water, telephones and a reliable transportation network linking the village with Kingstown. Social infrastructure facilities are also well developed, with a health clinic, police station, Protestant churches (Methodist, Pentecostal and New Testament), government primary school, nursery school, and a community centre. Housing provision has also improved substantially in the last 15 years, with the main type of shelter shifting from small wooden buildings to large, concrete structures.

The schools and community centre are the result of a pilot project on the role of women in rural development designed by the Women and Development Unit (WAND) of the University of the West Indies in 1981. Indeed, it was this project that led to the choice of the community as the study location for the current research. The project used participatory methodology (see below) and the entire community was involved, with women in particular playing a major leadership role. Besides the schools and community centre, one of the most important outcomes of the project was the establishment of the Rose Hall Community Working Group, which continues to develop and coordinate community projects including an adult education programme, training workshops, and economic livelihood projects such as a bakery.

Methodology

Based on an interpretative approach that explored the meanings of social realities from the personal experiences and perspectives of the informants themselves, the methodology employed in Rose Hall followed those of the other case studies in the text in involving in-depth, semi-structured interviews conducted with women and men from three generations. The Rose Hall Community Working Group was crucial to the research, with members helping to choose families to be interviewed. The conduct of the project was further eased by the fact that the coordinator had developed the pilot project of the WAND Women and Rural Development Project between 1980 and 1983, and the principal researcher had also worked on the project and was a native of the community.

The initial aim was to select a sample of 60 informants from ten families (three men and three women from each) representing different family types (nuclear, extended, and so on). However, given the small size of the community, overlapping families and a preponderance of young people, the final sample was based on 54 people, including grandmothers/fathers, mothers/fathers, and sons/daughters, as well as some cousins and daughters-in-law when certain family members were unavailable for interview. Information was collected through two main methods: first a baseline information schedule used to collect background information on each informant; and second, in-depth, open-ended interviews using a semi-structured interview schedule comprising questions on a range of topics. The initial intention to conduct focus group discussions to share preliminary findings was dropped when the majority of the informants declined to participate for fear of revealing personal and sensitive issues.

Profile of informants Of the 54 informants, 28 women and 26 men were interviewed, ranging from teenagers to a man of 90. The majority were aged under 35 (44 per cent), with 30 per cent between 36 and 45, a further 6 per cent between 46 and 64, and the remainder (20 per cent) over 65. As for the marital status of the group, a high proportion were legally married (17) or living in consensual unions (7). Among the rest, the majority were single (19), with seven widow/ers and four maintaining visiting unions.[2] The most prevalent household type was the nuclear structure, representing around 42 per cent (24), although extended families were almost as common (39 per cent or 21). Around 20 per cent of households were female-headed, with three living as single parents. Although the largest household comprised eleven members, most had four to five. The predominance of relatively small nuclear households contrasts with popular perceptions of large extended and/or single-parent families in rural areas of the Caribbean, as well as the notion that consensual unions are the norm (see, for example, Young, 1990 on St Vincent; see also below).[3] Only four of the informants had received no formal education, with more than half attaining primary level (28), and 19 completing secondary school. Of the latter, nine had obtained GCE 'O' levels and a further three had higher education qualifications (there were two trained teachers and one with a degree). Over one-third of the interviewees had full-time jobs (19), with a further three people working part-time in farming, six unemployed and six who had retired. Those working full-time were employed in a range of occupations including four teachers, four masons, a plumber, a librarian, a secretary and a pre-school worker. Around 20 per cent had worked abroad, with a further 14 having travelled outside the island for holidays, study or medical reasons.

Before moving on to discuss gender roles and relations in Rose Hall, it is worth highlighting the main changes that have occurred in the last few decades in the eyes of the informants, and particularly those of the older generation. These changes must, however, be seen in the light of the close-knit nature of the village, which has been dominated for years by certain families, and where a complex network of kinship ties exists resulting largely from intermarriage and child fostering. Bearing this in mind, the informants were unanimous in recognising that changes had occurred, both for better and for worse. The most positive changes were reported as lying in the improved material conditions in the community, especially in housing, infrastructure, incomes and diet. Education was singled out as the most important element in change; as one young man in his twenties pointed out: 'Without education, there would not be much upward mobility.' In contrast, the older generation lamented the deterioration in social and cultural aspects of community life. For example, older interviewees repeatedly said how they deplored the decline in moral values, the lack of respect for others (especially among the youth), and the rise of individualism and self-centredness. Compounding this was the disappearance of cultural traditions such as cricket, and dancing the quadrille (a typical dance in the Caribbean akin to a square dance). Perhaps most serious, however, was the perceived increase in violence related to political electioneering and drug use. Despite this, the community still maintains some form of cohesion and spirit. As one young man, Simon, pointed out: 'If someone from another community comes in and does something wrong, everybody is upset.'

Gender roles and relations

While the nature of gender roles and relations in Rose Hall reflects quite a high degree of adherence to traditional stereotypes (for example, the ideal of the male breadwinner and female housewife, and an association of aggressive, non-demonstrative behaviour with men and passive, subservient behaviour with women), it is also characterised by some blurring of the boundaries. Broadly speaking, this was delineated by generation, with the elderly expressing the most conservative attitudes, and the young being most likely to challenge traditional patterns. However, it was young men who were most resistant to change, and keenest to impose limits on female behaviour. One young man, Fred, stated: 'I would prefer to see girls playing with girls and not soccer.' At the same time, these ideas were by no means restricted to young men. A middle-aged man, George, thought that: 'Sometimes you can't tell the difference between men and women, sometimes you see a man and don't know that it's a man; the world is becoming confusing.'

Part of the reason for this 'confusion' lies in the fact that the majority of informants perceived the nature of differences between men and women to lie in biological factors and/or to be divinely ordained. Men and women were seen to behave differently and perform different roles because they were born with particular characteristics such as size and strength. As one middle-aged woman, Lucinda, noted: 'Men have more willpower, women are weaker, it has to do with strength.' Indeed, these views were held across the generations and among both sexes. One female teenager, Vicky, said: 'Strong aggressive women are tomboys.' A few people, particularly women of the middle and younger generations, did recognise that behavioural, emotional and psychological differences were the result of social conditioning. As Joyce, a middle-aged woman, put it: 'Boys tend to be more active than girls, it is the way they were brought up.' Moreover, younger women were most willing to recognise that everyone should possess qualities such as strength and tenderness regardless of their sex. In particular, it was thought that women should display strength of character as a defence against the vicissitudes of life. As expressed by one young woman: 'Women who are powerful get away from problems more than the type who are soft and cry a lot.' At the same time, this group thought that men should be allowed to express their vulnerability and that 'Men are human beings too, so when something hurts them they should cry too.' Indeed, this view was shared by men of all generations, who felt that to sanction and/or ridicule men for displaying emotion denies them their humanity. As one elderly man, Alfred, put it: 'When men cry and show their feelings I think it makes them feel free inside.'

In general, therefore, while gender stereotyping was much in evidence in Rose Hall, there was also quite a high degree of tolerance of those who challenged conventional behaviour. However, while all groups were willing to concede that men should be allowed freedom to express themselves emotionally, there was greater reluctance among men to accept women who did not conform with traditional stereotypes. Indeed, many men were concerned that women should retain their femininity. As one teenager, Ben, pointed out: 'I like strong women, but there is a limit, some women go over the limit and try to be men, dress the same way and so on.'

Socialisation and childhood Many of the views expressed above are related to the childhood experiences of the informants and how they perceive their own parental roles. Just as attitudes towards gender roles are contradictory and dependent on gender and generation, so too are beliefs about how children should be brought up. Older parents in Rose Hall have raised their children along 'traditional' gender lines, and although some younger parents are attempting to bring up their children differently, many are using their own upbringing as a model. In general, then, boys are encouraged to go to the mountain, tend to the yard and look after the animals, while girls are expected to do the housework. As one young man, Roy, noted: 'Girls should be raised to do things that are more woman-like, boys should be raised to be like their fathers.' While this was the dominant viewpoint, several informants from the younger generation stressed the

importance of teaching boys and girls the same tasks, especially encouraging boys to do housework. The main rationale for this was that
men could help their partners later in life, as well as fend for themselves.
In the words of one young man, Victor: 'It is important to teach boys the
same things as girls, so that when they get into a relationship they will be
able to help their partners.'

Childhood experiences in Rose Hall not only inform the nature of the
tasks boys and girls are expected to do, but also illustrate different attitudes
towards bringing up children of different sexes. In particular, women of
all ages said that their brothers, and boys in general, were given more
freedom, and that while both boys and girls were expected to be home by
a certain hour, rules were enforced more strictly for girls. The main reasons
cited for this were parents' concern for their safety, and attempts to prevent
them from getting into trouble, especially becoming pregnant at a young
age and/or falling into 'bad company'. As a young woman, Cherry, pointed
out: 'Parents are more concerned about their girl children, that's why they
send them to church, the boys can go to dance or do whatever they like.'
Part of this attitude was also based on the belief that it is difficult to
control male children, particularly when their peers put pressure on them.
Mary, a middle-aged mother, complained that:

> Girls can be accounted for but if you ask for the boys no-one knows where to
> find them ... If you try to keep them at home, it is difficult because they see
> their peers on the street and they want to be there as well.

Parental roles, parenthood and kin relationships   The informants talked
freely about their relationships with their parents and their own experiences
of parenthood. One particularly strong theme to emerge from the discussions was the centrality of mothers in people's lives. This was true
across all generations and among both women and men. Indeed, one
elderly man called Howard, in his nineties, remembered his deceased
mother as someone who was 'very strict but kind and caring, she taught
us right from wrong, instilled obedience and told us stories at the end of
the day'. Women felt the same bond with their mothers, and many also
picked up on the story-telling theme, as Flora, a middle-aged woman,
recounted: 'Mother was poor, she didn't stand for nonsense. She flogged
a lot, but she told us stories, now when my children want to hear stories
they go to her.' Mothers were commonly perceived as 'self-sacrificing',
managing to provide their children with emotional security and to instil
some basic values in the face of material hardship.[4] The mother–child
link stands in stark contrast to the frequent absence of fathers in the
childhoods of many informants from all generations. Not only were fathers

either absent or unknown, but in some cases where fathers were resident, they were perceived as indifferent and irresponsible. One elderly man in his seventies, George, commented: 'My father never gave me anything, my mother was nice and after she died I knocked about.' Nancy, a middle-aged woman, declared: 'My father never had time, he left most things to her [mother].'[5] Indeed, only in four cases did interviewees remember being raised by both parents equally.

While parenthood in Rose Hall most usually refers to the biological parents, it was not uncommon for people to be brought up by other relatives, or even family friends. Indeed, this pattern has contributed to the close network of kinship and friendship ties within the community, where childcare is frequently shared between families. This may be related to the prestige accorded to motherhood within St Vincent (and elsewhere in the Caribbean – see Besson, 1993; Ellis, 1986; Powell, 1984),[6] where childless women will 'borrow' children to raise, for status as well as financial reasons. However, while it was primarily women who took on the role of adoptive parent with 'borrowed' children, in a number of cases men too became surrogate fathers, particularly with stepchildren. As Edith, a middle-aged mother, pointed out: 'Any woman can be a mother, it doesn't have to be your child for you to be a mother. Once you have love you can be a mother, the same for the father.' Indeed, the bonds that developed between adoptive parents and children were often just as strong as with biological parents. Lewis, a young man in his twenties, recounted his feelings for his adoptive mother: 'The lady I live with is not related to me, but she is my mother, if anything goes wrong with me she is the one who takes care of me.' Patricia, who was middle-aged and in her second union, told how her partner cares for her children from her first union: 'He fusses over them, he acts just as though they are his.'

While most of the informants aspired to being parents, there was wide recognition that parenthood should not be entered into lightly. These views were most strongly expressed by women, perhaps because the major responsibility for raising children would fall on their shoulders. Genevieve, who was in her twenties, was particularly circumspect: 'Not everyone should be a parent. Parenting should be for people who care about children and want to take care of them.' Among those who were already mothers, there was a general feeling of regret at having too many children and not securing enough economic support beforehand. Muriel, who was in her forties and had five children, pointed out that: 'It is no sense having children you can't support; if I had my life to live again, I might have only had two children.'

Sex and sexuality Attitudes towards sex and sexuality in Rose Hall were conflicting and contradictory. While there was an increasing tendency to deal with these issues more openly, many fundamental beliefs on the rights and wrongs of sex had not changed over three generations. The greatest reluctance to talk about sexuality was evident in men over 35 years of age, and in both sexes over 50 years old.[7] Among this latter group, the main reason was ignorance about sex in their youth; they were brought up to believe that sex was taboo and to be secretive about it. Few from this generation had been told about sex before becoming parents, and any information they managed to obtain was from casual conversations or occasional experimentation. Eva, a woman in her fifties, recounted her former ignorance of these issues: 'Those days we were ignorant as nobody told us anything. Those days you could have told us that babies came in an aeroplane and we would have believed it.'

Although middle-aged women and the young were much less inhibited in talking about sexual relations, some still complained of not having been prepared for this kind of intimacy, and as a result, many described their first sexual encounter as a negative experience. For women in particular, fear of unwanted pregnancy, embarrassment or mistrust of men influenced their decision-making over intercourse and coloured their memories of their early sexual contacts. In the most extreme case, Margaret, who was in her forties, described how she was raped the first time she had sex: 'It wasn't good, I was forced to do it, I didn't want to. I was scared but he said that if I didn't he would stop speaking to me and wouldn't want to see me again, so to keep the relationship going I agreed.' While men were generally unwilling to refer to their first experiences, one young man, Eric, admitted that his first encounter was unpleasant: 'I felt guilty as if I had done something bad; I felt really bad and was embarrassed.'

Despite this, the consensus among interviewees was that attitudes had changed, with information on sex and sexuality more readily available for the younger generation than in their parents' or grandparents' day. The reasons given were sex education in schools and family planning programmes. However, although knowledge about sex had increased among the young, many informants commented that this had led to an increase in casual sexual encounters. Reactions to this varied according to generation, with the elderly complaining that sex had lost its primary purpose of procreation, and the young becoming increasingly concerned about early pregnancy and sexually transmitted diseases (STDs). Carla, who was in her teens, pointed out that: 'There are an increasing number of STDs, an increasing number of persons having sex and not paying attention to the consequences.' Concerns about casual sex, however, were strongly influenced by religious beliefs rather than generation *per se*, with those who attended church condemning casual sex as a sin.[8] Also interesting was the perception that premarital sex was sinful, especially among women and even among those living in visiting and consensual unions. At the same time, people realised that abstaining from sexual relations before marriage was an ideal that was difficult, if not impossible, to attain. Netty, who was in her thirties and a believer, said: 'I don't think that people should have sex before marriage, especially girls, but I don't think that people bother any more about whether a girl is a virgin.'

Marriage, family and fertility

Courtship Some aspects of courtship patterns in Rose Hall appear to have changed over the last three generations, although many of the fundamental tenets remain. Although one person, Harold, thought that girls these days were 'bold', it is still customary for men to pursue women until they give in. Among women, most still felt that they had to be coquettish in order to 'win their man'. Joy, a middle-aged woman living with her common-law husband, remembered: 'He asked me certain questions. I pretended not to be interested, but I was; he kept coming around until I accepted him, we hope to get married some time.' However, the formality of courtship has changed in two respects: first, in terms of a man using someone to intercede with a woman whom he likes on his behalf; and second, men or their intermediaries approaching a woman's parents to request permission for the continuation of the relationship or marriage. A number of the older and middle-aged informants reminisced about these customs. Howard, in his seventies, remembered: 'Someone talked to the lady for me. I had seen her and liked her,' and Jessie, in her fifties, recounted: 'We met and when we became friends I told him we can't always meet on the street, so he came to my mother and we started a relationship.' In contrast, younger informants noted a much more informal process of courtship bereft of these traditions.[9] In terms of how men and women interact at the courtship stage, men placed emphasis on physical attraction, while women were more interested in personal qualities such as understanding, companionship and commitment.

Partnerships and marital status While the profile of the informants would indicate that formal marriage was the norm in Rose Hall, this belies a more complex and dynamic system of marital relationships reflecting patterns found elsewhere in the Caribbean (see Ellis, 1986; Young, 1990). Indeed, the most common pattern among interviewees was where partnerships passed through three stages after initial courtship, from non-residential visiting unions, to common-law relationships, and finally to formal marriage. While these stages were often experienced with the same partner, it was not uncommon to have two to three serious relationships before marriage, and to have a number of children, possibly by different fathers. The main reason cited for this pattern was the belief that it takes money to get married – people had to be content with informal unions until they could afford a wedding, which was often only as they reached middle age. Formal marriage was still the ideal for all informants of all ages and was consistently aspired to (see also Ellis, 1986 and Powell, 1984 on the Caribbean in general). This contrast between ideal and reality created very contradictory sentiments, both among those currently living in visiting and consensual unions and among people who had done so in the past. In particular, those who lived in common-law unions often felt guilty and stigmatised, rooted in the Christian belief that they were 'living in sin'. The example of Gerald, in his forties and currently living with his partner and mother of his children, illustrates the contradictions inherent in these beliefs. He stated quite boldly that: 'The person you are living with might not be the one you marry because you don't want to live in sin all the days of your life.' He then went on to describe his relationship with his partner as stable and fulfilling, doing what he is supposed to do 'to keep things together, like being at home', sharing decisions with his partner, and trying to ensure that his children 'are better than me and are able to live comfortably later on'. While it was noted that more people were getting married nowadays because of improved financial status in the community, many also complained that there were still many young people involved in visiting and consensual unions. As Mary, a middle-aged married woman, pointed out: 'Young people are not getting married at an early age, they are living together. I think they should get married.' These ideas were expressed despite the fact that the vast majority of elderly and middle-aged people in the community had themselves experienced these types of partnerships. Overall, however, the prevalence of formal marriage in Rose Hall was seen to be increasing over time.

Family formation Among the informants of both sexes and all ages, there were diverging views of what constituted both a family and a household. Some considered a family to be the residential unit only – Evelyn, in her twenties, commented: 'It is a group of people living together in the same house even if they are not related by blood.' Others referred to family as the wider network of relatives, and even other members of the community. Henry, for example, who was in his seventies, said: 'Even if children are married and have their own house they are part of the family,' while Martin, a teenager, stated that 'Everybody in the community is my family.' Overall, however, the concept of family was seen to be fluid, and while it was primarily delineated by blood ties, it also depended on how people treated one another. In many cases, interviewees identified unrelated people as family because they had assisted them financially and otherwise. This was particularly true in instances where children had been fostered or 'borrowed'. All informants agreed that the family was important not only for procreation, but for care, companionship, support, and as an investment for old age (see below). Jessie, a middle-aged woman in her fifties, was adamant that: 'You need to have someone around you – an extended family looks after you.' Most informants gave the impression that intra-household relations among family members were good, with a relatively high degree of harmony. However, it was women of the younger generation who complained most about problems with families. Melissa, for example, in her twenties, complained that many of the problems in her family derived from its large size: 'My family is so large there is always quarrelling, but I love my family even though sometimes they get on my nerves.'

Fertility and childbearing   Related both to the issue of parenthood and to family formation is childbearing, which the informants discussed at length. Older and middle-aged respondents stressed the importance of children to provide security in old age – as Leticia, in her fifties, pointed out: 'If you don't have children, things might be difficult for you later.' Younger people, both male and female, on the other hand, emphasised the burden associated with having children. This was seen to be both financial and emotional. Edna, in her twenties, commented: 'Motherhood/ fatherhood should be for those who care about children and want to take care of them. Not every woman or man can take care of children and take on the responsibility.' Whether male or female, young or old, there was a general feeling that children were important; they all wanted children or believed they would have them. However, one theme that emerged from discussions among existing parents (of all generations) was that they had not been ready, had not planned the event, and that pregnancy and childbirth 'just happened'. As a result, the immediate reality of parenthood had often been accompanied by sadness, shock and disappointment. These sentiments were especially common among women. Jennifer, a mother in her early forties, described how she felt when she discovered her first pregnancy:

> When I found out I was in a state. I got pregnant when training to be a nurse so I had to leave. The father had gone away ... I don't know how I am still in my right mind.

These reactions stemmed primarily from fear of the pain of childbirth, their parents' anger, being deserted by the child's father and the hardships of bringing up a child alone. These fears seemed to be justified, as illustrated in such comments as: 'My mother was angry with me and gave me a rough time,' 'The father hid from me when he found out I was pregnant,' and 'Some people told my mother to put me out.' The physical effects of pregnancy were also difficult for many women; as Lilian, in her twenties, remembered: 'I was so sick that it led me to think that I must not walk down that road again, it was hard.' While the majority of the younger women had received advice on pre- and post-natal care and had given birth in hospital, women from the middle and older generations had received little information from medical personnel, or from parents or relatives, and birth was invariably at home with a midwife.

Men's experiences of parenthood differed substantially from women's. In contrast to women's negative reactions on discovering they were pregnant, men of all ages responded more positively to becoming fathers. This was related to their sense of manhood – as Harold, an elderly man, noted: 'When I found out I was going to be a father I was happy to become a full man.' Negative feelings were in some cases related to doubts about the paternity of the child and the impending responsibility. Indeed, this often led them to desert their partners/girlfriends. Overall, few men played a major role during women's pregnancy or lived up to their respons-ibilities. Indeed, this was a bone of contention among women of all ages, who turned to mothers, grandmothers and other relatives for emotional and financial support. Elizabeth, now in her sixties, recounted how her sister helped her through her pregnancy at a time when 'I didn't even have a nightgown'. However, discussions with younger men revealed that some were increasingly recognising their responsibilities, and being aware of the importance of such things as nutrition and emotional support. As Arnie, in his late twenties, stated: 'I made sure that she had the right foods and was well taken care of. At first it was a financial burden but I adjusted.'

Decision-making and domestic labour   When considering patterns of decision-making and the division of labour within the home, it emerged that the household was a female domain, as noted elsewhere in the Caribbean (see Anderson, 1986; Powell, 1984), and that women wield a high degree of power at this level. Only a couple of informants believed that men should be heads of the household, with the majority believing that headship should be shared. These notions were expressed by both men and women. As Ronald, in his forties, admitted: 'People say the man is the head, but that doesn't mean he is the boss.' Most considered there to be joint decision-making within households, especially in dealing with disagreements and resolving conflicts. However, there was almost unanimous agreement that women managed the finances and decided how the family income was spent, with only five men saying they were in charge of the family budget. Indeed, men willingly accepted women's authority in this sphere on the grounds that they 'do a better job'. Edward, in his late fifties, pointed out that: 'Before I did a lot of bad things with my money, drinking and so on, but now I give it to my wife to keep.'

Despite women's apparent control at the household level, they also recognised their domestic responsibilities as extremely burdensome. Indeed, most viewed housework as harder than work outside the home. As Elvie, who was in her sixties and had worked in the fields all her life, said: 'Housework is hard work, every day you do the same things, you get no rest … in the field it is easier, if you go to weed, if you go to plant, you do one thing at a time.' Moreover, most women said they received little help from men in their daily tasks in the home. Some changes were apparent in men's views of housework, with one young man telling of his change in attitude: 'I used to think of housework as girls' work, but now I see it as boys' work as well.' Nevertheless, old ideas die hard, as illustrated by the words of another man of the same generation who was adamant that: 'Housework is not a job, it is easy.' The burden of domestic labour for women, however, must also be viewed in the context that every woman interviewed had worked outside the home at some time in her life (see below).

Education and work

So far the discussion has centred primarily on gender roles and relations at the household level. However, gender ideologies also pervade men and women's behaviour beyond the home, and can be examined through looking at educational attainment and paid employment.

Education There have been dramatic improvements in levels of educational attainment in Rose Hall over the past few decades. This is related to changes in the educational system in St Vincent as a whole, particularly since the 1970s (see McKenzie, 1986), and is reflected in the fact that the only four people with no formal schooling were over 60 years of age. Men and women have benefited equally from increased educational opportunities, although those under 35 years of age had the most formal education and had obtained higher qualifications than those from the middle and older generations (see page 25 for attainment levels among informants). Overall, education was highly valued in Rose Hall and seen as a prerequisite for securing a job and 'getting on in life'.

The experiences of schooling among the older generation contrasted strongly with those who had attended school more recently. The elderly respondents (those over 60) recounted how they usually entered school at the age of nine or ten, attended erratically and remained for only four or five years. Several factors were responsible for this, with poverty being the most crucial. Not only did lack of financial resources mean that parents had little money to buy books, clothes and lunches, but children were also required to work full-time on the farm by the age of 15 in order to contribute to family income. Moreover, there was no primary school in Rose Hall 40 years ago, with the result that children had to walk long distances to neighbouring villages. The experiences of the elderly at school were couched largely in a negative light. Strict discipline and corporal punishment were the order of the day, with some expressing the view that there had been 'too much beating', that 'children were afraid of teachers', and that today's system is much more conducive to learning in that 'teachers and pupils can now have fun together'. Moreover, there was a broad consensus that the subjects they learned (reading, English, arithmetic and general knowledge) rarely equipped them for securing employment, although many felt that they had learned some basic values. As one woman, Elsie, said, the only lesson she learned at school was: 'If you want people to respect you, you must first respect yourself.'[10] Another negative factor was that teachers allegedly paid more attention to children who dressed better and came from wealthier families, while the poor were left to struggle, regardless of their academic ability. As Jimmy remembered: 'I was a "dunce", so even when I gave the correct answer the teacher would keep on asking until a "bright" child answered.'

The elderly agreed that standards of education had improved substantially, and that as a result young people have many more opportunities than previously. As Winnie, in her sixties, pointed out: 'If I had the opportunities that some of these children have now, life would have been better for me.' The oldest generation identified that whereas in former years only a few residents were policemen, nurses and teachers, now there were a large number of qualified and professional people in the community, including teachers, agronomists and doctors. While the young generation agreed, they also made the point that competition was fierce and that possession of six or seven 'O' levels was no guarantee of obtaining employment. In addition, they felt that although technical and vocational courses were now offered, more emphasis needed to be put on teaching skills that would generate employment.

In terms of gender stereotyping in education, all the informants mentioned the importance of girls and boys having equal access to schooling. However, some of the younger generation noted that while everyone takes the same subjects until Form 3, the choices made in Form 4 (for 'O'

levels) reflect a high degree of gender bias, with most boys choosing subjects thought to be 'male', such as sciences, and girls choosing 'female'
subjects such as the arts. While a few students did venture into non-
traditional areas, they were often ridiculed, with boys, for example, being
called 'sissies' for taking domestic science-related subjects. Representing a
minority viewpoint, however, one teenager, Edwin, who was studying food
and nutrition, declared: 'I feel great getting to do things girls usually do.
To me it seems like you are exchanging.' Despite this, the norm among all
generations was for streaming girls and boys into gender-typed subjects,
albeit that children made these choices themselves (see also McKenzie,
1986 on St Vincent). This was reflected in the occupations they later
moved into.

Work and economic livelihood While agriculture remains the backbone
of the economy, economic opportunities have become more diversified
over time. As the community has developed there has been increased
demand for labour in non-agricultural activities, especially health and
education, and in artisanal occupations. Moreover, given the improvements
in educational attainment, there is a pool of qualified people to take
advantage of these new openings. However, unemployment remains a
problem in the village, with people complaining of the lack of jobs for
young people, as well as reduced returns from agriculture. Despite these
changes, work patterns have remained remarkably similar over time. In
particular, women in the community have always worked outside the home,
with only four women never having worked at some point in their lives
(see also Massiah, 1986 on the Caribbean in general).[11]

Hardly surprisingly, the elderly stressed the importance of agriculture
in their lives. Many remembered starting work as farm labourers as young
as 12 or 13, earning as little as 12 cents a day. Although men and women
worked alongside one another, tasks were divided, with men doing the
digging, and women the planting and weeding. While some non-agricultural
jobs were available for this generation, low levels of educational achievement meant that few avenues were open to them beyond construction
jobs for men, and domestic service for women. As Emily, in her forties,
stated: 'I did not pass school leaving, so I knew I wouldn't get a good
job.' Many of the elderly stressed the economic hardships they endured,
recalling how they had often had to do without, practically stealing to
feed their children, and how they had to depend on landowners for whom
they worked for food, as well as on alms from family and friends. Most
agreed that they only survived by 'the Grace of God'.

Although the situation has improved, those from the middle generation
in particular complained that farming was no longer as lucrative. While

everyone in the community was involved in the production of food crops and/or animal husbandry of some kind, this was now often seen as a way of generating supplementary income. In the light of the diversification of economic activities and the generally low incomes derived from farming, more than half the informants had held more than one type of job over their lifetimes. Among women, these non-agricultural occupations ranged from domestic service and childminding among the middle and older generations and those with few educational qualifications, to teaching, nursing and secretarial work among the younger generation, and those with more education. Among men, the most common non-agricultural jobs across all generations were in the construction sector and they worked as masons, plumbers and electricians, while of the younger men who had pursued education a few worked as teachers and one as a librarian. This reflects a high degree of gender segregation, with men and women choosing to work in jobs traditionally thought of as 'male' or 'female' domains, the latter in particular representing an extension of women's caring and nurturing roles. Furthermore, it was generally agreed that women earned less than men, and faced considerable pressures in merging their reproductive and productive roles (see page 39).

Also important in the work histories of the residents was labour migration: to other Caribbean countries, England, North America and even Saudi Arabia. Prompted by economic hardship, international migration has always been widespread in the community among both men and women, with the former working mainly as sailors, construction workers and farm labourers, and the latter as domestic servants and childminders (see also Young, 1990). However, views were divided as to whether women or men migrated more. Some felt that women had more reason to leave, as Virginia, in her forties, thought: 'Women think differently, they are the ones who look after the children and have the bills to pay.' Others felt that men had more opportunities. In any case, most migrants returned to St Vincent, and although most gained financially from their sojourns abroad, many had been dissatisfied with their wages and working conditions. Charles, who was in his seventies, had worked in England in a factory and complained: 'The job was too hard, for three years I worked nights, from eight to eight.'

For those who could not afford to migrate, or were not able to secure employment in the community, unemployment was their fate. While six of the informants were unemployed (of whom five were men), several had experienced periods of unemployment during their working lives. Furthermore, unemployment was considered a serious problem as it was thought to be linked with the increase in violence and drug use. As Betty, in her forties, declared: 'There are many young people snorting [cocaine] because they cannot get work.' While some thought nothing could be done about this, others believed the government should be responsible for providing jobs. Indeed, many made suggestions as to how to deal with unemployment, with one woman in her seventies declaring: 'We need more factories to give people work,' and another in her thirties arguing: 'The government should set up a skills training centre in Rose Hall.'

Female employment and domestic responsibilities Not only was female employment coloured by women's domestic roles in terms of their seg-regation into jobs that were extensions of nurturing and caring, but the practical realities of working were constrained by family responsibilities. A significant number, young and old, commented on how their ability to continue working was affected by family responsibilities. These constraints were imposed regardless of their position in the family; the fact that they were women automatically conferred domestic responsibilities upon them. Molly, who was in her seventies, had been training to be a seamstress when she was in her teens, but 'had to stop after a time because my mother took sick and I was the only girl'. Betty, in her twenties, left her job as a receptionist to 'stay home and take care of my grandparents'. After they died she returned to work as a pre-school helper, and even though she received a low salary she saw it as an alternative to 'staying at home and doing nothing'. Interestingly, Betty perceived her work at home and in the pre-school centre as similar and as having equal value: 'Taking care of children and my grandparents is the same, both are important work.'

The pressure imposed on women in trying to balance work and domestic responsibilities was recognised by both sexes, although it was younger men rather than the elderly or middle-aged who voiced their sympathy. Ernie, who was in his twenties, declared: 'When the woman returns home she is tired and this causes a strain.' Hannah, a middle-aged mother who also worked on the family farm, illustrated the difficulties she faced: 'It is difficult, especially with a lot of children who need you around. I go to the farm on three days. When I come home at night I try to get as much work done as I possibly can.'

Despite these difficulties, it was generally agreed among men and women of all ages that it was good for women to work outside the home. However, this was largely for financial reasons and to supplement male wages, as Joy, in her forties, pointed out: 'Some have children and the husband is not getting enough money so the mother could go out and bring in some money to help with the children, especially with education, clothing and food and paying bills, I think it is right.' Henry, also in his forties, noted: 'I know that if some mothers don't work, their families would not survive'. However, a few women from the younger generation recognised that employment was important for women's independence, as Jenny, in her thirties, said: 'I feel women should be independent, I don't believe in them staying at home to do the washing, cooking, and cleaning while the husband goes off, they should both work.' This was at odds with the views of some men, who felt that, although it was good for women to work, they did not want their own partner to do so. Indeed, these sentiments were expressed by men from all age groups. Kenny, in his twenties, stated: 'It is good for women to work, but if I had a wife I wouldn't want her to work … I like it the old way, let the wife stay at home and take care of the children and the house.' These views were based on men's fears that their role as breadwinner would be usurped, that they would have to depend on women, and that women's ability to perform household chores would be affected.

On balance, while it seems that women are beginning to embrace the notion that paid work is fulfilling, many men are still of the opinion that women should work to assist in generating family income, and that their primary responsibility is the home. Indeed, this association of women with familial roles strongly influences people's expectations of women in the world of work, reinforcing the notion that women are only capable of doing jobs that are effectively extensions of their domestic roles.

Conclusion

Twentieth-century transformation in Rose Hall, St Vincent has had a mixed response among the local population. Many of the changes in material well-being are welcomed by all regardless of age or sex. While these are partly related to developments in physical infrastructure provision, they are also influenced by increased educational attainment and some diversification of economic opportunities. Although quick to highlight the benefits of socio-economic change, the elderly in particular bemoan the adverse impacts on the community in terms of the loss of cultural traditions. Marriage might be on the increase, but young and old alike are concerned with the rise in drug use and violence, both associated with high levels of unemployment.

In tandem with these changes is the transformation of attitudes and beliefs, which are seen to have changed much more slowly. While this relates to a deterioration of moral standards in the eyes of the elderly, the ways in which men and women perceive and construct their womanhood and manhood, as well as the general nature of gender roles and relations, are also seen to have altered. The words of Hetty, in her middle age, perhaps best describe these changes:

Men abused women ... sometimes they drink, smoke weed and have a good time with friends. He gives the woman no money but when he comes home he wants supper on the table. Sometimes there is no money to buy supper so he start to beat his wife. There is less abuse now. Before when women got beaten they ran into the street and everybody in the village would know. Now ... they stay at home and confront their husbands and talk it out. They [the men] don't want everybody on the street to laugh in their face and say that they are abusing their wife, they don't want their children to tell their friend daddy has beaten mummy.

This illustrates not only how women are increasingly confronting and negotiating the injustices of their lives, but suggests how some men are responding to peer and community pressure to change their behaviour. However, while there was evidence of a diminution of gender inequalities across the divides of the community, some were more open to change than others. Indeed, it was among some of the middle-aged and the majority of younger women where the most serious efforts to force change were being made. As Lucy, in her twenties, pointed out: 'Women were tired of being pushed around and with doing only one kind of work, mostly housework, so they got together and talked about it.' While these women recognised that changes in wider Vincentian society with respect to the status of women had an important impact on their desire to push for greater equality, increased educational attainment and improved economic opportunities were also influential.

Although this paints a largely positive picture, resistance was encountered among other groups. Older men and women tended to conform with gender stereotypes and tacitly performed the roles assigned to them by society. The same could not be said, however, of many younger men under 35 years, who were the most trenchant in their unwillingness to embrace shifts in gender roles and relations. This may be related to their feelings of powerlessness in the face of increasing unemployment, compounded by a realisation that many women in the community are striving ahead of them educationally and in the jobs they are able to secure. With their traditional role as breadwinner becoming more elusive, they perhaps felt resentful of women's attempts to challenge existing power structures in other spheres such as the family.[12] Ironically, however, when men were given the opportunity to shoulder responsibilities, many refused, particularly with respect to children. Indeed, women across all generations repeatedly recounted experiences of men who refused to accept responsibility for their actions. The situation in Rose Hall is thus one of manifold contradictions. Inroads towards gender equality have been made, and there are many examples of men and women living together in relative harmony. On the other hand, there are many tales of injustices against women, illustrating that change has been, and will continue to be, gradual. More-over, the mismatch between young women's attempts to challenge gender inequalities and young men's resistance to change may be a major source of conflict in times to come.

Recommendations

On the basis of interviews with informants and interviewers in the field, a number of recommendations for policy can be made:

• Vocational training programmes to teach the young, and especially young men, a range of transferable skills to increase their chances of securing employment.

• Recreational facilities aimed at unemployed people to discourage drug use and violence in the community.

• A broad-based adult education programme to meet the needs of all community members with a focus on vocational and technical training.

• A comprehensive family life education programme to expose young men and women to topics such as sex and sexuality, family planning, safe sex, and pregnancy.

• A parent education programme to help women and men, especially those under 35, acquire knowledge and skills of parenting with an emphasis on sharing responsibilities.

• A community-based gender training programme to raise awareness about gender roles and relationships, particularly with respect to gender stereotyping, discrimination, and domestic violence. Attempts should be made to allay the fears of young men in particular as a way of trying to combat their resistance to increasing gender equality.

Notes

1. Compiled from a report prepared by Pat Ellis Associates, Inc., St. Philip, Barbados.

2. Visting unions refer to semi-permanent relationships where the man does not live in the same household but visits several times a week. Such unions often involve the birth of children and some financial support from the man (Ellis, 1986; Pulsipher, 1993a). Visiting relationships are common throughout the Caribbean, and St Vincent is no exception (see Rubenstein, 1991; Young, 1990).

3. In a study of a rural settlement, Windward Valley, in St Vincent, Young (1990: 154) found that 46 per cent of households were female-headed. Moreover, Pulsipher (1993a: 114) points out that 70 per cent of children born in the Eastern Caribbean are born to non-married parents. Momsen (1993: 243) notes that families in St Vincent are smaller than those in other Eastern Caribbean countries and less likely to be extended (only 18 per cent).

4. Powell (1984: 122) describes a similar parental style for the Caribbean as a whole, which she characterises as 'a sacrificial giving of self to the service of children'.

5. These patterns echo those found elsewhere in the Caribbean. Shorey-Bryan (1986: 70) points out for the region as a whole that 'men often play a limited role in family life and child-rearing and in that sense they are "marginal" to their families'. The reason identified for this is related to economic marginality and the fact that 'men feel alienated from their families precisely because they feel a subconscious guilt in not being able to live up to their own, and society's, ideal of being the provider' (ibid.).

6. Referring to the Caribbean as a whole, Powell (1984: 110) points out that, 'whereas men are more favourably set to derive their power and authority, prestige and status from direct links to the economy, women derive theirs from the family, mainly through their children'.

7. This contrasts with Gearing's (1995: 191) findings in the capital, Kingstown, St Vincent, where she noted that sexuality was frequently and openly discussed in daily gossip or 'comess' and that sexual activity was seen as good and pleasurable.

8. It should also be noted that more women attended church than men and that attendance increased with age. Indeed, even women of the younger generation often felt they had to choose between boyfriends and church.

9. By contrast, Gearing (1995) noted that in Kingstown, St Vincent, such formalities still prevail, at least among the middle classes.

10. This echoes the point by McKenzie (1986) that education in St Vincent, Barbados and Antigua is oriented towards personal development rather than vocational relevance.

11. As Massiah (1986: 177) points out: ' ... women in the Caribbean have always worked. They have done so in their homes, in the several sectors of the economy of their territories and in every stratum of society.' This stretches back to the days of slavery when female slaves were required to work alongside men in the plantations, and later, in the face of economic hardship, when men were rarely able to secure employment, women often took on the role of breadwinner.

12. Another viewpoint of relevance in St Vincent is that of Pat Ellis (1986: 8), who notes that young men in the Caribbean are not taught survival strategies in the same way as women, and as a result are heavily dependent on their mothers, other female relatives and later on their partners. At the same time, they have been socialised in the ideology of male dominance and resent this dependence. This may cause considerable conflict among men and women in adult life.

CHAPTER 3

BARBADOS[1]

This analysis is based on interviews conducted by female sociology students from the University of the West Indies with their brothers, parents and grandparents. While the interviewers represent an upwardly mobile segment of Barbadian society, many of their older kin came from humbler origins. As such, impressions of changing gender roles and relations on the island should be viewed within a context in which successive generations have received greater education and attained higher socio-economic status than their predecessors.

As in St Vincent, gender roles and relations are marked by overlapping tendencies: continuities and changes interweave with divisions and convergence, and, as in most of the countries in this volume, perceptions and reactions among respondents range from resistance, through tolerance and/or acceptance, to enthusiastic support. Narrowing gaps between men and women in Barbados are evident in a wide range of domains including the home, education and the labour market, and are reflected in rising female visibility and status. In contrast to St Vincent, however, where reluctance to embrace these changes was most in evidence among young men, in Barbados, older males (fathers and grandfathers) expressed greater disquiet about 'female emancipation'. Indeed, given the very rich testimonial material contained within the report on Barbados, the 'raw' views of informants are given as much space as possible.[2]

Country profile

Barbados is a small but densely settled island state in the south-east Caribbean, with a population of around 300,000, and a GNP per capita of US$6,210 in 1992 (UNDP, 1995: Tables 2 and 16). Although, like St Vincent, Barbados is heavily dependent on agriculture (sugar and rum being its main exports), the fact that its per capita GNP is three times higher is largely a result of the foreign exchange generated by international tourism. Although international tourism is widely adjudged to be a 'fickle' industry (see Jud, 1974: 34; McKee, 1988; Potter, 1983), and Barbados is facing increasingly stiff competition from neighbouring islands, visitor arrivals exceeded 900,000 during 1995, and represented a 4.8 per cent increase on 1994 (EIU, 1996b: 46).

The ethnically mixed population of Barbados reflects its roots as a British colonial plantation economy, and comprises groups of European and African descent, along with more recently settled minorities from India, Syria and the Lebanon.[3] Although whites are clearly only a tiny minority on the island, formal societal institutions such as law, state and religion continue to bear the stamp of three centuries of British rule, and imperial influences on Barbados' architectural and urban forms have earned it the title of 'Little England' or 'Bimshire'.[4] Reflecting the majority black population, however, Afro-Caribbean culture dominates at family and community levels, and citizens of Indian descent have also tended to retain their own beliefs and forms of social organisation.

European settlement in Barbados dates back to 1627, marking the initiation of its conversion into a monocultural cash-crop economy in which sugar and slavery served the interests of British imperial expansion. Although full emancipation of slaves came in 1838, it was not until 1966 that Barbados secured political independence. Even now that politics are in the hands of the black population, descendants of the British planter class have retained their control over strategic sectors of the economy, and social stratification is much in evidence. This is not to diminish, however, the major achievements of raised living standards and widening access to education and social services. Indeed, adult literacy in Barbados in 1993 was 99 per cent (on a par with most industrialised nations), life expectancy for women is 77 years and men 72 years (1990 data), and its composite HDI stood in 1992 at 0.900. The latter placed it twenty-fifth out of the 174 countries included in the UNDP's ranking for human development, and, significantly, positioned it above 'Northern' nations such as Luxembourg, Portugal and Malta (see UNDP, 1995: Table 1). Whether or not the social advances made by Barbados (including progress in gender equality) will hold into the twenty-first century is in question, however. Recession and structural adjustment programmes over the last ten to fifteen years have dealt serious blows to the economy. Although inflation has been in the order of only 2–3 per cent per annum since 1995 and the exchange rate has been stable, external debt currently stands at $US587 million, and there are disturbingly high rates of unemployment (EIU, 1996b: 42). Official labour force statistics place the unemployment rate at around one-quarter of the economically active population, and women seem to be worse affected than men. In 1992, for example, female unemployment amounted to 25.7 per cent, whereas the male equivalent was 20.5 per cent.

One reason given for higher unemployment among women is that they sometimes prefer not to disclose the fact they are working because they feel there is more prestige attached to being 'housewives' than to being engaged in informal occupations such as 'hustling' (petty trading), where many of them are concentrated. In this way, a number of women actively involved in generating income do not appear in official labour force figures. Yet even if women are disproportionately concentrated in informal commerce, alongside other 'feminised' activities such as services and clerical work, they were still recorded as 46 per cent of Barbados' national adult labour force in 1992 (UNDP, 1995: Table 11).

Moreover, adult women's economic participation is critical since over 40 per cent of households in the country are defined as 'female-headed', i.e. headed by a woman without a co-resident spouse, or other 'significant' male such as a father or brother. What is also important is that, whether women are partnered or not, their labour in the 'unpaid' domain of housework and childcare has long been greater than men's. Coupled with this, women's greater responsibility for financial provisioning may be burdensome when low salaries give rise to stringency measures and the management of debt. Indeed, in 1992, the share of earned income among women in the country (39.4 per cent) was still lower than their share of the labour force (UNDP, 1995: Table 3.5).

Politically, women's representation is also lagging behind, despite the fact that independence in 1966 carried the slogan of 'equality' alongside those of 'individualism' and 'black nationalism'. Barbados has a UK-style system of government, with Queen Elizabeth as head of state; her representative in Barbados, the governor-general, appoints the leader of the largest party in parliament (see EIU, 1996b: 40). The leader is currently Owen Seymour Arthur of the Barbados Labour Party (BLP) whose electoral victory in 1994 was marked by a majority of over 50 per cent of the seats in the government assembly. The other main parties are the Democratic Labour Party (DLP) (which under Errol Barrow's leadership was the first black party in power), and the National Democratic Party (NDP). Although the 1994 elections saw the voting in of an unprecedented number of women candidates, and three into ministerial positions (one as deputy prime minister), women's share of parliamentary seats in the same year was only 14.3 per cent (UNDP, 1995: Table 3.5). However, a number of female respondents in the current study expressed optimism about increased female participation in formal politics. In order to contextualise these perspectives and women's and men's views on other matters relating to gender, it is first necessary to provide a brief résumé of the sample population and methodological aspects of the Barbadian survey.

Methodology

As mentioned earlier, the interviewers for the project were current or recently graduated female students from the Sociology Department of the University of the West Indies. All were in their early twenties (with a mean age of 22 years), and identified themselves as 'black'. Where the students did not have access to a brother, both parents and/or grandparents, relatives of the same sex and generation were substituted. Between them they interviewed a total of 50 informants, among whom grandmothers (or gender/generation equivalents) had a mean age of 73 years, grandfathers 75 years, mothers 49 years, fathers 46 years, and brothers 25 years.

The interview process itself was found by respondents to be as interesting as the research output, although reactions were not always positive. While many interviewers found the experience of delving into their family histories illuminating and rewarding, others claimed to have felt pain in the process, especially where their childhoods had been unhappy. For some young women, the project provided a pathway to greater emotional closeness with their kin (especially grandparents with whom contact had been somewhat sporadic). For others, frustration held sway, especially where the stories recounted by relatives did not dovetail with the interviewers' own interpretations of events. Beyond this, time, distance, inconvenience, physical discomfort, and the hard graft attached to transcribing circuitous responses and/or extended soliloquies on certain topics presented pressures common to most types of social research work. In retrospect, however, these difficulties tended to be eclipsed by the intellectual and emotional gains.

One drawback of the project as it affects this chapter is that the voices and opinions of the young women on the substantive research topics were not presented in the report. Instead, others speak about younger women. Further omissions include a lack of detailed discussion of topics such as childhood, courtship and marriage. These caveats should be borne in mind as we look through the respondents' own eyes at changes in gender roles and relations in Barbados.

Gender roles and relations

No review of gender roles and relations in Barbados would be complete without reference to its creation as a plantation- and slave-based colonial economy in the late seventeenth century. By 1680, less than four decades after white settlement, male and female slaves from West Africa numbered nearly forty thousand, with around three-quarters engaged in sugar cane production. Another quarter of the slave population provided domestic services to the white planters, and for many women this extended to childminding and nursing. The remaining number of African descent (mainly male) engaged in traditional artisanal work such as carpentry and blacksmithing.

Although there was clearly some distinction by gender in what men and women did, the key feature is that, along with their counterparts throughout the Caribbean (see Chapter 2; also Massiah, 1986), black women in Barbados have always worked outside the home.[5] Indeed, in many respects class differences were probably more marked than gender differences during the slavery era insofar as the hard physical labour of black women contrasted starkly with the enforced idleness of their élite white counterparts. Whereas black women toiled long hours, worked in the fields alongside men, reared the children of white women, but enjoyed some measure of personal worth and power, white women were enslaved to Eurocentric modes of femininity. The latter both confined them to the home and subjected them to male dictates, their main role being the bearers of cultural respectability and morality for a group of men who themselves were subject to authority from Britain. The notion of a 'homogeneous Barbadian woman' was thus as tenuous three centuries ago as it is today.

Following emancipation in 1838, black women's high economic activity intensified in the early twentieth century, when men began to migrate overseas in large numbers (see page 56) and female household headship became established as a feature of Barbadian family life. These factors seem to have been critically important in the construction of contemporary gender identities. Breadwinning, for example, is by no means an exclusive preserve of men. Although this is partly a function of poverty, women's right to work as a marker of self-worth and autonomy seems to be accepted by both sexes and across three generations. Although older men are generally less convinced of this than younger males, one grandfather, Selwyn, conceded:

> Yes, women should work ... a man needs independence and a woman needs independence. A woman is no chattel and she should not be dependent on any man for her upkeeping, by prostitution or by marriage ... So, making a woman a slave, keeping her in a house, picking rice for one man and washing diapers for one child is nonsense.

While women's labour-force participation is accepted as part of their gender roles, there is less evidence that participation in domestic labour or childcare is an actual or normative component of men's responsibilities. The notion that reproductive work is essentially 'women's work' is most apparent among the middle and oldest generations, which is not to say that women in these age groups accepted the full weight of this burden contentedly. Lorna, a mother in her forties, reported:

> I think I was a bit disappointed when I first became a mother in that my husband was not the kind of father who got up in the night to help change nappies or to give bottles or that kind of thing ... Where money was concerned, okay, but not that kind of help, even in the house. He has the idea that a man's place is to do the outside jobs, while the woman is to be responsible for the children and for everything inside the house.

Women's primary responsibility for childcare and domestic work among older generations meant that employment was often undertaken at the cost of a heavy 'double day' of labour. Although vestiges of this pattern are still in evidence, the gradual increase in men's contributions to domestic life is recognised (if not always welcomed) by men of all generations. As one grandfather, Sidney, put it:

> Years ago ... it became an accepted fact that women really was the family, family was her business. Particularly here in Barbados where men would have their sprees and drink their liquor and leave everything to the woman of the house. But things have changed over the last few years and they are changing rapidly. Right now men are doing things, all sorts of things in the home and the women are not contented to do all of the work and they are making their husbands or their men share in even cooking. Everybody would say he is a sissy. But today it is an accepted fact. Men are telling you boldly today how good they can cook ... And even, some men are even involved in washing. They are taking their full load in the household. Not all men but some.

Younger men not only acknowledge these shifts towards greater complementarity between the sexes, but also seem to be more prepared to act as agents in the process. Sean, the 20-year-old brother of one of the interviewers, claimed:

> I don't believe this housewife thing works any more ... Both people should run a house. It is good when a woman could get out there and look for work and hold down a job because it helps a lot ... All two work together. Then come home and share the responsibility home. They clean the house and look after the kids together. I think that is how it should be.

Part of the reason why what 'should be' may not always be found in practice is that men and women seem to share the view that regardless of many similarities between the sexes, there are also differences. Beyond simple observations that men's physical build and capabilities distinguish them from women, many respondents seemed to believe there were psychological and emotional distinctions, particularly that women are temperamentally better suited to parenting, are more able to show their feelings, and are more sympathetic to the needs of others. As one mother, Pearl, declared:

> I think when it comes to comforting and sympathising and being gentle and able to be there for you, I think women seem to manage better. Even handling children, women seem to have that tenderness and that patience.

Childhood and socialisation   Views varied on the extent to which masculine and feminine identities are natural or 'God-given', or are created from a young age within the family, the community, in schools and so on. However, there was fairly widespread recognition that socialisation at least played a part. Indeed, one father, Tom, felt that what he termed 'training' was an all-important factor in shaping character and behaviour:

> I find, I think, personalities is basically, or usually reflect the kind of training received. I don't know if I can say women are always more gentler and nicer and sweeter, sometimes they are. As far as intelligence is concerned, I believe it's another fifty–fifty. I believe there are men and women alike who are blessed with lesser degrees, but I don't perceive any one set as being more intelligent than the other. I think it has to do with opportunities, sometimes it has to do with parental background, or has to do with property and riches.

On top of this kind of observation, a number of respondents pointed to the way in which socialisation could often be at odds with people's 'natural' tendencies. This was particularly applied to men, with some respondents pointing to the way in which stereotypical ideals of masculinity could pressurise men into hiding their true instincts, preferences and/or aptitudes. Andrew, from the youngest generation, summarised this notion:

> Emotionally, men are looked upon in society to be tough, not afraid of anything, not to be sissies, have no emotion, while the women are the opposite you know. They say that it's OK for a woman to cry, but for a man it is not ... I think that's where the problem is, right? Because they accuse men of being cold, heartless, not showing any affection towards the female species at all. And it's a funny thing you know, some women are so used to the rough, bang type that they can't tell the difference. They would see a good fella and they would say, 'Nah, he too quiet, he too soft.' And they would go with a guy who would beat them and curse them and abuse them. And people would say that she loves him no matter what. That is the truth.

At the same time, there was acknowledgement that such stereotypes were in the process of dissolution. Although respondents rarely pinpointed the precise mechanisms involved, the most important seem to revolve around changes in the roles of men and women within the household, and expansion and reform of the Barbadian education system.

We have already noted that gender roles and relations within the home have undergone transformations in recent decades, particularly in terms of a greater readiness among men to share the responsibilities of household life, and a more visible participation of women in waged work. This has not only presented new role models for children but has also provoked changes in generational divisions of labour, important in numerous ways to gendered socialisation. For example, although boys and girls have long been expected to help their parents out in activities related to household survival, there was possibly more pressure in the past for boys to assume a 'grown-up' male breadwinner role if their fathers died or deserted. Vere, a grandfather, whose father died when he was seven years old, was unable to finish primary school because of his mother's need for economic assistance:

> I left primary school at age eleven, and I worked, I had to get bread, work so that my sisters and brothers could go to school. And work for me was just four cents a day, for pay. The old lady [mother] drew my money and it was all right for me.

As for daughters in these situations, they were usually drawn out of school in order to take on reproductive responsibilities. As Eudora, a grandmother, reported:

> When I get in second standard and coming up to third, I really then was picking up. And I was the last girl so everything was going good. But then my mother, she get in contact with some friend and she had a little boy and so life change. I had to stop home and keep this little boy. And the children meet me and tell me, 'You don't know you pass for third.' And I would have been glad to go, but she din' think. So therefore I had to done school early. I couldn't complain for the little bit but I was sorry that I had to leave at that early age.

Nowadays, however, the growing expectation that both women and men will work in later life, coupled with more intense competition for jobs, seems to have led most parents to try to keep their offspring in education as long as possible. Indeed, some of the young male respondents felt that daughters are even more likely than sons to be encouraged to remain in education and/or to work harder at their studies. Sean, for example, declared:

> I would probably say they pushed the girls more than the boys. Because they think that they guys all they do is run from home and play dominoes and pass the exam easy. While the girls can't do that. They probably put more pressure on the girls than the boys ... In all my years the first place was mostly girls. There was one girl that I know that was bright right through. She came first in everything, even games.

This opinion contrasts sharply with the experiences of older women, who felt their own education had suffered because men's primacy as household breadwinners had led their parents to prioritise the schooling of sons.

The closing gap between the educational component of sons' and daughters' socialisation needs to be set within the context of widening educational provision and concomitant changes such as the de-gendering of subjects in school curricula (both discussed later in the chapter). However, the movement of men into particular types of teaching jobs (especially those once occupied almost exclusively by women) is also noteworthy, particularly in respect of challenging the idea that behavioural attributes are inherently gendered, and that it is impossible (not to mention undesirable) for men to act in a 'feminine' manner. One middle-aged woman, Pearl, remembered that in the past she associated

> the milder jobs with ... like women being secretaries and being teachers and so forth. Even in the school situation, well before you would never find a man, a male teacher teaching small children ... The men would teach the higher-ups, the seniors. Because we don't seem to think that males have the patience, that women would have the younger ones, you know, to get down on the floor and be one with the little ones.

Shifts towards a blurring of divisions between men's and women's roles and behaviour at home, in schools and at work were enthusiastically supported by a number of respondents, particularly women, and even those from the oldest generation. One of the grandmothers, Myrtle, said how much she admired the fact that women nowadays were driving buses, exclaiming: 'I does feel proud when I see a woman doing these things, masculine things so!'

Parental roles and parenthood Not all changes have been equally acceptable to all respondents, with older men in particular expressing concern about women's diminished time for parenting and family life. One middle-aged father, Lyle, felt that precocious sexual behaviour among the young and failure to obey their elders owed a lot to mothers' increased abandonment of the home for involvement in the labour force:

> Nobody at all don't have no discipline today. Discipline is what would keep the family together in the olden days ... from the time children begin getting children there is no discipline, because children can't discipline children. So if you check back yourself, you can see that all the hooliganism began when the children start having children ... When I was a boy the things that happening now couldn't happen. When the night close in, you had to be in your parents' house. As the sun gone down, you inside. You could only go out in the road if you mother send you at the shop or if somebody in the village pass and say: 'Miss

so and so I going down the road and I want your little girl come and go with me or your little boy.' But otherwise you in. You around the table reading with not even a light, a lamp and you there squinting your eyes reading, you either reading the ABC book or the Bible or something about there. Everybody in the house, but not now.

Eric, another father, had similar views:

And yuh know, if the woman is out working and that is what is causing children to be bad behave, nobody there to discipline. And most women today, some only want one child, some want two and some don't even want any. And this is the independence coming back where the family is concerned.

Some respondents clearly felt that other factors beyond women working outside the home had made parenting and discipline more difficult. One such factor was secularisation and an associated decline in religious observance, the latter being regarded as a cause as well as a consequence of unruly behaviour in children. One mother, Joan, talked about how children used to go to Sunday School, do their chores in the home, and listen to their elders, whereas nowadays boys in particular tend to take to the streets.

Another factor mentioned was the decline in authority in schools, with its quasi-parental function conceivably having become more significant in the light of the increased amount of education in children's lives. One of the grandmothers, Doris, maintained:

I think there is a lot of difference between those days and now because you had to be very disciplined. But today it seems to me like the children could do whatever they like to do and nobody is to say anything.

Similar sentiments were shared by a father, Tom, who declared:

You were always told, 'You must always have respect for those in authority.' And we had to have that respect. Regardless to whether you pitching marbles or playing a game of cricket and you see a teacher or head-teacher pass, you stop till he pass by.

The negative effects of declining school discipline are even felt by the youngest generation, with one young man, Antonio, stating:

Nowadays when I was at secondary school nothing like that was done. The teacher didn't care how you came to school, no kind of attention was paid to that. The strictness wasn't there 'cause the teachers couldn't lash you anymore like years ago.

Yet although some respondents in all generations clearly felt that corporal punishment was a necessary component of discipline, its value met with mixed reactions. Many of the middle-aged and elderly interviewees who had been subject to a range of humiliating, not to mention painful, modes of correction (including standing one-legged on a 'fool's bench' for hours, and being flogged with a cane), claimed that learning had been difficult in a climate of fear. This applied to Sidney, one of the grandfathers:

> In those days they used to man-handle you. When I say man-handle, I mean your teacher would tell you something and, if you did not get a hold of it, he would beat you, beat something into your head ... Nowadays we have better methods. The thing was to fear your teacher, which to my mind is wrong.

At the same time, links were drawn between effective discipline at school and within the home, and the diminishing authority of parents and parent figures alike was in some cases attributed a role in rising crime rates, with an elderly respondent, Myrtle, declaring:

> Mr F— would stuff the boys with licks. And you could not tell anybody that the school teacher beat you. Somebody on the road could lick you and send you to your parents and your parents would lick you again. We had strict rules and we did not have any lawlessness or bad behave children like what is stirring today.

While the above discussion reveals a diversity of viewpoints about issues of parenting and parental authority, on questions of sexual identity and sexuality, particularly men's, informants were virtually unanimous in their opinions.

Sex and sexuality   Although there was little discussion in the report of sexual behaviour among men or women in the 1990s, it is clear that in previous decades sexual relations outside marriage met with more stringent social penalties for women than men, and that sexuality was a taboo topic. Between emancipation and independence, for example, sexual propriety was implicit in moral teaching in the schools administered by the Anglican church, yet explicit instruction about how to avoid 'transgression' (in the form of scientific instruction on the facts of life) was absent from the curriculum. As one of the grandmothers, Maureen, recalled:

> We had to learn it our way, de hard way. Nobody explain how you get pregnant, yuh know, about the birds and the bees. No, you would have to fly and catch them for yourself. Nobody tell you that because that seem as it was a bad word, a nasty word. And you couldn't ask 'cause that was shameful.

Even in the subsequent generation, any single female teacher who got pregnant was dismissed from her job, and pregnancy among pupils was a rare and shocking event. As a middle-aged woman, Lorna, a former convent schoolgirl, recalled:

> We were never told the dos and don'ts and that sort of thing. I mean there was one girl who got pregnant while at school and that was a big thing. I mean the sisters were flabbergasted. And I will always remember them ... telling the school that she had a tumour. They never admitted that she was pregnant you know.

While men's licence for heterosexual freedom has always been much greater, increases in non-marital pregnancy and greater acceptance of this in the public domain indicate that there is some relaxation of the social mores that previously restricted women's sexual behaviour. Yet lest men's sexual freedom is imagined to be free of any gendered constraints in Barbados, it is important to note that considerable resistance is voiced about non-heterosexual activity.[6] At one end of the spectrum, some respondents expressed concern about the way in which men's appearance was becoming increasingly 'effeminate'. Maureen, a grandmother, declared that:

> Today things change so much that if you don't look at a person good, you won't know the man from the woman ... They have they hair plait, and earring and they do up all kind of different thing. So you have to be very careful between a man and a woman today.

At the other end of the spectrum, homosexuality is represented as an aberration contravening the rules of nature and Christianity alike. Indeed, many people made reference to God and to the Bible as a means of underlining their discomfort about, if not outright hostility to, gay sexual behaviour. One father, Lyle, expressed his opinion thus:

> I believe that homosexuality is a perverted activity and it's wrong. I do not believe God created anybody to be a homosexual, even though I hear this idea being pushed here and yonder. Ah, I believe that, like every other sin, it can, God can give the power to overcome, I believe that in many cases people become homosexual by choice, sometimes for money, sometimes for other reasons. Some were subtly drawn into it, they were young men abused by olders and sometimes they themselves become abusers. But I don't think nobody is destined to be a homosexual.

Similar views were articulated by one of the middle-aged female respondents, Grace:

> From the Bible's perspective, God made Adam and then he made Eve, which shows that God made man for a woman and woman for a man. As somebody said, if God wanted man to have a male partner, instead of making Eve, he would have made Steve.

While female homosexuality was not touched upon by respondents, women's increased independence within (and in some cases from) male-headed family life attracted a range of negative reactions.

Marriage, family and fertility

As noted previously, Barbadian family patterns incorporate a significant proportion of households headed by women. In the earlier part of the twentieth century, a major catalyst for female household headship was the gender-selectivity of international migration, with men being the majority of overseas migrants. Since the 1950s, however, increasing numbers of women have joined the ranks of those looking for work abroad and imbalanced sex ratios no longer play the role they did in giving rise to households headed by women.[7] Nevertheless, high levels of female house-hold headship persist, and respondents across all generations tend to have similar views of the corollaries, with particular links being drawn with women's rising levels of labour-force participation and greater self-assertion. Marriage also seems to be less common, even if people might aspire to it as an ideal.

While there was wide awareness that women of every generation have probably always 'sacrificed' more for their families than men, anxiety was clearly felt in some quarters that women's independence and demands for gender equality were going 'too far'. Such qualms found their most forceful expression in the words of older men, who were concerned that changes in women's lives were weakening the institution of the family and, as noted earlier, undermining women's allegiances to their homes, their children, and their spouses. George, a man in his seventies, argued: 'Family is the business of both the fathers and the mothers. The women have a role and the men. God made it like that. Women must never get it in their heads that they are men.' Eric, a father in his forties, subscribed to similar views:

> Family life has changed ... in fact now that the female is working and there is more exposure for them to, if I should say, temptations or even other relation-ships, and this has caused a lot of problems within the family. Not that I'm saying women shouldn't work. You can't turn back the clock.

Fertility Whether or not women's desire to devote less of their lives to childcare than in the past has been primarily responsible, Barbados has experienced a sharp drop in fertility since the mid-1950s. Since the creation of the Barbados Family Planning Association in 1955, the crude birth rate has fallen by two-thirds to a level of 16 per 1,000 (1992 figures), and

Barbados' success in this arena places it ahead of many other Caribbean nations.

Yet 'success' is time and culture specific, and it is important to note that multiple births have been a source of satisfaction and social prestige for women. While most younger women are restricting births to one or two in their lifetime, older women may boast of their virtually dynastic numbers of descendants. Agnes, a proud great-grandmother, is a prime example:

> Well, my family is very large ... I had seven boys and five girls, and then they produce children which give me, in my last reckoning, about 55 grandchildren and then 40-plus great-grands. And then they gone more now since the last reckoning that I had. You see, my grandchildren had children, and I don't even know how much they are now.

It should also be noted that women's smaller burdens of childcare may be offset by having to spend more time caring for senior household members as the elderly begin to replace the young as the major dependants in the population.[8]

Family organisation and links with kin The problems of how to care for a growing number of elderly people in the wake of declining population replacement levels may also be compounded by a widely recognised diminution of extended family units. Many respondents felt that the kinship networks within which households have traditionally been embedded (even for years and across the great distances created by international migration) are also on the wane in terms of the amount of contact they now have with their more distant relatives.[9] One father, John, reported:

> Family is not what it used to be before. When I was a boy, family used to be closely knitted. One problem in a family would affect the whole family from yonder, the far family. According to the old people, even the pumpkin vine part of the family would be affected by one problem. Today all that change. Family now like strangers nowadays. They live apart, live far apart ... They just like they ain't no more family.

Changing residential arrangements seem to have played a major role in the declining extended family unity perceived by the older generations. In the past relatives tended to live, if not in the same house, then nearby, and this facilitated interaction and mutual support. Currently, the tendency is for the youngest generation to establish independent living arrangements near educational institutions or sources of employment. While such trends are undoubtedly the result of labour market changes and the fact that increasing numbers of young people are pursuing higher education, the social and psychological corollaries of these shifts are viewed with some regret. One of the mothers, Pearl, lamented:

> Extended family life is no longer like it was in the old days. There was always an old grandmother or an elderly relative, usually female. She was in the house, sort of in charge of everything, even if she was very old. Apart from that, I think that more family used to live closer together. When I say closer, I mean physically as well as emotionally. You know, like when a niece or nephew would build a home closer to the grandmother. I think now that they are spreading their wings, they have moved away from the old home and the family unit has broken down, yes. And I think more people depended on one another for different things, like certain items were shared which would be unthought of today. Families shared washcloths and hair combs and things like that, something like that would not happen at all today.

Although the diminution of extended family contact may have made life more difficult for households in which both parents are employed, this may be offset by men's increased participation in housework and childcare. For lone mothers, however, scope to spread these responsibilities is less. The trend towards independent living arrangements has conceivably cut off important sources of help that in the past underpinned the efforts of women to raise families without a partner. One middle-aged woman, Pearl, noted that when she was growing up, lone mothers tended to remain in their natal homes and were able to cope better with the pressures of single parenthood: 'Even in them days if you had a single parent, she still lived with her mother. And the aunties and uncles and cousins were there. So that she had extra help bringing up the children.' This is not to say, however, that women nowadays do not cope with single parenthood. As a brother of one of the interviewers put it:

> Well, from what I can see, as far as raising the children, women are doing better than the men, and now the men are taking a battering as far as society is concerned. Because sometimes the woman has to be the mother and the father, yuh know, while the male only pop in once in a while and give the woman money and that's all. The single-parent woman has to deal with the bills, the needs of the baby, the needs of herself, the needs of the house and it seems as though they are doing pretty well too, yeah.

If lone mothers today have less support from kin, part of their success may be due to the greater prospects of independent survival fostered by the progressive removal of gendered barriers to education and employment.

Education and work

Changes in education and livelihood over the course of the twentieth
century in Barbados have been dramatic, and in many respects constitute
the bedrock in which other changes have been grounded. They have
certainly been key in shaping the life courses of men and women from
the three generations, and are keenly felt by older respondents as having
undergone immense transformation in their own lifetimes.

Education Two prominent shifts in education over the last 60–70 years
have been, first, the rising quality of educational provision, and second,
the extension of education to a much wider section of the Barbadian
population.

Education in the pre-independence period Unlike the youngest generation, most
mothers, fathers and grandparents had not proceeded beyond primary
school. This was mainly due to poverty. Low incomes meant severe
hardship for parents who endeavoured to keep their children in school.
Schoolchildren from poor households often had to suffer the humiliation
of taking assistance from outside parties. For example, during the childhoods of middle-aged respondents, a system of charity meals was set up
for poor children attending schools in urban areas. Although this potentially
equipped children with the health and stamina to endure their lessons, the
desire to maintain 'face' was such that children often went hungry instead.
Marcia, a middle-aged woman, described the pressures of being a poor
schoolgirl in the pre-independence period:

> And if you could not afford lunch, dem had dis system where de children had
> tuh walk to de park and collect lunch. And it used to be embarrassing fuh poor
> children because yuh would watch dem line up going to de park and coming
> back because you know dat these are children dat had to go and get lunch, dat
> duh parents cannot provide for them. Never mind de ones dat go home and
> sometimes get sweet water and biscuit 'cause dey parents can't afford tuh give
> dem lunch. But de parents don' want no person to see their children going to
> the park. So yuh go home and come back tuh school hungry.

Primary education provided by the British colonial administration at this
time took place in so-called 'all-age' schools. Most of these were single-
sex, disciplinarian, and offered very limited instruction beyond rote learning
of facts. The schools were also rudimentary in terms of physical structure,
teaching aids and books. One of the grandfathers, Alfred, whose school
had an earth floor, recalls his mother having to pull chiggers (parasites)
out of his feet at night, and a middle-aged mother, Joan, reported:

> Yuh didn't have any books to carry to school. Yuh wrote on slate or chalkboard in the early school and then further up you just needed exercise books and you leave them at school ... Yuh went to school with yuh two long hands and a pencil push in your hair.

Following two introductory years at an all-age school, pupils were expected to progress though seven 'standards'. If children passed their annual examinations, they could expect to complete their primary education at around 10 or 11 years old, although the majority did not graduate until around 14 or 15. Only a small minority of the black population proceeded to secondary schools (especially prestigious establishments such as Harrison College), because of colour and class barriers. As Sidney, one of the grandfathers, explained:

> Sometimes you get to seventh. I got to third, you know, and that was it ... In those days it wasn't like what you have now, your secondary school and all that. Like Harrison College that was for the high ones. You would have to be known. Your application give them the backgrounds of your parents. So it was only the real high upper-ups could get into them schools. In the elementary, when you got to the seventh that was that.

Similar restrictions applied to the middle generation, with Richard declaring:

> A fellow like me would had to be real bright, had to get 'bout a hundred and somebody marks to go to Harrison College. And if you had the right colour and ten marks you would still go because of the type of family yuh come out of. Today, de children lucky because a fellow could come from nowhere and as long as he get 85 marks he could go.

Discrimination was also prevalent in the pre-independence era, with several respondents noting bias and favouritism towards the better-off and lighter-skinned pupils. This undoubtedly disadvantaged the learning of poorer children, as well as reinforcing racial and class hierarchies. A mother, Joan, recalled:

> There were teachers at that time and from Monday to Friday and they know that you have de breed, that they know that you some person's daughter, that you have a little above some other person, they would pay more attention to dem sort of children. Put them at the helm of the realm. They'd be like head girls, form captain and prefect and all of dat. And don't care how good you do in class, and you are not some person daughter, they would leave you down there.

Gender discrimination was also present. This mainly took the form of channelling students into gender-stereotypical subjects aimed at grooming women for the roles of mother, wife and homemaker, and men for work in the fields. Thus while boys and girls alike were given a basic smattering of English and mathematics, the curriculum in female schools usually involved instruction in needlework and cooking, and in male schools, gardening and manual skills.

Education in the post-independence period It was only with independence in 1966 that gender, race and class discrimination were challenged and over-turned, as equal educational opportunity became enshrined in the policies of successive black majority governments. Education was seen as a means of preparing society for greater equality, democracy and mobility on the basis of merit rather than privilege. An important pre-independence step towards this came with the introduction of free secondary education in 1962, and compulsory school attendance until the age of 16.

The remainder of the 1960s saw the replacement of individual school entrance examinations with a government-administered common entrance exam to all public and private secondary schools, the introduction of book loans and student bursaries, free school meals at primary level, and grants for school uniforms. Extremely important from the perspective of gender was the introduction of co-education at all levels of the school and college system. This carried in its wake the attempt to eradicate gender-typing of subjects. Even if reality did not always match rhetoric, and deeply embedded assumptions proved persistent, Ryan, a young man in his twenties who grew up in the aftermath of the revolution in Barbadian education, reveals that considerable shifts were made at this time:

> Actually, we did all the same courses, especially at secondary school. But when a choice came up between art and home economics, it was felt that the girls should take home economics and the boys should take art ... in practice it was totally different because a great deal of the boys took home economics and actually had a great time and the art class was pretty well mixed between boys and girls. And you were always surprised, although you really shouldn't be, when you see a girl doing technical drawing, doing TD, or a boy doing needle-work up to fifth form. I mean it was weird because basically it's not what we've been taught. But if you're really open-minded you have to understand the world is changing and distinctions like that don't matter any more. So actually it's rather enlightening when you see the different genders breaking the barriers that were put up years ago.

Yet despite the fact that adult literacy is now as high as 99 per cent in Barbados, and more and more children are moving into tertiary and higher education, educational reforms have not escaped some criticism. A number of the older respondents feel that the emphasis on free, critical and independent thought, and the relaxation of corporal punishment, has prompted an erosion of standards and discipline. Beyond this, the morale of the teaching profession is low, and structural adjustment policies have put such a squeeze on educational resources that there is currently talk of introducing fees for higher education. Moreover, despite the persistence of social democratic ideals, the children of the poor still tend to do less well than those of the better off. The one rather striking feature in all this is that girls tend to be doing better than boys in examination results, and from some quarters this has given rise to demands for the return of single-sex schools. At the same time, even educated males (those who have completed secondary education or more) are understandably demotivated when the job market offers them a shrinking range of opportunities. As one grandfather, Vere, complained:

> Today these young Barbadians are so damn proud that them don't want to do nothing. Dey don't want dem foot or dem hand tuh touch de earth. When dem come from school wid one or two certificates dey going say, dem don't want go fishing, won't weed nobody place, mix nuh cement ... De money is out there, but a lot of youngsters don't give two hells about dat.

Limited prospects of what young men may deem worthwhile employment might be one reason for declining commitment to educational achievement. It possibly also suggests a need for greater integration between educational and employment policies on the part of the Barbadian government, although the current economic climate is likely to make this difficult.

Employment and livelihood As already noted, recession and structural adjustment have placed such strain on the Barbadian economy that unemployment is escalating sharply. This represents a major change from the middle years of the twentieth century, when economic modernisation was accompanied by an opening up of the formal labour force to the black population. Employment expansion and improvement was catalysed by the foundation in 1941 of the Barbados Workers' Union, which aimed to better the conditions of black workers and their access to jobs. Given the continued grip of the white population over private business, most new opportunities were created in the public sector, and during the 1950s blacks started moving into posts in the police force, the fire service and the post office. While men tended to occupy these positions, a few women were able to secure jobs as teachers, nurses and clerical workers. Post-independence, the traditional barriers to black male and female workers were eroded further, partly in response to rising educational attainment. Marcia, one of the mothers, was fulsome in her support of these changes:

> Well, I must say dat now de black race have really, really excelled in all fields, 'cause there's no barriers now, no place dat de black people can't go so long as

dey have de education. Before dey would have de education and still it was a barrier, just because of colour. And I would say, although we have a lot of people dat would not understand dis, we owe a lot to de prime minister, Mr Errol Barrow, who at dat time started when he got into power he pushed for de blacks tuh take a greater part in de society. Like when dem have all white schools, he pushed for black children tuh get into these schools, let them break down de barriers. But de jobs now is very good fuh black people, de black children once they learn, and I am very proud of dat.

Yet, while racial inequalities in the labour market may have reduced over time, it is clear that women's occupational mobility is not all that it might be. As noted earlier, female unemployment rates are higher than men's, their average earnings are less, women are more heavily concentrated in tertiary activities than their male counterparts, and more women than men are in informal sector occupations. However, the fact that women and men currently have almost equal shares in the labour force places Barbados well ahead of the majority of countries in the South, and many of those in the North as well. This is not just a function of labour market modernisation and restructuring, but the result of household patterns where all members are expected to play an active role in contributing to the well-being of the unit.

Beyond this, there is evidence that women aspire to better jobs than in the past, much of which is to do with a gradual diminution of gender stereotypes. This applies more to younger than older women, with middle- and older-generation female respondents largely of the opinion that light employment or jobs utilising domestic skills were inappropriate for men, and heavy, physically demanding work inappropriate for women. One middle-aged woman, Joan, summed up the situation thus:

> Yuh have certain jobs fuh women and certain jobs dat just suit fuh men. Like I think a man should never be a secretary ... Dat is a woman's job, dat is a soft job. And I don't think a man should be doing nurse work. Dat is a soffie job tuh me, for a man. A man shouldn't be a dancer, dat is a woman job. But I wouldn't want to see nuh woman 'pon top a building painting. Dat is degrading fuh her, but a man got de stomach and everything for dat.

Overseas migration Similar assumptions affected older and middle-aged women's views on, and experiences of, overseas migration, which has long been an important livelihood strategy for Barbadian families. In the early part of the twentieth century, international migration was heavily male-dominated and represented an escape route for men barred from ascending the occupational ladder in Barbados itself due to colour and class discrimination. As Agnes, one of the grandmothers, observed:

They go to better their position, to get more money. They didn't have enough jobs here in Barbados for people to stay here so they had to go out. If not, I don't know what would have happened to the island all like now.

For many of the older male respondents, migration had not only been a means of upward mobility, the saving of money and self-improvement, but also became a symbolic *rite de passage* to full manhood. As Eric, one of the fathers, who had worked as a ship's crew, pointed out:

I was in England, and I been to Australia, Canada too. Dem is places dat I like. Yes, and I spent 21 days in Thailand and 21 days in Spain. Man, I been all over de world already and it was beautiful ... I'd do it all over again. Make a man out o' yuh.

Although women also started to migrate in large numbers from the 1950s onwards, their spells abroad were usually shorter than men's because of their reluctance to leave home and family for too long.

Nowadays, younger people of both sexes, while mobile, also tend to spend less time away than older male respondents did, which may be partly because of the imposition of restrictions by receiving countries. As it is, return migration to Barbados is relatively common. Once people start getting older, they are less able to stand the cold climate in places like Britain, the northern United States and Canada, and/or desire to see their place of birth before they die. As one of the brothers, Terry, claimed:

Well, they come back because it's home sweet home. There is no other place like Barbados, yuh know. Although it's getting pretty horrible these days, it still is home.

Conclusion

The rapid erosion of major inequalities based on class, colour and gender in Barbados in the space of relatively few decades testifies to the importance of policy in reducing social injustice.[10] The progressive 'Caribbeanisation' of major bastions of colonial culture, particularly politics and education, have brought benefits to a broad section of the population, and for the most part, shifts in Barbadian society have been welcomed by respondents. This includes changes in the sphere of gender, although the delinking of women from primary responsibility for household labour seems to have perturbed some older men, especially where they have seen this as having contributed to undermining the institution of the family and parental discipline. Another cause for concern, felt by a much wider range of informants, is the declining willingness on the part of younger men to 'demean' themselves by taking work for which they deem themselves over-qualified. Such tendencies may be a product of the demoralisation imposed by high levels of unemployment and the stress felt by men who, for many years, have regarded employment as a central component of manhood. While renewed economic growth could help to generate a wider range of employment more attuned to the rising educational attainment of the male population, another solution to a potential 'crisis' of masculine identity could be the continued tendency for men and women to take more equal shares in family and household life. This is likely to benefit women as much as men, and could rank Barbados even higher as a country where women's rights have been more than a politically expedient item on policy agendas.

Recommendations

On the basis of the informants' views, the following recommendations might be made:

- Free or subsidised childcare facilities to enable women's full access to employment and to address some of the difficulties of children being left to their own devices through the work-induced absence of parents. This could include pre- and after-school care, as well as daycare for infants.
- Investment in vocational training and micro-entrepreneurship to capitalise on the higher educational standards of the population.
- Emphasis in formal and informal education on the desirability of equal sharing between the sexes of parenting responsibilities and housework to support and endorse current tendencies for younger men to play a greater role in these tasks.
- Consciousness-raising initiatives at the community level and within schools to sensitise people to alternative sexualities and to create greater tolerance towards individuals with gay and lesbian orientations.

Notes

1. Compiled from a report prepared by Christine Barrow, Faculty of Social Sciences, University of the West Indies, Cave Hill Campus, Bridgetown, Barbados.
2. Creole terms and phraseology used by respondents are left in their original form. Creole is Caribbeanised English and is most widely spoken by lower income groups. Anglicised English tends to be more common among more privileged groups with higher levels of formal education.
3. The black population of Barbados amounts to 95 per cent of the total, whites 4 per cent, and other racial groups 1 per cent.
4. *Bim* is a slang term for Barbados.
5. 'Work outside the home' is not a particularly appropriate term when many

female slaves were live-in domestics, and given that in contemporary Barbadian society some women conduct income-generating ventures *within* their homes. However, the main alternative term, 'economically active', would have been less appropriate in a cross-temporal sense given that slaves did not receive a market wage for their labour.

6. We have to remember here that we are dealing with a non-random sample of respondents who, by virtue of their familial links with the interviewers, are more likely to give a strong heterosexual bias to the sample than would a broader cross-section of Barbadian society.

7. In 1921, following three decades of heavily male-dominated international migration (mainly to Panama), the sex ratio was highly feminised, with only 675 men per 1,000 women. Nowadays women only slightly outnumber men on the island. It should also be noted that even though women's participation in overseas migration flows increased in the second part of the twentieth century, migration from the island as a whole slowed due to clamp-downs on the entry of foreign migrants into receiving countries such as the UK and USA.

8. Barbados has now reached the so-called 'advanced' stage of the demographic transition inasmuch as the elderly are living so long that set against the declining birth rate, the growth of the elderly population is now outpacing that of the young.

9. 'Distant' is clearly a flexible term open to subjective definition. For some respondents, distant relatives may refer to second cousins, for others, aunts, uncles, nieces and nephews, and for others, any kin beyond the parent–child dyad or siblings. Some interviewers saw the present project as a means of forging closer ties with grandparents with whom they felt contact had been limited. Some also perceived the interview as an opportunity to re-establish communication with absent fathers.

10. Clearly government policy is not the only factor accounting for changes in Barbadian society since the post-war period, as demonstrated by many other cases in this volume. Nevertheless, it is conceivable that without the strong commitment of post-independence black governments on the island to increasing opportunities for disadvantaged groups, the process of diminishing various forms of social polarisation may have taken far longer and/or even failed to occur.

CHAPTER 4

MALAYSIA[1]

Malaysia has experienced high levels of economic growth in the last few decades, due mainly to export-oriented industrialisation. As one of the fastest-growing economies in Asia, Malaysia accordingly presents an interesting backdrop against which to examine changing gender roles and relations. Beyond this, greater consciousness of women's rights seems to be growing across all ethnic divides in this pluralistic society (Karim, 1995: 40).

While the present discussion includes some indication of changes in gender roles, relations and attitudes among three generations from a range of states within Malaysia, the bulk of the analysis is drawn from the perceptions of younger age groups, notably university students and their peers. From their perspective, it appears that Malaysia has undergone substantial economic transformation, reflected in a marked expansion of employment opportunities. Linked with this have been improvements in the standard of living which, in turn, have influenced social values and practices. Evidence of increasing gender equality is apparent, although this has occurred neither in a uniform manner nor without resistance. Men seem to have benefited more from the rapid advances, and to have made greater socio-economic strides than women. Men also appear to be reluctant to challenge inequalities in male–female relationships, and this has given rise to resentment among many younger women.

Country profile

Only since the Second World War have Malaysia, Singapore and Brunei been independent nations. Prior to this, they formed one colony under British rule, although the Portuguese and the Dutch had colonial interests in the state of Melaka (now Malacca) before the arrival of the British in 1786. After a turbulent period during the Second World War with the short-lived Japanese occupation of Malaya (currently Peninsular Malaysia), the British had to contend with a twelve-year independence struggle on the part of the guerrilla Malayan Communist Party, which ended officially in 1960, but continued sporadically until 1989. While Malaya achieved formal *merdeka* (independence) in 1957, Malaysia came into existence in 1963 and included Sarawak, Sabah, Singapore and Brunei. However, no sooner was this agreed than the Philippines laid claim to Sabah, and Indonesia to all the eastern states. To complicate the situation further, political and ethnic power struggles between Singapore and Malaya (Singapore was social democratic and Chinese-dominated, while Malaya was conservative and Malay-dominated) led to Singapore being expelled from the union in 1965. Brunei also refused to be incorporated into the Malaysian union and remained a British protectorate until complete independence in 1984.

Following this chequered history, contemporary Malaysia now comprises Peninsular Malaysia, extending south from Thailand, and East Malaysia, representing 50 per cent of the total land area situated in the northern part of the island of Borneo, which is divided between Sarawak and Sabah (with the enclave of Brunei in between).[2] Officially called the Federation of Malaysia, the nation operates as a federated constitutional monarchy ruled by the king (Yang di-Pertuan Agong), who is elected by the Conference of Rulers from one of nine hereditary rulers. The national legislature is based on a bicameral federal parliament comprising a senate (Dewan Negara) and House of Representatives (Dewan Rakyat) (EIU, 1996c: 3). Each of the 13 states has its own government and constitution ruled in nine cases by a hereditary sultan, and in the remaining four states by a governor (Yang Dipertuan Negeri), who is appointed by the federal government for four years.

According to the 1991 census, the population of Malaysia stood at 18.3 million, although this had increased to 19.9 million by 1995 (EIU, 1996c: 4), with a projected rate of growth of 2.2 per cent between 1992 and 2000 (UNDP, 1995: Table 16). However, the population is strongly concentrated in Peninsular Malaysia, with only around 15 per cent of the total living in Sarawak and Sabah. The varied ethnic composition of the population – Malays, Chinese, Indians, indigenous Orang Asli, and various tribes of Sarawak and Sabah – has been a major source of conflict past and present. On the establishment of the nation in the 1960s, for example, there was concern amongst the government that the indigenous Malays were socio-economically disadvantaged vis-à-vis other ethnic groups, especially the Chinese. Following race riots in 1969, the government adopted the New Economic Policy (NEP) as part of the Second Malaysia Plan, which in general aimed to reduce poverty for all Malaysians and restructure the economy and, specifically, attempted to overcome Malay disadvantage. This involved various types of affirmative action, such as making Bahasa Kebangsaan (also known as Bahasa Melayu) the official language in order to foster national consciousness, establishing land ownership schemes for the landless (mainly Malays), and giving Malays preferential access to the civil service, education and scholarships (see Rigg, 1994). In addition, the government conferred the title of *bumiputra* (sons of the soil) to all indigenous Malays and tribal groups in Sarawak and Sabah. Hardly surprisingly, this created tension with Chinese and Indian groups, which still exists today. In 1991, 60.6 per cent of the Malaysian population were *bumiputeras* (mainly Malays), 28.1 per cent Chinese, and 7.9 per cent Indian. As a direct result of government interventions, Malays, constituting only around 55 per cent of the population in Peninsular Malaysia, dominate the political scene, while the minority Chinese tend to control the economy.[3] The Indian population, who are mainly Tamils, represent around 10 per cent of the population in Peninsular Malaysia, concentrated on the west coast. Finally, in East Malaysia, Malays make up only around 25 per cent of the population, with the remainder comprising a range of 25 different ethnic groups.

This diversity of ethnic groups is also reflected in the plurality of religions practised in Malaysia, which more or less coincide with racial groupings. Beyond Islam, practised by most Malays, the Chinese are followers of Taoism, Buddhism and to a lesser extent, Christianity, while the Indians are mainly Hindu with a minority of Muslims and Sikhs. Despite these formal religions, and the dominance of Islamic law (Shari'a) in the government, Malaysian culture is also strongly influenced by Malay customs (*adat*) based on indigenous belief systems. Coexisting with other religious customs within the Malay community, *adat* determines kinship systems in both villages (*kampungs*) and in urban areas, stressing complementarity in social relations (particularly gender relations) and often acting as a counterweight to more hierarchical systems found in Islam (see Chapter 6). For example, *adat* influences patron–client and employer–employee relations in economic and political life through the use of intimate kinship terms of address such as *pa'cik* (uncle) and *ma'cik* (aunt), which serve to dilute authority patterns and emphasise informality (see, for example, Karim, 1995: 37).

As for Malaysia's economy, rapid growth in recent decades has raised its status to that of an upper middle-income country, and heralded it as an emerging 'tiger' to join others such as Singapore, Taiwan and South Korea. In 1992, Malaysia had a GNP per capita of US$2,830, with a per capita GDP of US$7,790 (UNDP, 1995: Tables 2 and 20). Real GDP growth has been high since the 1970s, with a rate of 7.9 per cent between 1970 and 1980 and 6.2 per cent between 1980 and 1993 (World Bank, 1995: Table 2). In the 1990s, however, GDP growth was particularly remarkable, with a rate of 8.7 per cent in 1994 and 9.6 per cent in 1995

(EIU, 1996 c: 4). In fact, growth was so rapid that there are now concerns that the economy will 'overheat', especially given continuing balance of payments and inflation problems (ibid.: 6). While all sectors of the economy have grown since the 1970s, it is industry, and particularly manufacturing, that has experienced most expansion. Between 1980 and 1993 manufacturing grew at 10.3 per cent (World Bank, 1995: Table 2), and in 1994 this sector represented 31.7 per cent of GDP (EIU, 1996c: 4). Reflecting the dominance of manufacturing over the economy, electronics and electrical machinery constituted the principal export in 1994 (US$29.1 billion). More recently agriculture has become increasingly important for the Malaysian economy with the promotion of agro-exports such as palm oil and logs and timber, boosting agriculture's contribution to GDP to 14.5 per cent in 1994 (EIU, 1996c: 4).

Social indicators in Malaysia reflect relatively high levels of human development, with a life expectancy at birth of 70.8 in 1992, and an adult literacy rate of 81.1 per cent. Moreover, 78 per cent of the population had access to safe water and 94 per cent to sanitation in 1993 (UNDP, 1995: Table 2). When these are differentiated by gender, however, it appears that men have made greater gains than women in some areas. For example, the adult literacy rate among women is 75.4 per cent compared with 87.8 per cent among men (ibid.: Table 3.1). In terms of political participation, in 1994 women represented only 10 per cent of seats at local and parliamentary levels and 7 per cent of ministerial posts (ibid.: Table A2.4).[4] In contrast, women's share of the adult labour force in the same year was 36 per cent (ibid.: Table 11), representing an increase from 1970 when it stood at 31 per cent (World Bank, 1995: Table 29). The latter is, in part, related to the increased demand for female labour in the manufacturing sector, although there is evidence that women face considerable discrimination in factory jobs in terms of wage levels, gender stereotyping and poor working conditions (see Ong, 1987). Among female Malay factory workers, this discrimination may also extend to moral stigmatisation in that they are often perceived to be flouting Muslim norms of modesty and propriety (Buang, 1993). In all economic sectors women remain largely excluded from the upper echelons, and tend to be concentrated in jobs considered inferior to men's and receiving lower wages (Karim, 1995). For example, in 1992 only 8.3 per cent of adminstrators and managers were women, although they represented 38.2 per cent of professional and technical workers (UNDP, 1995: Table 3.5). Therefore, despite improvements in women's access to employment, economic development does not seem to have benefited women in a uniform manner.[5] However, it is important to point out that Malaysian women have actively resisted subordination, as illustrated by Aihwa Ong's groundbreaking study of spirit possession among Malay factory women as a means to resist male authority (see Ong, 1987). In addition, the endurance of *adat* customs, in which women play an important role, and their integration into Islam, arguably makes the Malay social system less restrictive than other Muslim societies in Asia (see, for example, Karim, 1992; also Chapter 6 of this book).[6]

Methodology

Following the methodology employed in the other case studies in the text, the study in Malaysia focused particularly on how the process of social and cultural change has affected people in the younger generation, using information from middle-aged and elderly people as points of comparison. The study was conducted by the Department of Anthropology and Sociology at the University of Malaya in Kuala Lumpur. The researchers were drawn from students who had completed undergraduate studies in sociology, who had practical experience of sociological theories and methodologies, and who had taken courses on youth and gender studies. Ten female university students were involved in the project, all in their twenties, and from a range of ethnic groups (Malay, Chinese and Indian).

The research was conducted between April and December 1995, during which time researchers returned to their home towns to conduct interviews. Informants were drawn from a range of states in Malaysia and from both rural and urban areas. Each student was required to select five to six family members, ideally a grandmother, grandfather, father, mother and brother, with the researchers themselves filling in for sisters. Depending on the availability of informants, aunts, uncles and stepmothers were substituted when necessary. Sixty people were interviewed across the three generations, split evenly between the groups. An open-ended interview format was used, covering a range of issues (see Chapter 1), yet focusing on three core questions: What does it mean to be a Malaysian man or woman? How have the lives of women and men been shaped by the social and ideological context, and how have these affected opportunities and constraints? How do personal experiences of men and women differ over the generations?

The researchers encountered a number of problems. These included a lack of privacy, with people often being shy to talk in front of other family members. In turn, many were reluctant to discuss sensitive issues such as sex, sexuality and love, especially given their relationship to the researchers. Finally, the interviews were conducted in the local language, and researchers often found it difficult to translate their own and others' experiences into English. For this reason, the informants' comments are largely paraphrased rather than using direct quotations. While the profile of informants includes all three generations and allows us to see how basic socio-economic factors have changed over time, the in-depth analysis of informants' perceptions is drawn primarily from the younger generation; changes are therefore seen mainly through the eyes of the young.

Profile of informants   Of the 60 informants, 30 women and 30 men were interviewed, with the oldest generation aged mainly between 61 and 70, the middle generation aged between 41 and 55, and the youngest generation concentrated in the 21–30 age group. Grandfathers tended to be older than grandmothers, fathers older than mothers, and brothers older than sisters. All the informants lived in Peninsular Malaysia, with one grandmother from Singapore. Of those from Peninsular Malaysia, 5 informants were from Kuala Lumpur itself or in the states closest to the capital, with 16 from Kelantan (the least developed province in the country) and 12 from Selangor, and the remainder living in 6 other states (Kedah, Malacca, Johore, Pahang, Penang and Perak). Most were from urban areas, although the older generation were most likely to be residing in the countryside. In ethnic terms, informants were mainly Chinese (30) or Malay (24), with a minority of Indians (4). Religious affiliation broadly reflected these ethnic groupings, with the majority practising Islam (24), followed by Buddhism (22), and small minorities of Hindus (6) and Christians (8).

All the oldest generation were married, as were the middle generation except for one mother and one father, who were divorced and widowed respectively. Only two of the young generation were married. Respondents were classified according to their attendance at religious schools (*pondok*),[7] primary level, lower and upper secondary, and university level. Eleven respondents had received no education (all among the older generation), with 4 having attended religious schools. Reflecting the nature of the study carried out by university students, 18 informants had reached tertiary level, with 14 educated to primary level, and 13 to secondary level (8 at lower secondary and 5 at upper secondary). Information on employment was not available across all three generations, although among the youngest generation, male occupations included carpentry, engineering, sales, and own businesses with a concentration in the manufacturing sector. Young women were concentrated in administrative and clerical jobs, with a few working in industry.

In order to contextualise the changes that have occurred in gender roles and relations in Malaysia, it is important to outline respondents' general views about changes in Malaysian society in general. Socio-economic transformation was generally welcomed by the informants as it has opened up many opportunities, particularly in education and employment, and has improved living standards. However, negative aspects were also recognised, including the loss of some cultural traditions, such as Malay games most common in Kelantan, particularly top-spinning (*main gasing* – an adult game using tops weighing up to seven kilogrammes with players arranged in teams) and kite-flying (again, an adult pastime involving competitions). Other consequences were reported as an increase in materialism and individualism in society and loss of community spirit. At the same time, increased religious fervour, especially among Muslims, was noted. According to informants, this has been manifested through an increase in women wearing headscarves, the construction of more mosques and a rise in the number of religious programmes on television. In line with this has been a decline in animism, formerly common among the middle and older generations. The contradictions inherent in these positive and negative influences are reflected in the nature of gender roles and relations.

Gender roles and relations

Gender roles and relations among the informants appear to be fairly asymmetrical among all generations. In the minds of most informants male and female spheres are distinct, with men consigned to economic, breadwinning roles, and women to domestic, reproductive responsibilities. However, these beliefs have not been static over time, with evidence of change among women in particular. While both sexes of the older generation believed in a strict delineation between men and women's roles based on the notion of the male provider and female homemaker, changing perceptions were evident among the middle and youngest generation. However, this was primarily among women, with men tending to adhere to traditional beliefs. While women of the middle generation expressed a belief in shared responsibility for bringing up children, women of the younger generation had built up resentment to men's resistance to more egalitarian relations. Indeed, one young woman, Yau, believed that men always wanted to be better than women, while another, Zarina, thought that men wanted to dominate women in all aspects of life.

Perceived differences between men and women extended beyond role expectations, with the majority attributing different characteristics to each sex. Men were thought to be brave, strong and protective, with one young man, Ang, saying that they were 'faster', 'naughty', and 'well-built'. On the other hand, men considered women to be 'gentle', 'soft', and 'kind'. Moreover, a number of men perceived themselves to be more intelligent than women, although some conceded that women 'have the ability to remember better'. Some male informants were more willing to admit to men's failings. Lim, for example, thought that men were selfish, reckless and anxious to maintain their freedom, whereas women were mature, responsible and loving. Young women tended to be more balanced in their attitudes, with most considering men and women to possess similar abilities and to be 'equally good'. However, they still believed that men and women had different responsibilities in life. As a 20-year-old woman, Rajini, pointed out, men prefer challenging jobs while women are content to control the household (even though men are seen as the head of the family). Both sexes, however, thought there were strong biological differences between men and women that influenced their behaviour and personalities, and only some young women thought socialisation was responsible for gender differentials. While one young man, Ting, thought that gender stereotyping was increasing over time, the majority felt that it was lessening. Women were keen to embrace these changes, with two informants thinking that men and women would have equal status within their lifetime. Men were reluctant to accept change, although many felt that changes were occurring regardless of what they thought.

Socialisation and childhood   Seeds of change seem to be firmly rooted in shifting socialisation patterns and childhood experiences over time. One of the main areas is that of discipline. Half the informants from the younger generation, for example, thought that in the past, children were brought up more strictly. While most saw this increased freedom as beneficial, some considered it detrimental to children's value systems. Aishah, for example, thought that children these days are pampered too much, to the point that they have lost respect for their elders and are disobedient. Nevertheless, it was felt that this more relaxed attitude benefited girls in particular. Formerly girls were rarely given any freedom of movement outside the family home, but now they are allowed similar privileges to boys.

Differential treatment of girls and boys is the other major area of change identified by informants. Both sexes thought that in the past, especially in the days of their grandparents, boys received preferential treatment from parents, not only with respect to freedom, but in terms of educational opportunities. While boys were sent to school and encouraged in their studies, girls were expected to help with housework, with only a few sent to school. Attitudes among the middle and younger generations had changed substantially such that sons and daughters attended school, with girls in particular urged to study hard. One woman, Vasanthi, remembered how throughout her childhood her mother forbade her to do any housework so that she could study, and never took her on holidays to allow maximum study time. Another woman, Rossnita, recounted how her father would throw her school books around if she did not study.

Interestingly, the childhood experiences of men from the younger generation were recounted in less favourable terms. While most women remembered receiving relatively strict, yet supportive, treatment from their parents, men's childhood memories were dominated by tales of punishments experienced at the hands of their parents, particularly fathers. One man, Azaharuddin, recounted how he was tied to a tree by his father when he was naughty, while another, Syed, remembered how his father beat him when he was too lazy to go to school or failed to read the Qur'an. Men were, however, aware that these punishments were in response to the freedom they were allowed. Azaharuddin, for example, pointed out that lack of parental control led him to steal and fight with his friends.

While in the past, therefore, girls and boys were treated differently by parents, more than half the younger generation thought that sons and daughters should be raised in the same way. Among the minority who were in favour of having different upbringings one woman, Fatimah, thought that girls should be taught 'womanly skills'. Another, Mukarah, thought that daughters should receive more attention than sons in order to redress the imbalance of son preference in the past. Overall, however, attitudes towards raising children seem to have become more egalitarian over time. This has benefited women in terms of improving their access to education and allowing them greater freedom, and men by making their childhoods happier by relaxing discipline and punishments.

Parental roles, parenthood and kin relationships Perceptions of motherhood and fatherhood tended to reflect more traditional attitudes than those expressed in relation to socialisation. This was possibly because since none was a parent, their views were shaped by their own mothers and fathers. Descriptions of parents revealed that mothers were generally held in high esteem, often being described as kind, loving and gentle. One young man, Lim, felt such affection for his mother that he said he always liked to see her face. A young woman, Aishah, depicted her mother as kind-hearted and fair-minded, with curly hair, always dressed in a *baju kurung* (a long, loose blouse worn over a sarong)[8] and eating fried mushrooms. Although a number of respondents considered their mothers to be strict, it was mainly fathers who were seen in this light. While fathers were also viewed as caring, they were also commonly seen as busy and fierce. Anwar, for example, described his father as having a huge body, being hot-tempered, eating spicy food and being strict with his children. There was therefore a greater feeling of closeness with mothers.

These patterns were further illustrated when informants discussed motherhood and fatherhood in more general terms. Being a mother was seen as integral to women's identity. Half the respondents noted that women with no children 'will feel sad'. It was also recognised that motherhood brought many responsibilities, with a couple of respondents stating that not having children was not a bad thing because of freedom from many worries. Fatherhood was also seen as important for men, from the point of view of being the head of the family and major decision-maker. Fathers were also seen as the main breadwinners with responsibility for ensuring the families' financial well-being, as well as playing a role in educating children.

While biological parenthood has important symbolic implications for gender identities, other relatives also play a part in bringing up children. Although the majority were raised by both parents, six informants noted how other family members had been involved. One brother and sister reported how they were raised by their mother, sister and teacher, while another grew up with his parents, grandmother and foster family. Interestingly, in three of these six cases brothers rather than sisters were mentioned as assisting with childcare.

Sex and sexuality   Attitudes towards sex and sexuality have changed considerably over the past three generations. Both the older and middle generations of both sexes considered it a taboo subject, which they were unwilling to discuss either in public or in more intimate circles. One response from parents to their daughter, Fatimah's, enquiries about sex was: 'We cannot tell you because you are young ... You must get married first and then we can discuss this.' However, embarrassment had largely disappeared among the young, who were open and frank in their discussions of sex. They attributed this openness to greater maturity among young people, as well as the influence of the West, and the international media. Information about sex and sexuality was rarely supplied by parents, but was gained from books, magazines, television and videos, with some learning from brothers and sisters. Seeking information in this manner was essential as there was no sex education in schools.

Most of the young informants considered sex to be very important, although those who discussed their first sexual experience did not express great enthusiasm. While both a young man, Roslee, and Samundeeswari, a young woman, said that they were nervous, Roslee went on to say that he and his partner had got closer, but that he got bored if he had sex too often. Samundeeswari thought sex was interesting, but preferred to have it when she was not busy. Among those who had no sexual experience, they were still aware of their sexual identity from puberty onwards. While men remembered physical changes in terms of their voices deepening and the growth of body hair, women discussed the arrival of menstruation in psychological terms, with one woman, Vasanthi, describing how she felt more independent and rational, and started paying more attention to how she dressed and projected her personality.

The broad consensus among young people was therefore that sex has changed from a personal to a public issue, which many attributed to the modernisation of the country. They also felt that the older and middle generations were gradually coming to terms with more liberal attitudes, although the process was a slow one. Greater sexual freedom was also felt most acutely by women – as Fatimah pointed out, women are no longer afraid to make the first move, while men continue to act in the same way as before. However, it is interesting that the majority of young informants still considered it 'unnecessary' to have sexual relations before marriage. Moreover, those who were in favour of premarital sex thought it was acceptable only when the couple were in love and had plans to marry. Apparently liberal attitudes were therefore tempered with more con-servative beliefs.

Marriage, family and fertility

Courtship, partnerships and marriage Courtship patterns in Malaysia also appear to be more open than in the past. The major change reported by informants was that today people were able to choose their own partners. While arranged marriages still occur, there is no longer any pressure to enter into them. Only one female informant was planning to marry someone chosen by her parents, and while she accepted it, she also commented that she did not fantasise about her wedding as a result. Freed from parental control in choosing partners, young men and women met boyfriends and girlfriends in different places. Men reported how they met girlfriends at school or university, while women were more likely to meet boyfriends through social activities such as volleyball competitions, or through friends and sisters. Both sexes considered the personalities of partners as being more important than physical appearance, with trust being a crucial issue.

Relationships were generally treated seriously, and often as a precursor to marriage. For example, Loo commented that she was attracted to men who were loving, caring, responsible and willing to take responsibility for her – characteristics of a prospective husband rather than someone with whom she would have a frivolous relationship. The difference between relationships and marriage was seen as legal, identified as the signing of documents and taking of oaths. Moreover, marriage was generally venerated and aspired to, as reflected in the predominance of marriage among informants across the three generations. Only two people from the middle and older generations were not married (one being a widow and the other divorced). However, the young felt that one should establish a career before getting married. Six people, both men and women, from this generation wanted to develop their careers before they considered looking for a partner.

Fertility and childbearing   Fertility rates have declined substantially in Malaysia since the 1970s, with a total fertility rate of 5.5 in 1970, dropping to 3.5 in 1993 (World Bank, 1995: Table 26). Nevertheless, the desire to have offspring was expressed by all but two female informants. One woman, Ros, saw children as important in order to 'ensure the family line', and another, Loo, as a form of 'guaranteeing people's futures'. Children were thus seen as insurance for old age, as well as providing a sense of continuity in people's lives. Among those who did not want children, one woman felt that motherhood was too 'sacred' to enter into, while another saw raising children as too burdensome. Indeed, all inform-ants were aware of the emotional and financial responsibilities involved. Partly for this reason, many wanted to have fewer children than their parents, although the desire to maintain a career (especially among women) also influenced their desire to limit births. Most women and men expressed a desire for two to four children, with only two female respondents wanting to have six. Again, the demands of living in a rapidly developing country were felt by the younger generation and manifested through the recognition of the costs involved in raising children.

Family and community relations   While there was no specific information on the types of households in which the informants resided, most of the younger generation said they came from large (around seven to eight members) or medium-sized (around five to six) families. Nevertheless, a number thought that household size was declining due to rising costs of living.[9] Concepts of the family converged around the notion of a mother, father and their children, acting as a source of love and care. While some saw the family as the smallest social unit in the country, one man, Samy, poetically referred to the family as a book, with each part having its function. Family ties were seen as more enduring than friendship, with one respondent claiming that one could never be sure of a friend's sincerity, yet could always depend on family.

All men and most women admitted to having close family ties involving participation in regular gatherings during festivals, such as Hari Raya Pasua (marking the end of Ramadan) or Chinese New Year. Despite this, a recurrent theme was the danger of familial dissolution. Two main reasons were given, one being a perceived increase in materialism and individualism among parents, related to the rapid economic development of the country and Western influence, which had led to disharmony within families. One man, Roslee, thought that parents nowadays were more interested in making money than in caring for their children, with wives going out to work and both parents being busy all the time. The second main factor was a perceived decline in religious knowledge among parents, leading to a neglect of religious teaching and ultimately to a loss in 'family values'.[10]

Increasing individualism was also mentioned in relation to changes in community life. A common opinion was that of one woman, Rajini, who thought that people's self-interest was leading to a breakdown in community ties, with individuals no longer wanting to know their neighbours or to help out. However, these attitudes were sharply differentiated according to urban and rural residence. There was a broad consensus that 'community spirit' had been kept alive in rural areas or what the Indian informants generally referred to as 'the estates'. In contrast, urban living was seen as unfriendly and even hostile, particularly in the capital, Kuala Lumpur, where people only had time for work and neglected all other forms of social interaction.

Decision-making and domestic labour Although the informants made few comments relating to domestic labour and decision-making within households, there was a general feeling that patterns had become more egalitarian, or at least that the younger generation planned a more equal division of responsibilities. At the same time, perceptions of the division of labour reflected quite a high degree of complementarity over the three generations. From a more 'traditional' perspective, two men and four women felt that household chores and childcare were strictly women's domain. However, around half thought that women were the main decision-makers within the household, with the remainder commenting that decisions were shared. Both sexes thought men should take a more active role in household tasks and management, and both thought that there was some move towards this.

Education and work

Education and work are both crucial in explaining the manifold changes that have occurred in Malaysian society with respect to traditional norms and customs in general, and in gender roles and relations more specifically.

Education Educational attainment has improved dramatically, with women in particular benefiting from increased access to schooling. Among the older generation over one-third had received no formal education, with those who had attended school mainly reaching only primary level. Grandfathers were better educated than grandmothers, with only half of the latter having gone to school (one to an informal religious school or *pondok*). Achievement levels among the middle generation reflected some improvement, although women still lagged behind, with less than half the mothers having attended formal school (two having gone to *pondoks*). It was among the younger generation where most significant advances had been made, with the majority of women and men having a college or university education. Although this is related to the nature of the sample survey (using university students as researchers), it also reflects more general trends in Malaysia, where educational opportunities have opened up dramatically, especially for women. Moreover, striving for a good education is now seen as central to the lives of boys and girls, and is encouraged by parents.

Although men and women from the younger generation reported having equal access to schooling, evidence of strong gender stereotyping emerges with respect to the subjects taken in secondary school. Men tend to prefer science and mathematics, while women are more interested in social sciences and languages (especially Malay and English). However, men are more likely to do a range of subjects from the humanities as well as sciences, whereas women rarely take science subjects. Another gender difference is that boys are more likely to take part in extra-curricular activities, mainly sports, whereas girls have little interest in these. It was generally agreed that girls tend to work harder at school and are more disciplined than boys. Boys receive more frequent punishment, which is usually more severe than that meted out to girls. One woman, Fatimah, remembered how boys would have to stand on their chairs for punishments, whereas girls had only to stand on the floor. Overall, informants considered their school-days as extremely important, and thought that without a sound academic background it was impossible to 'get on' in contemporary Malaysia.

Work and economic livelihood   In the context of rapid industrialisation and upward economic mobility, employment opportunities have increased and diversified significantly. It was generally agreed that jobs in both the private and public sectors are relatively easy to secure (with a good education), and that salaries are competitive. This is just as well since there is a strong stigma attached to being unemployed. Indeed, many stated that it was 'embarrassing' to be out of work and to depend on one's parents. Both men and women considered work as a way to ensure future happiness. One woman, Zarina, stated that by working a person could acquire new knowledge, learn how to communicate, and cease being dependent on others, especially parents. High rates of female labour-force participation are now commonplace, signalling an important change. Most of the young women felt that paid work was important for women to assert their independence from parents and husbands. In contrast to their mothers and grandmothers this group stated a strong preference for entering the labour force as opposed to becoming housewives. Young men tended to be supportive of women working, also representing a shift from the past (when husbands often prohibited women from working). However, their reasons for encouraging women to work were financial – it was a way to help support their families, rather than a way to attain economic autonomy.

Reflecting the importance of the manufacturing sector in Malaysia's economy, half of the informants were currently working, or had previously worked, in factories. For example, five men had jobs in the electronics industry in engineering and technical positions, while three women had worked as production operators on assembly lines of electronics companies. Factory work was considered easy to secure, and was often used as a stepping-stone to other, higher-status, jobs or further education. One woman, Loo, had worked as a production operator in the quality control department of an electronics factory in Singapore, where she received S$180 per month (around US$120), as well as free accommodation and transport. She was able to save enough money to study teacher training at university.[11] The rest of the women tended to be concentrated in clerical and administrative jobs in both private and public sectors, with one working as a teacher, while the remainder of the men were working in sales or teaching. This distribution among the young reflects a high degree of gender stereotyping in that women tend to be clustered in lower-status jobs, receiving less remuneration than men. However, this does not necessarily reflect the educational qualifications of women, which are broadly similar to those of men. Indeed, it is women who feel that a tertiary education gives people a much better chance of obtaining employment, regardless of the type of job. Thus, while at first glance the economic lot of Malaysian women seems to have improved dramatically, they still have a long way to go before reaching parity with men.

Although there was little in-depth comment from informants on how Malaysian women balance their work and domestic responsibilities, it was agreed that working wives and mothers continue to shoulder the bulk of reproductive responsibilities. While the trend among the younger generation is towards a greater commitment to sharing domestic tasks, some female informants reported how women, for example, have to maintain their role as drivers (of cars) for husbands and children, regardless of whether or not they are working. Moreover, one woman, Aishah, said that women who are educated have a particularly hard time as they are expected to liaise with government officials on issues relating to the home, as well as assist husbands with any work problems. In many ways, therefore, women's improved position has actually increased their responsibilities.

Conclusion

Economic change and improvements in social infrastructure in Malaysia, particularly since the 1970s, have had both beneficial and deleterious implications. Many new choices have opened up in education and employment, especially for the Malay population, who have been granted preferential access to opportunities. While these changes have been welcomed, the young are also concerned about the more negative ramifications of progress. The rise of materialism and individualism related to increased wealth of the population have been identified as potentially undermining the family and community cohesion. In this culturally diverse country, Malaysians therefore find themselves caught between modernising influences, and a reluctance to relinquish their cultural identity. Indeed, the Islamic religious revival since the 1970s arguably stands as testimony to these processes (see for example, Nagata, 1995, on the popularity of 'veiling' among professional middle-class women as a way of asserting their cultural identity).

While belief systems and attitudes tend to change more slowly than material circumstances, there is evidence of shifts in constructions of womanhood and manhood across the generations and ethnic divides. Although the older generations continue to adhere to tradition, with men as breadwinners and women as homemakers, there is evidence of a blurring of gender asymmetry among both the middle and younger generations. While most advances have been made among youth, the fact that parents have so willingly embraced the importance of daughters' education, for example, indicates how shifts in the nature of gender relations have been in motion for some time. Indeed, it is important to remember that traditional Malay culture is based on complementarity between the sexes, suggesting that rather than new forms of gender relations emerging with economic development, submerged forms are re-emerging.

It also appears that men have made more rapid gains from wider socio-economic improvements than women. While educational attainment, for example, has increased among both sexes, men have consistently achieved higher levels (although there has been greater parity more recently). Moreover, women are still not incorporated into the labour market on an equal footing with men, and are concentrated in lower-status occupations even when they have similar qualifications. Perhaps for this reason, women of the younger generation expressed feelings of resentment against men. Although some men from the younger generation were conceding to changes in gender roles and relations, the underlying sentiment was one of reluctance to embrace gender equality. Women therefore appear to have been granted many opportunities to improve their position, but have yet to reap full benefits. They have been allowed to break the traditional norms, yet have met opposition when they fundamentally challenge men's expectations. At present, women seem to be blaming this impasse on men's slower acceptance of changing attitudes.

Finally, it is important to emphasise that women's desire for change does not necessarily involve a wholesale acceptance of what might be perceived as 'Western feminist ideals'. Women are also keen to maintain their cultural identity (as Malays, Chinese or Indian). This is reflected in their belief in greater openness about sex and sexuality and their simultaneous wish to confine sexual relations to long-term relationships, as well as in their disapproval of the loss of community spirit in the country, and maintenance of Malay styles of dress.

Recommendations

A number of recommendations can be made, following up suggestions made by interviewees and interviewers. These include:

- The introduction of sex education in secondary schools.
- A family life education programme, aimed at the young, to deal with issues such as sex and sexuality, family planning, safe sex and pregnancy.
- A parent education programme to assist women and men in acquiring parenting skills, with emphasis on sharing responsibilities.
- A community-based gender training programme to raise consciousness about gender roles and relations between men and women, with particular focus on young men.
- A national-level programme to raise awareness among employers about gender stereotyping and discrimination.

Notes

1. Compiled from a report by Professor Fatimah Daud, Department of Anthropology and Sociology, University of Malaya, Kuala Lumpur.
2. Peninsular Malaysia comprises the 11 states of Perlis, Kedah, Penang, Kelantan, Perak, Terengganu, Pahang, Selangor, Negeri Sembilan, Malacca, and Johore (the 13 states also include Sarawak and Sabah, as well as the federal districts of Kuala Lumpur and Labuan Island).
3. In national politics, for example, the Barisan Nasional, the governing co-

alition, is dominated by the United Malays' National Organisation (UMNO) Baru, winning 164 of the 194 seats in the Dewan Rakyat in 1995. The remaining political parties are strongly delineated along ethnic lines – for example, the Malaysian Chinese Association (MCA) and the Malaysia Indian Congress (MIC) (EIU, 1996c: 3).

4. While this proportion might appear small, it compares favourably with the United Kingdom, for example, where women held 7 per cent of parliamentary seats and 9 per cent of ministerial positions in 1994 (UNDP, 1995: A2.4). Furthermore, Wazir Jahan Karim (1995: 45) points out how Malay women (more than Chinese or Indian) have managed to safeguard political representation despite Islamic law. Karim also notes how they have become 'the hands and feet' of the government, campaigning at the grassroots (ibid.).

5. Cecilia Ng (1991), for example, found that agricultural mechanisation in a rice-growing area in Selangor in West Malaysia had undermined women's productive role, leading to a loss of status in the community.

6. While other ethnic and religious groups do not necessarily conform with elements of *adat*, there is some evidence of change in gender relations among the Chinese and Tamil populations. In the former it has been suggested that women are asserting greater economic autonomy through taking over family businesses while men are engaged in newly established high-status professions in computer science. Among the Tamil community there has been a decline in the dowry system, as well as greater acceptance of divorce and condemnation of keeping mistresses (Karim, 1995: 40).

7. Religious schools (*pondok*) are attended by Malay Muslims and focus on teaching the Qur'an. Instruction is in Jawi (the Malay language written in Arabic script), using Kitab Jawi (Jawi books) written by Malay scholars who interpret Islam from a Malay perspective.

8. *Baju kurung* is traditional dress for Muslim Malay women, often worn with a *selendang* (long veil/headscarf) and with roots in *adat* customs rather than in Islam (Karim, 1995: 41).

9. While informants did not refer specifically to household structure, the perceived decline in household size suggests the increased importance of nuclear households in Malaysia (see Karim, 1995: 40). Indeed, in a study of Malay households in various villages in Kelantan, Ingrid Rudie (1995: 241) found a shift from extended households to nuclear structures between 1965 and 1987.

10. This contradicts the views expressed by informants when asked directly about the importance of religion in Malaysian society. Although a few thought modernisation was making people less interested in religion, most thought religions (especially Islam and Buddhism) were being followed more strongly today (see also Nagata, 1995: 104–6 on Islamic revivalist or *dakwah* movements). Moreover, the majority were strong believers and attended a mosque, temple or church on a regular basis (although men were said to attend more frequently). Perhaps informants were expressing their fears, rather than the realities of religious life.

11. This salary was lower than that of another woman, Alison, who also worked in a Malaysian factory in Penang as a production operator. She earned RM18 a day (Malaysian Ringgit) which is equivalent to around US$150 per month, although she did not receive free accommodation.

CHAPTER 5

SOLOMON ISLANDS[1]

While the Solomon Islands remains a largely rural society, urbanisation, coupled with a shift towards a cash economy and the spread of Western influence, have engendered wider changes in belief systems and societal institutions. Many pressures are placed upon people's lifestyles, which are both resisted and embraced by the population. In the opinions of 51 informants, both male and female, there was a general regret at many of the changes, especially in relation to family life. The effects of these changes on gender roles and relations have been ambiguous, and are cross-cut by generation. Broadly speaking, the elderly were the most vocal in their resistance to change. The middle generation perceived themselves to be in a transitional position, both welcoming and challenging the improved status of women in particular. The young were the most keen to stress the benefits of more relaxed social attitudes, as well as improvements in educational and economic opportunities. Overall, however, it is important to emphasise the variations in the relative status of men and women in the Solomon Islands. Partly explained by a range of matrilineal and patrilineal kinship systems, the diversity of experience among informants makes generalisation difficult. However, despite an underlying desire to halt the erosion of traditional culture, it appears that there are moves towards greater gender parity.

Country profile

The Solomon Islands form an archipelago in the South Western Pacific, about 1,920 km north east of Australia and stretching 1,400 km south east from Papua New Guinea across the Coral Sea to Vanuatu. The third largest archipelago in the Southern Pacific, the Solomon Islands covers 25,556 km^2 in terms of land area and 1.35 million km^2 of sea. These comprise six major islands and hundreds of small volcanic and raised atolls, with 347 of a total of 922 being populated.[2] Long settled by Melanesians (with some settlement by Polynesians), the Solomon Islands were given their name by the navigator and nephew of Peru's Spanish viceroy, Alvaro de Mendaña y Neyra, in 1568. Mendaña left Peru in search of the islands, which supposedly appeared in the legends of the Inca king, Tupac Yupanqui. Despite a number of expeditions by Portuguese, British, French and American explorers in the sixteenth and seventeenth centuries, European missionaries and traders did not reach the islands until the nineteenth century. The Northern part of the Islands became a German protectorate in 1885, and the Southern became part of a British protectorate in 1893. Rennel Island and the Santa Cruz Islands were added to the British protectorate in 1898 and 1899. Between 1898 and 1900, Germany ceded most of the Northern Solomons and Ontong Java Islands to the United Kingdom in exchange for freedom to acquire Samoa. Subsequently, the entire archipelago was named the British Solomon Islands Protectorate. The aim of British colonial rule was to maintain order, control tribal warfare and European headhunting (for slaves to work on plantations in Australia and Fiji), and to prevent cannibalism. In 1942, the Japanese invaded the Solomons and caused near total destruction in the former capital, Tulagi, and elsewhere. After US forces reclaimed the Solomons in 1943, the returning British administration chose to establish a new capital at Honiara to take advantage of the infrastructure built by American forces during the Second World War.

The country gained self-government in 1976, and in July 1978 became an independent member of the Commonwealth based on a constitutional monarchy. The national legislature is unicameral, with a 47-member parliament, and an executive comprising a UK-style cabinet chosen from within parliament and headed by a prime minister (currently Solomon Mamaloni). Local government takes the form of eight provincial assemblies, each with its own premier and ministers, and one town council (Honiara Municipal Authority). Governments are elected for four-year terms and the current ruling political party is the Solomon Islands National Unity, Reconciliation and Progressive party (SINURP), with the National Coalition Partners (NCP) in opposition (EIU, 1996d: 32).

The third largest Pacific Island area after Fiji and Papua New Guinea, the Solomon Islands had a population of 285,176 at the last census (1986), with current estimates standing at around 400,000. Indeed, population growth rates are among the highest in the world at 3.4 per cent between 1960 and 1993, with a projected rate of 3.3 per cent between 1993 and 2000 (UNDP, 1996: Table 21). Most people reside in rural areas, with approximately 80 per cent living in villages of under two hundred inhabitants, and only 10 per cent in the capital, Honiara. Urban population growth rates are increasing, however, with rates of 5.4 per cent between 1960 and 1993, and estimates of 6.4 per cent beween 1993 and 2000 (ibid.: Table 20). The majority of islanders are Melanesian (94.2 per cent), with the remainder comprising Polynesians, Micronesians, as well as some Europeans and Asians (Chinese). Although the Pacific region contains only 0.1 per cent of the world's population, between one-quarter and one-third of the world's languages are spoken here, with more than one hundred being spoken in the Solomon Islands alone. Most Solomon Islanders are trilingual, speaking their home area language, the lingua franca, Solomon Islands Pijin, and English (South Pacific Commission, 1994). While over 90 per cent of the population are Christians, the rest are either ancestor worshippers or other non-Christian sects. With most islanders following a so-called 'traditional' way of life, island identities are often stronger than national allegiance. Within this, there is also a broad differentiation within islands between *man blong solwata* (coastal dwellers) and *man blong bus* (people from the interior).

The third most impoverished country included in this volume (after Zimbabwe and Pakistan), the Solomon Islands had a per capita GNP in 1993 of US$740. While GNP per capita annual growth rate between 1965 and 1980 was high at 5.0 per cent, it fell to 2.6 per cent between 1980 and 1993 (UNDP, 1996: Tables 4 and 25). While 75 per cent of the population depend on subsistence agriculture, the country's economy is dominated by commercial agriculture, which makes up almost half the country's exports. While agricultural exports have traditionally focused on copra, palm oil and cocoa, in recent years fishing (mainly tuna) and timber have overtaken these as the main exports (with the latter constituting 80 per cent of all exports) (EIU, 1996d: 33). Unfortunately, the shift towards logging has had little regard for environmental protection. Timber extraction began in 1961, and half of the viable (non-steep-sloped) resource has now been logged. Indeed, timber reserves are likely to be depleted within the next 15 years, with potentially devastating effects on the national income. The ramifications of this are already being felt, with the Australian government withdrawing US$1.5 million per year in aid to the timber sector in 1996 in protest over the government's forestry policy (ibid.: 36). Related to this, the economy receives significant income from foreign aid. While initially the United Kingdom was the major donor, in the last five years Australia and to a lesser extent New Zealand have played more active roles.

In line with relatively low levels of economic development, there is still much progress to be achieved in human development. Although ranked above Zimbabwe and Pakistan, the Solomon Islands lies in 118th place in the UNDP's HDI (UNDP, 1996: Table 1). Although life expectancy at birth is quite high (70.5 years in 1993), adult literacy is only 62 per cent, with an educational enrolment rate of only 46 per cent (ibid.). In terms of gender inequalities, the situation appears to be even worse. While figures for the GDI are not available, comparison between the GEM and the

HDI shows that the Solomon Islands drops 25 places (ibid.: Table 3; see also Chapter 1). It should also be noted that the Solomon Islands has not yet signed the UN Convention on the Elimination of Discrimination Against Women (CEDAW) (UNDP, 1995: 103; see also Chapters 1 and 6). Participation by women in political life is particularly low, with only 2.1 per cent of seats in parliament held by women in 1995 (ibid.), although surprisingly, in 1994, 5 per cent of the executive comprised female ministers (UNDP, 1995: Table A2.4). Despite this, women's economic activity rates are high, with 51 per cent of women aged 15 and over involved in the labour force in 1990 (ibid.: Table A2.3). While there has been a gradual shift towards women's involvement in cash-crop agriculture and the formal sector, their incorporation has been mainly into the lower echelons of the labour market. For example, only 2.6 per cent of women are employed in administrative and managerial posts, compared with almost 40 per cent working in services, and a further 27 per cent in professional, and clerical and sales occupations respectively (ibid.: Table A2.7).

Methodology

The project on which this chapter is based was coordinated by the Commonwealth Youth Programme in the South Pacific in Honiara. Following the methodology employed throughout the volume, in-depth interviews were conducted by eleven Solomon Islanders (six women and five men) who were currently undertaking, or had just completed, their university education (in Australia, New Zealand and Papua New Guinea). A total of 51 informants were included, and interviews were carried out with five people in ten different families, with the female researchers also participating in the focus group discussions. Although two researchers returned to their home provinces to interview their families, the majority interviewed relatives who were currently living in, or passing through, Honiara in January 1996. Therefore, only one or two researchers actually interviewed their siblings, blood parents and grandparents, with most including cousins, uncles and aunts to complete the generational picture.

While the project was generally perceived to be worthwhile by both the researchers and informants alike, a number of problems were encountered. Many of these revolved around the need to contextualise the topics under discussion within the local situation. A major barrier was the translation of 'Western' concepts into Solomon Pijin. Each interviewer had to develop rather particularistic strategies of communication to elicit information – one researcher noted: 'The real nightmare was that I had to keep twisting questions until they understood and answered my questions.' These problems were particularly marked among the elderly

residing in rural areas, who often lacked sufficient education to comprehend the issues under discussion. Beyond communication problems,
issues of sex, childbearing, and womanhood and manhood were difficult
to approach in that custom deems these private matters. Some elderly and
middle-aged informants refused to discuss them. The use of tape-recorders
was often a source of bewilderment among the elderly, often making
them shy or reserved, or as one researcher pointed out: 'The women I
interviewed laughed and giggled most of the time. I think they are
conscious of the recording so they are a bit shy.' Despite these problems,
the researchers found the project very rewarding. In the words of one
young woman, Julie: 'The whole exercise was an eye-opening experience.'

In terms of the characteristics of the informants, the mean age of
women in the eldest generation was 61.5, and that of men 68.[3] Among
the middle generation, men had an average age of 41, and women 40.
The younger generation of both sexes were around 25. The majority of
the eldest and middle generations were formally married, with more than
half living in extended family arrangements. There were marked differences
in educational levels between the generations, with many of the older
informants having no formal schooling at all, or only a few years of
attendance at primary level. Attainment rose among the middle generation,
who were more likely to have attended secondary school, with many of
the younger informants having some form of tertiary-level qualifications
(either completed or in the process). Occupational differences were notable
across the generations, although in general women were more likely to be
involved in the non-money economy than men. Accepting this, the elderly
tended to be engaged in activities requiring no formal qualifications, or
even literacy in many cases, such as farming and fishing in the case of
men, and domestic service for women. Among the middle generation a
higher proportion of informants were employed in formal occupations
such as administrative or secretarial work, teaching, nursing, or the police
force. Many of the younger generation were unemployed or still pursuing
their education in a range of disciplines such as dental therapy, biology,
journalism and psychology.

Before discussing the nature of gender roles and relations in the
Solomon Islands, it is important to point out the main changes that have
occurred in society over the last fifty or so years. As mentioned earlier,
the shift towards a monetised economy, burgeoning urbanisation and
Western influence have been regarded in a largely negative light by informants. As one elderly woman, Rose, put it:

> It has changed so much because of the increase in the influence of Western
> society and the breaking up of community life in the Solomons. That means it

changed politically, economically, and socially and spiritually ... [before] the
society just stays simple. It doesn't change, the only change was [the colonisers]
converting them to Christianity, and a conversion from old hunting days and
tribal wars.

Interestingly, the conversion to Christianity (which was instigated mainly
by the British, both through religion itself and through the provision of
education and health facilities) was generally viewed in a positive light.
Indeed, the church (mainly Anglican and Roman Catholic) remains one of
the most important institutions in society.[4] While many noted the decline
in rates of observance, Christian beliefs still dominate the culture, as one
young man, David, pointed out: 'I think it [religion] is growing. People are
now turning to Christianity and before a lot of people were heathens;
more are being converted.' Rather than Christianity being blamed for the
erosion of tradition, however, most people cited urbanisation, with many
speaking disparagingly about life in Honiara in particular. One elderly
man, Walter, noted:

> When you come to a place like Honiara, your culture breaks down. That is why
> you see people in Honiara getting married in one month and divorcing in the
> next ... it is not real Solomon Island society, having been influenced by Western
> societies.

While the Solomon Islands remains a society bound by traditional *kastom*
(customs) based on tribal groupings, it is also a society in a state of flux.
Social and economic changes have had important ramifications for the
nature of gender roles and relations, as detailed below.

Gender roles and relations

Gender roles and relations are contradictory, characterised by both complementarity and hierarchies. While people are expected to adhere to
traditional stereotypes of the female wife and mother and male breadwinner, informants continually referred to an ideology of sharing between
the sexes. Although there have been some changes in the status of women
over the generations, especially with respect to courtship and sexuality,
many of the youngest generation still hold traditional attitudes towards
women's place in society. These patterns are partly related to variations
within the Solomon Islands where some tribes and islands are based on
matrilineal kinship systems, while others are bilateral or patrilineal.[5] In
relation to intra-national differences in gender roles and relations, Myra,
a middle-aged woman, commented:

> In the Solomons our culture differs in various provinces. For example, in Malaita,

men are treated as superiors and they tend to burden the women with all the family responsibilities. But in the province where I come from, that is the Makira province, women are respected, like, when a woman gives birth, neighbours or people living in nearby houses take care not to make loud noises because the mother needs rest. Also, we have a matrilineal system.

Bearing in mind these variations, certain patterns prevailed across all generations, such as the broad consensus that the differences between men and women were based on biological factors. This was discussed mainly with respect to male strength and female weakness in physical terms. One elderly man, Filipo, noted: 'This is because of the differences in their genetic systems. A woman is slower, more feminine, a man's genes make him stronger and rougher.' Tracy, a middle-aged woman, commented: 'I think it is their anatomy. Yes, especially when it comes to manual things that might require physical strength.' Recourse to biological factors was also made when describing variations in the emotional states of men and women, as Bradley, a young man, noted:

I think biologically they are different altogether, I think their personalities are quite different also. Women tend to be more loving and boys tend to have a 'don't care' attitude. They don't show their emotions.

While biology was taken as the fundamental starting point for gender differences, many informants were keen to point out that upbringing played an important role and that men and women had equal mental capacities. Chris, an elderly man, expressed these sentiments:

Women think differently from men. Also the way males and females are raised is quite different too. But I don't think in terms of intelligence man and woman are different.

It is also important to stress that many men recognised that social attitudes contributed to notions of female inferiority. As Martin, a middle-aged man, opined: 'The only thing that spoiled us males is our mentality that women are lower than us. For instance, I do not see any difference in the performance of male and female doctors.' Overall, informants discussed how men and women excelled in different areas, which were often complementary, as exemplified by Ruth, a middle-aged woman:

Both women and men have the same ability to do things. But I still believe that some jobs are better done by men than women, or vice versa … For instance, with looking after the baby, women do better because they are more attached to the baby than to the man. In the future, I'm sure these differences will decrease as more women take on the roles traditionally played by men.

Ruth's comment was reiterated by others, with men and women of all generations expressing their faith in the fact that inequalities would gradually disappear in the future, or that the process of change had already been set in motion. Margaret, another middle-aged woman, observed that:

> In many areas I think that men are superior to women but I think that women have not had a chance to prove themselves in these fields … these days women are starting to break down these barriers and are going into fields that were once considered for men only.

Socialisation and childhood Variations in patterns of gender roles and relations, and the seeds of change that appear to have already been planted, are reflected in the nature of socialisation patterns in the Solomon Islands. Across the generations, most respondents agreed that girls and boys should be raised in the same manner, although some elderly and middle-aged men emphasised the need to treat sons and daughters differently. Frank, an elderly man, stated: 'The girl must be taught differently from boys when it comes to domestic duties.' A perceived need to ingrain in girls the responsibilities of reproductive labour was reiterated by Collin, from the middle generation:

> Girls need more attention, they need more love, they need guidance, for example, cooking, housekeeping, and sewing to keep them occupied. Boy don't really need that sort of thing; they'll find out as they go along.

Women tended to emphasise the need for girls and boys to share in tasks around the home. Freda, an elderly woman, pointed out: 'Both sides must work. It is wrong to say "girls do the dishes, boys just sit and wait for your food".' Although many agreed with Freda, a number of informants discussed how girls had less freedom beyond the confines of the home. Steve, a middle-aged man, stated:

> I think we all got raised in the same way, me and my three sisters, there was no favouritism. The girls had less freedom maybe in the sense that they couldn't go out like I did in canoes and walk though the plantation or climb the hills. They were sort of kept home with my mother.

Women themselves recalled the restrictions imposed upon them by parents, especially when they wanted to go out in the evenings with their friends. Myra, a middle-aged woman, remembered how her parents forbade her to go to Sisi dances (traditional dances), although she sometimes disobeyed, going to watch rather than participate. Indeed, it was in the area of discipline that informants had the most to discuss in relation to socialisation patterns. Many of the strongest memories among the elderly and middle-aged informants related to the strict rules and punishments enforced by parents. Gillian, from the middle generation, told how: 'There were many rules, and you would get whipped if you broke them. I would wash clothes, clean around the house and cook.' In the light of these memories, many felt that levels of discipline had declined dramatically, with people across all the generations lamenting these relaxations. The older generation in particular felt that children did much less work around the home nowadays. Namoi, an elderly woman, noted:

> In my time we were taught discipline, to respect our parents and all those kinds of things. But these days ... I see young people drinking, smoking, fighting and causing a lot of trouble.

While the youngest generation were less likely to complain about lax standards of discipline, they still worried about the erosion of traditional values among children. One young man, Matthias, discussed this:

> There are girls now that try to act like men. They should be disciplined by their parents. Usually it's the boys that stay up late with their mates, but girls do that now, even to 1 a.m. Girls did not do that sort of thing back then.

There was a broad shift towards more equal treatment of boys and girls both inside and outside the home. A break in the tradition of handing down socialisation practices through the generations was noted: while the elderly tended to follow in their own parents' footsteps, middle-aged informants were more inclined to challenge rules laid down during their own upbringing. One elderly man, Terry, recalled:

> I took my father's teachings and used it on my children. I teach the girls differently, for example, when the boys are sitting in the house they can't go past or lay down in front of them or play. The boys do these things and they can say excuse me before they pass. The girls do the cooking and clean the house. The boys would work outside and cutting trees down and weeding the grass.

Tracy, a middle-aged woman, was determined to instil more egalitarian values into her children:

> I tried not to do the same things my parents did to us. I used to try my best to make the girls and boys do the same work. Now my son is already big, and he can cook as well as do dishes. Above all he sometimes takes care of the girls as well.

Parental roles, parenthood and kin relationships Parenthood in the Solomon Islands was viewed as one of the most important responsibilities of adult life. All the informants, regardless of gender or age, expressed a strong desire to be parents. While the centrality of parenthood was felt by both men and women, motherhood was particularly revered. This was reflected not only in the way in which motherhood was integral to women's identity, but also in the importance mothers played in the lives of men and women. One young man, Simon, remembered how: 'When I got sick she usually helped me and when I needed anything I would run to my mother and ask her. She has really helped me a lot.' At the other end of the generational spectrum, Dorothy, an elderly woman, recounted: 'My mother was a really wonderful person, she was no doubt strict, but she really was very kind to us and brought us up like how we should have been brought up.' Perhaps because mothers were perceived as pivotal during informants' childhood years, many emphasised their desire to reciprocate by caring for their mothers in old age. Jack, an elderly man, stated: 'My mother tells me a lot of things, I obey. When she grew old, I love her. Whatever I have, I give her because she supported me when I was little.'

While fathers also figured strongly in the recollections of informants, their role was more marginal. The emphasis was often on their contributions as breadwinners, disciplinarians and decision-makers within families, or as Namoi, an elderly woman, pointed out: 'They help to build families and give advice to children.' Mary, a middle-aged woman, recalled:

> My mother played a very important role in my life. My father was working and she was running the whole show by herself. When I came home from school she was always there … I do not think I can survive without my mother. I saw my father as a financier.

Despite this distancing, fatherhood was seen as important for men. Collin, a middle-aged man, asserted: 'Being a father is a big thing. You are the key in the home … If you downplay your role, you'll lose your pride.' Some of the youngest generation thought that fathers were increasingly playing more interventionist roles in family life. As Karen pointed out: 'Sometimes they help mothers. They contribute in sharing ideas. They balance the family.' While parenthood was viewed as a great source of satisfaction among both men and women, some also recognised the difficulties of parenting. Joan, from the middle generation, emphasised this:

> Being a parent is the most difficult thing I have ever done in my whole life. It is even more difficult than sitting a university exam. I told my mother if I were to retrace my steps I would never dare. Once you decide to be a parent it is something you die with.

Such was the importance of parenthood among informants, those unable to have children would invariably adopt offspring. Indeed, many reported how they had been raised by adoptive parents. Cecilia, an elderly woman, remembered:

> I was not raised by my real parents. I was raised by my adopted mother. She was a very kind and hardworking person. She died after I started running around, then I went back to my real mother.

Beyond the substitution of blood parents through adoption, other family members were extremely active in helping to raise children, as highlighted by Frank, from the eldest generation:

> I was raised in three different villages ... by my grandmother in Ngamanie, my mother's sister in Otambe and my uncles in Lipe. They all treated me differently. I didn't like how my uncles treated me ... my grandmother and mother's sister took very good care of me.

Across all generations, however, it was grandparents who most commonly assisted in looking after children. One young man, Ted, discussed the role his grandparents played:

> I was raised by my parents, as well as my grandparents from my mother's side. I have been raised with discipline, and I've been fortunate to have such spiritually grounded parents and grandparents.

Sex and sexuality While the subject of sex and sexuality was flagged as an area of *tabu* or *tapu* (equivalent to the English taboo), especially among informants from the older generation, who refused to discuss the issue, a number of people from the middle and younger generations spoke more openly about sexual behaviour. This in itself is indicative of the changes that have occurred in attitudes towards sex and sexuality over time. In the words of one young woman, Sarah:

> Like for now ... and in the past as well, sex is a taboo thing. No-one talks openly about it. It was a 'no-no' in the family and even in conversations. But now, people are starting to be more open about it, and even free to express themselves and their feelings openly.

Despite this, there was general concern over the relaxation in attitudes. In particular, the older and middle generations expressed their misgivings that sexual activity was becoming divorced from love. As Margaret, a middle-aged woman, asserted: 'It comes with love and then it is stronger and more meaningful and it is there forever a bond ... [now] it's com-mercialised. It has lost its meaning.'

Beyond this, the dangers of greater openness towards sexuality revolved around fear of an increase in unplanned pregnancies, as Myra, a middle-aged woman warned: 'A lot of young people nowadays take it as something for pleasure and it has resulted in a lot of unwanted pregnancies.' In addition, the concern over the spread of HIV/AIDS was also cited. As Kori, also from the middle generation, stated:

> I think it is more public now because all of a sudden we are caught in this AIDS thing and people are dishing out condoms ... The village people, they've just jumped from one extreme to another. First it is taboo, then they hear it on the radio and they say you can come and get free condoms and people think you are going to use them.

Premarital sex was generally condemned by the older and middle genera-tions. Rose, an elderly woman, said: 'I don't think it is right because it is against our customs and religious beliefs. Sex before marriage is not applicable but I think it has changed a lot nowadays, probably because of this sort of boy/girlfriend business.' Indeed, religion was continually cited as a reason to limit sexual relations outside marriage, as David, an elderly man, pointed out: 'People should not sleep together before marriage as the Bible does not allow it.' Tracy, from the middle generation, reiterated religious grounds for abstinence, but also highlighted the importance of the 'bride-price' in determining whether or not people were permitted to have sexual relations before marriage:

> It is not a good idea because the doctrines I learn at Church go against this. What people think and do have changed. For instance, when a girl is bought with a bride-price, she is not allowed to sleep with the boy until the ceremony of handing her over to the boy is done.

Indeed, the payment of the bride-price before sexual relations was men-tioned by a number of older and middle-aged informants. Tom, from the older generation, recalled how: 'If you had a friend, according to custom, money would have to be paid "over" the girl, then they would have to be blessed in church, before they could go together.' The importance of bride-price was ingrained in children by their parents – Cecilia, an elderly woman, remembered how her mother had told her not to sleep with a man until he had paid for her.

The custom of the bride-price was much less common among the youngest generation, none of whom cited it as a prerequisite for engaging in premarital sex. However, while they were generally more in favour of sexual relations before marriage, it was condoned only within the context of a stable relationship. One young man, Bradley, noted: 'Sometimes, the girl delivers before marriage, or the marriage happens as soon as the girls gets pregnant. I think it's all right if they keep to themselves and are not promiscuous.' Indeed, promiscuity was condemned by this group, particularly by women. One young woman, Jennifer, considered students to be most culpable:

> Students don't care what they do. The girls here get pregnant but the boys don't care about what they've done ... They should try to control themselves.

Related to the taboo surrounding sex and sexuality in the past was the fact that the elderly had received no sex education. As John, an elderly man, said quite bluntly: 'I learned about it when I was doing agriculture ... through animals' behaviour.' Among the middle generation, informants learned about sex either from books, or from discussions with their peers, although most agreed they did not fully comprehend their sexuality until after marriage. Ruth, a middle-aged woman, noted how:

> I read a book, *What a Young Woman Should Know About Sex.* The book was very explicit, telling all the things about sex. However, the information I gathered from that book didn't help me much, until I got married and experienced it myself.

While sex education is now part of the school curriculum, some of the youngest generation felt there should be more emphasis on values rather than a narrow focus on biology. Karen, a young woman, discussed how her parents outlined the dangers of sexual contact, something not covered in school: 'My parents told me to be aware ... At school they didn't warn you, it was just teaching.' The lack of knowledge about sex and sexuality affected people's first sexual experiences, which were largely viewed in a negative light. This was particularly notable among young women, who often felt their value as prospective marriage partners was undermined as a result. Joy, for example, recounted losing her virginity with much regret:

> My first experience wasn't that great, like everyone painted it to be. It was very painful and uncomfortable. I wasn't married at that time and also it was sad after it finished because I realised that this is it, I've lost my virginity and whoever comes along later ... would find that I'm not worthy. I think I feel that I'm just dirty after that.

While the issue of homosexuality was rarely discussed, it was mentioned by a few men and was viewed with much antipathy. As Richard, an elderly man, pointed out: 'In our custom, men go with women not men ... Homosexuality is seen as a disgrace in the Solomons.' The middle generation also viewed it in a negative light, with one man, Collin, considering homosexuals to be dangerous in that: 'They could mentally disturb whoever they decide to live with.' In contrast, the younger generation were more broad-minded in their views, with Bradley stating that: 'It depends on each individual and what their values are, what they think is right for them ... If they don't disturb me then I think it's up to them.'

Marriage, family and fertility

Courtship　Courtship patterns have undergone quite marked changes from one generation to another. In the past, there were very strict codes of behaviour. This usually involved obtaining parents' permission before making contact, as well as being accompanied by a chaperone once a relationship was formalised. In some instances, formal courtship was allowed only once an engagement had been announced and the bride-price had been paid. Jack, an elderly man, recalled: 'Before, only after money had been passed, to make them "engaged", could they sit openly together, but only in the house of either of the relatives.' Many of the elderly felt that the loss of courtship traditions was detrimental to the moral well-being of the young. Dorothy, an elderly woman, complained:

> I think the old ways were better. You would ask the parents openly, and things were clear. But that was only for talking together ... Now, things aren't straight yet, when they start going together. Then you hear, 'She's three months pregnant already.'

Courtship patterns among the middle and young generations were more relaxed, usually based on mutual attraction and love. Couples often met through school or college, although even then contact was minimal, often involving letter-writing rather than one-to-one contact. Olive, a middle-aged woman, remembered:

> I knew my husband when we were still single at school, but we did not go out. He wrote to me for a relationship while I was at nursing school. At school I had other boyfriends but I did not mean to marry them at all.

Partnerships and marriage　Marriage is one of the most important institutions in the Solomon Islands. Rates of formal marriage, either in church or *kastom* partnerships (traditional ceremonies), are high. However, although marriage remains the bedrock of relationships, there have been changes. Most notably, there has been a shift from arranged marriages on economic grounds among the elderly and some of the middle generation, towards the free choice of marriage partners among the young. Nua, an elderly woman, remembered her arranged marriage:

> My deceased husband's parents came to my parents and asked their permission so that I could marry their son. However, I didn't see their son and we hadn't met before. The boy came to my parents' house three times. On the third time my husband-to-be came with his parents, and later we got married.

Often, however, couples did not know each other before their wedding day, as in the case of Philip, a middle-aged man, whose parents arranged his *kastom* wedding with a woman he had never met. Not only did arranged marriages take place when the couples were very young (they were often no more than 12 or 13 years old),[6] but they were usually viewed as an economic transaction rather than a union of love. Mary, an elderly woman, reminisces:

> Before the boy must come and ask for the girl and put down money in advance. When we get married they pay for us first then prepare the food. When I got married, we went to church first. I wore a white dress, I did not have a veil … I did not wear shoes … I was not excited because he was not the guy that I fell in love with.

Overall, there was broad agreement among the elderly and middle generations that the sanctity of marriage was declining. One elderly woman, Lily, felt this was because the financial pressure of the bride-price had been removed, making people less likely to stay together:

> Some marriages now are not serious. There is no thought of 'this is my woman, and I can't leave her, my money has been spent on her'. Often, they just leave their wife for a younger one, especially the men who marry without bride-price. They don't care, because they have gotten a free wife.

The increasing incidence of marital break-up was widely mentioned. Beyond the decline of the bride-price, urbanisation and the spread of Western culture were cited as major factors in marital dissolution. Jack, an elderly man, talking of Honiara, noted how: 'We are joining other more affluent countries who have high rates of marital separation.' Cecilia, also from the older generation, reiterates this: 'People working in towns see new faces and think "mine is getting old, maybe I should get a new one".' The middle generation shared these views, as John pointed out:

> I think divorce is coming up very strong in urban areas where social life is very strong. For example, anyone of the partners goes to the club and comes back late from doing bad things. Trouble like fighting would happen that would end up in divorce.

Despite the concern over increasing rates of marital separation and divorce among the older and middle generations, the young continue to aspire to marriage. Indeed, all wished to get married at some point. As one young man, Christian, said: 'I'd like to settle down and have kids and raise a family.' Across all generations, marriage was seen as central to the formation of families, and a central force binding people together.

Family formation The importance of family for the functioning of society was continually mentioned by informants. David, an elderly man, said: 'Those people who don't have a family are not always happy. People who have a family are always happy.' Myra, a middle-aged woman, said: 'Family gives a sense of belonging to a group,' and Olive, also from the middle generation, pointed out: 'One's personality is shaped by the kind of family one is brought up in.' Family was also seen as a source of support, especially during times of distress, as Jennifer, a young woman, asserted: 'It is these people that I can always fall back on if anything goes wrong in my life or whenever I need help.'

The interpretation of what family means to people centres around the extended rather than nuclear family. Indeed, a collectivist family culture dominates the country, based on the *wantok* system. Broadly speaking, this refers to people who share the same dialect (and therefore have the same 'one-talk'), although in its strictest sense it is defined by everyone belonging to an extended family. While the *wantok* system was viewed as extremely important, many regretted the decline in extended families. Joan, an elderly woman, stated:

> Family lifestyle in the Solomons is gradually changing. In the past we live in communities and all we owned is for the community or extended family tree. However, this is changing with the introduction of cash economy. Parents tend to care for their own nuclear family and not the extended family.

As well as blaming the introduction of the cash economy on the decline of the extended family, many cited urbanisation and the influence of the West. Namoi, an elderly woman, said:

> Before our old people respect our custom and uphold it very high. But now it is not ... The social issues that are creeping in from the Western world into our Melanesian society have a big impact on the family life style, especially in Honiara.

A shift towards greater individualism was noted by many – as Tony, an elderly man, said: 'More families are becoming individualistic, basically due to jealousy and capitalism.' Linked with these wider structural changes, many identified increased alcohol abuse as contributing to family breakdown. Jack, an elderly man, asserted:

> The family break-up is due to alcohol. Sometimes, when the father gets his pay, he does not think of his family. He gets his friends and they go and spend money on beer. The money which should have been spent on his family.

This was reinforced by Gillian, a middle-aged woman, who stressed the effects of alcohol on children, as well as on parents, whom she considered as increasingly neglectful of their family duties in favour of social activities:

> Family ties and the *wantok* system is still strong but the behaviour of families is not the same. There are problems with children drinking, smoking, fighting and going to clubs with friends ... some children give up school because of these things ... There are parents who are contributing to these problems also, they go drinking and dancing in the clubs and gamble in the casinos and the children are neglected.

Similar patterns were identified with respect to the demise of community ties, also blamed on the influence of the West and individualism. One elderly man, Richard, said:

> Many people are becoming more individualistic. If you ask someone to help you with some work, you have to pay him some money. Also people do not cooperate in doing some community work; there are also many village rows now.

The increase in village disputes was widely mentioned, related mainly to issues of land ownership (with people making claims on communal land), as well as the erosion of traditional networks of reciprocity. As Olive, a middle-aged woman, stated:

> Village life has changed a lot over the years; people are not as friendly and caring to strangers or visitors ... In fact, the last time I was in the village, I was shocked as people were charging anyone who wanted to climb their coconut trees to get a coconut to drink. Also, I noticed that everybody seemed to be in competition with each other about who was wealthier or had the better possessions.

Fertility and childbearing While fertility levels have fallen slightly, from 126 per 1,000 among women aged between 15 and 19 in 1970, to 103 in 1992 (UNDP, 1995: Table A2.5), they remain high. While some informants thought people were having fewer children, others thought they were having more. Collin, a middle-aged man, noted: 'There was a change in the past; there were less children for any couple because workloads were less, but now the family size is increasing because of more workload.' However, people from all generations were brought up in large families. Christian, a young man, was one of nine brothers, while Tracy, a middle-aged woman, was one of six children.

Children and marriage go hand-in-hand in the Solomon Islands. Especially among the older generation, they are seen both as a validation of marriage and proof of money well spent through the bride-price. Dorothy, an elderly woman, discusses this:

When you marry, you mean to have children. In our custom, where they buy women into marriage, women without children feel bad about and sad about not having children. When men marry they expect to have children from their wives, to show they are worth the price they were bought for.

Indeed, among men, in particular, children were the primary reason for marriage, as Harold, an elderly man, said: 'I got married because I wanted children. When my wife got pregnant, I started looking forward to our child's birth so that we can raise them up and when I grow older they would look after me.' The role of children as a source of support in old age was mentioned by the majority of informants. As one elderly woman, Freda, pointed out: 'It's good to have children, because when we get old they are the ones to be looking after us.' Jane, a young woman, said: 'I want to have children so that I can send them to get betel nuts for me. Otherwise I won't have anyone to send around when I get older.'

Such are the pressures to have children that both women and men lose respect in the eyes of their relatives and friends if they do not. Tom, an elderly man, noted: 'They are the saddest people because when they grow older they won't be able to have anybody to take care of them. Villagers also have disregard for such people.' It was frequently pointed out that it was 'embarrassing' for those people unable to bear children. Myra, a middle-aged woman, asserted:

> The nature of women is to bear children and it is one of the most important things in a woman's life. Here in the Solomons to be childless is embarrassing, so it is in our culture to adopt children from relatives.

This was reinforced by Bernard, a middle-aged man:

> It is important that women become mothers as it can be embarrassing if they don't have children. Their blood dries up and they become skinny. Those that are married grow big and so do their husbands.

While the responsibility for childbearing falls heavily on women, there are also pressures on men. Charles, an elderly man, recounted: 'Men who don't have children worry. A man needs children to carry on his line, and replace him.' Another middle-aged man, Philip, said:

> Sometimes it is the men who are infertile. Some men fight about this with their wives. They blame their wives for not bearing them children. As it is an expectation that once they are bought with a bride-price, they must bear children.

The only group to be more circumspect about the importance of offspring were younger women, who considered it a matter of individual choice. They nevertheless emphasised the importance of children for women's identity. Karen, for example, said:

> If they don't have children because they decided not to, then it's up to them ...
> But if they don't have children because they can't bear any or are barren, then
> I feel sorry for them.

As for childbirth itself, this was perceived as a shared experience for
women and men. Men from all generations stressed the importance of
assisting women during pregnancy and childbirth, mostly with household
chores. Richard, an elderly man, remembered how:

> I helped her in and around the house ... I would let her have her rest while I
> attended to the housework. Often I took her to hospital for her check-ups and
> treatments.

The delegation of domestic labour to men was not just confined to periods
when women were pregnant. While many elderly men still said household
chores were women's responsibility, those from the middle and younger
generations were increasingly likely to help out. Brian, a middle-aged man,
stated: 'It's not fair for women to do the job alone. It must be shared
since man and woman when they are married become one.' This was
most notable among the younger informants, who noticed a shift in gender
divisions of labour within the home. As Alison pointed out: 'I think
males are not so dominant now. They also tend to help the women with
the household chores and everything.'

Education and work

Education Primary and pre-primary school education are not yet compulsory, as reflected in low literacy and enrolment rates. This is mainly
because the education system has been in the hands of religious institutions
rather than the state since colonial days. Despite this, there was a broad
consensus that education is important both for the development of the
country and for the pursuit of greater gender equality. Jennifer, a young
woman, said:

> At home, only women are expected to do most of the work. But in schools, the
> rules say that everybody is equal and should do the same thing and should
> work together. Also, at home men have more share at mealtimes than women,
> but at school we share equally.

However, both school enrolment and the equal treatment of boys and
girls in education are recent phenomena. Many of the older generation
had not attended school at all, or often only for a few years at primary
level, as Freda, a grandmother, recalled: 'Schools were quite scarce in
those days and then we had the war so I had no chance to go to school.'

Freda also pointed out how she learned all she needed to know from her mother and aunts in terms of housekeeping. There was also a strong gender bias in school attendance during the 'olden days', with parents often preferring to send their sons rather than daughters to school. The experience of one elderly woman, Nua, illustrates this. Although she attended school until she was a teenager, she remembered: 'Mum and dad used to think that only boys should be the ones to be educated and not the girls because girls can't make it anywhere.' In some instances, parents saw female education as empowering girls to break accepted codes of morality. This is reflected in the comment of one elderly woman, Ruth, on the dangers of literacy: 'Only men were looked upon to be educated, fearing that girls go to school and when they learn to read and write they start writing letters to their boyfriends.' Even among the men schooling was seen as a chore, and, interestingly, as an imposition of the colonial regime. Filipo, an elderly man, maintained that: 'In those days all the children in the village had to go to school because the colonial masters wanted them to and parents felt that I too must go to school.' Enrolment was more broad-based among the middle generation, with increasing numbers proceeding to secondary school. However, not until the last 20 years or so has education beyond secondary level been accepted or expected by Solomon Island society. However, fewer women than men stay on in the education system, with financial constraints meaning that boys' education is still perceived to be better value than girls'.

Across all the generations, people spoke of their attendance at mission schools, which were predominantly Roman Catholic, Anglican or Evangelical. Many remembered foreign teachers; Simon, a young man, recalled how:

> In primary school [the teachers] were locals. For my first three years we were taught by sisters [nuns]. In secondary school, I was taught by teachers from all over the world. Both Solomon Islanders, and Australian, American and other nationalities. We were also taught mainly by brothers and fathers [monks and priests].

Education has also changed. The elderly spoke of learning basic arithmetic and literacy (in English), with science for the boys and home economics for the girls. One elderly woman recalls the gender-typing of subjects, but also stresses their importance: 'Home economics moulded my life to be what I am today. I can sew, I can cook, I know how to make sure the house is clean.' Among the middle and younger generations, there was less gender differentiation, as John, a middle-aged man, remembered: 'We all did everything. The girls learnt woodwork with the boys.' Teaching methods were dominated by rote learning among all informants, with one young man, Christian, stating how he was taught 'mostly [by teachers] speaking and writing on the blackboard and we take down notes'.

It was in the arena of discipline that informants had the most vivid memories. Everyone spoke of strict rules, which, if broken, were punished by various methods. One elderly woman, Namoi, remembered how, 'We were punished by being made to stand on one leg, or write a sentence a hundred times,' while an elderly man recalled how he was made to go for one day without food for missing a church service. The most common punishments, however, were weeding or brushing the school grounds, as one middle-aged woman, Gillian, noted: 'We had to carry stones and pull the sensitive *nila* grass [mimosa] out from the gardens or footpaths as punishment for misbehaving.'

Although education has expanded, especially for women, only a minority today go to university. This is primarily because of the lack of tertiary institutions in the country, in that there is only one Institute of Higher Education (SIHE), and an extension unit of the University of the South Pacific (USP). As a result, higher education can often be obtained only by going overseas (usually to Australia, New Zealand or Papua New Guinea), and at a high financial cost. However, another barrier is the paucity of employment opportunities for the educated population.

Work and economic livelihood While there has been some change in employment opportunities in the Solomon Islands, the country remains an agricultural society, with many making a living from subsistence farming. However, the majority of informants were employed in a range of jobs, from farming and fishing to administrative positions and medicine. Gender-typing still characterises employment, with fewer opportunities open to women than men of all age groups, and with women more likely to be working in the non-money economy.

While many of the elderly today are dependent on their children for their livelihood, they were also the most constrained by the lack of employment opportunities. Elderly women, in particular, had problems finding paid work, with domestic service often the only option. Dorothy, for example, noted: 'After leaving school and getting married, the only work was being a housewife. Occasionally I would be required to baby-sit for some Europeans in town [Honiara].' Many felt this was due to their lack of education, as Lily pointed out: 'If I want to work I work as a housegirl. I think to myself, if I had gone to school I would have been able to get a good job.' Elderly men, on the other hand, worked in a variety of jobs in farming and fishing, with some employed as doctors, ministers, teachers, policemen, or shop assistants.

While higher levels of educational attainment among the middle generation ensured greater diversity of occupations, many still noted the difficulties in securing jobs. One middle-aged man, Tony, a former government clerk, discussed how:

> When I left school there were many jobs available in the government, office work ... now I find it very difficult; work is not readily available ... If you do not hit a certain category then you'll miss out, whether it is for form six or five level or for specific jobs. How I see it now is that some job areas are already saturated.

Women from the middle generation also expressed their concern over securing employment. Again, the only available jobs were in feminised public service positions such as nursing or low-level secretarial positions. However, at least this was seen to represent an improvement in that these occupations were in the formal sector and required relatively high levels of schooling. This generation also noted that the future for women was considerably brighter. As Sarah pointed out:

> At the time if I had left school teaching and nursing would have been available to me as a female. But now there is hotel catering and other male orienting [sic] things like doctors ... Before the economy was narrow, it was based on an agricultural baseline.

Unfortunately, this view was not reinforced by young women themselves, as Janine, a young woman, pointed out: 'I think students find it very hard these days to get a job after leaving school. A lot of them are *master lius* (jobless and street rovers) in town.' Indeed, the lack of opportunities was also felt by young men such as Christian, who complained: 'When I left school the most available work was manual work; jobs like construction, or labourer in a cocoa shed.' Young people were concerned about their future, and many felt it was not worth investing in their education if they could not secure work.

Although employment was obviously important in underpinning the material survival of many informants, it did not hold a central position in the formation of their identities, whether male or female. Both viewed work as an economic necessity, although one middle-aged man, Martin, who was unemployed, said: 'When I had a job I felt happy that I could clothe myself and my children.' Among women, the financial element was also stressed, as Vera, a middle-aged woman, noted: 'I think it is good because we will both help our family, especially on the financial side.' Few women reported any resistance from partners, although the majority mentioned that their economic autonomy had little bearing on the amount of reproductive labour they carried out in the home. As Margaret, from the middle generation, stated: 'My husband does not mind me working.

But even if I have a job, I still do most of the housework like washing and cooking.'

Conclusion

The Solomon Islands are currently undergoing an uneasy transition towards a more urbanised and monetised society. This has been greeted with dismay by many islanders, who are nostalgic for the past and opposed to the erosion of tradition. Resistance to these transformations, especially the demise of the extended family, the weakening of community ties and the increase in marital dissolution, was voiced across all generations. Indeed, it was significant that everyone, regardless of generation or age, continued to define themselves in terms of their families (through their kin ties or children), rather than through their achievements in the so-called 'public sphere'. Nevertheless, there was a general welcoming of other changes that were perceived to benefit women, especially the enhanced educational and economic opportunities. Furthermore, although gender inequalities have been prevalent throughout the Solomon Islands in the twentieth century, there was also evidence among some of the elderly of a desire to accommodate greater parity. With some of the more blatant gender disparities on the decline, especially arranged marriages and the bride-price, it appears that there is considerable scope for improvements to be made.

Recommendations

The informants suggested a number of policy recommendations. The most common ones revolved around suggestions on how to maintain traditional customs, especially conserving the extended family. One elderly woman, Dorothy, said:

> We would be looking at a big education programme to be carried out among our own homes. Then if our own homes are taught to respect our custom and culture it will carry them all throughout their life.

With such considerations in mind, specific recommendations could encompass:

- A wide-ranging community education programme to celebrate Solomon Islands culture, with particular emphasis on urban areas.
- A community-based gender training programme focusing on consciousness-raising activities, to include information on sharing responsibilities within the home.

- A community-based programme on the dangers of alcohol abuse among adolescents.
- Educational training programmes to encourage the development of transferable skills among the educated youth.

Notes

1. Compiled from transcripts prepared by Susan Hewlett, programme officer of the Commonwealth Youth Programme, South Pacific Regional Centre, Honiara.

2. These include Malaita (the most heavily populated), Guadalcanal, Isabel, Choiseul, Makira and New Georgia.

3. Many people in the Solomon Islands, particularly among the older and middle generations, do not know precisely when they were born. Instead, they often relate their age as being before or after a certain event in the community.

4. Around 34 per cent of Christians in the Solomon Islands are Anglican, belonging to the Church of Melanesia (COM), while around 19 per cent practise the Roman Catholic faith. A further 18 per cent belong to the South Seas Evangelical Church, with 11 per cent belonging to the United Church (Methodist), and 10 per cent to the Seventh Day Adventists.

5. In the past, matrilineal kinship systems were prevalent in parts of Guadalcanal Province, Savo (in Central Province), Vella Lavella (in Western Province), and parts of Makira, where political power and control over customary land lay in the hands of female clan leaders. Women still maintain considerable power in these areas.

6. This is considerably lower than official estimates, which put women's average age at marriage at 22.3 in 1970, with a decline to 21.2 in 1990 (UNDP, 1995: Table A2.5).

CHAPTER 6

PAKISTAN[1]

Pakistan is the only country in this volume that has had a female political leader (former Prime Minister Benazir Bhutto). However, along with the Solomon Islands (see Chapter 5), it is also one of 41 nations that has not yet signed the United Nations Convention on the Elimination of All Forms of Discrimination Against Women (CEDAW) (UNDP, 1995: 43). These apparent contradictions undoubtedly result in part from the country's Islamic inheritance. Although women's rights are acknowledged in some aspects of Muslim religion and culture, these exist alongside 'models of hierarchical relationships and sexual inequality' (Mernissi, 1996: 14; see also Ingrams, 1983; El Saadawi, 1980). Indeed, it is 'commonly held that women's legal status and social position is often worse in Muslim countries than anywhere else' (Beall, 1997: Chapter 1). Having said this, Islam is arguably no more discriminatory than other monotheistic religions such as Judaism and Christianity. Moreover, despite the embeddedness of Islam within Pakistan's strong cultural nationalism, this is not the only factor responsible for women's disadvantage in the country (ibid.; also Mernissi, 1996). In the opinion of Benazir Bhutto (1995: 112), it is more likely that the 'backwardness of women is rooted in male prejudice and non-religious cultural taboos'.

While the term 'backwardness' never featured in the accounts of male or female respondents, nor is it one we ourselves would use, one of the most striking aspects of the Pakistan study compared with the other countries in the book is the limited evidence of positive change in gender roles and relations during this century. In fact, more generally, it has been argued that the position of women has deteriorated as gender relations have been harnessed to the post-colonial project of Islamisation, particularly from the 1980s onwards (see page 113). Although improvements have occurred in some elements of men's and women's lives over three generations, notably in literacy and educational attainment, they are regionally uneven and differ across class/income groups. Moreover, in beliefs, attitudes and socio-cultural practices, particularly those pertaining to gender, people seem to have adhered closely to the customs of their forebears. In this way, the voices of people in the different generational groups appear to echo, even celebrate, the past, rather than sound a rallying cry for future transformation. One possible reason is that Pakistan is still struggling to create national stability in the wake of its inheritance of profoundly divisive legacies from colonial rule and the early post-colonial era.

Country profile

The Islamic Republic of Pakistan is a relatively young country, created in 1947 and referred to by its present name only since 1971.[2] Occupying an area of 803,940 km[2] in the lands around the Indus river basin, the nation came into being in the wake of independence from Britain, and the partition of India. The state initially established as Pakistan represented an attempt to grant sovereignty to the Muslim majority areas of the sub-continent. Today 95 per cent of Pakistan's approximately 130 million inhabitants are Muslims.[3] Yet despite shared religious belief among the majority of its citizens, Pakistan is by no means a unified society.

Administratively Pakistan comprises four provinces – the Punjab, Sindh, Baluchistan, and North-West Frontier provinces, each of which is inhabited by different ethnic groups (the Punjabis, Sindhis, Baluchis and Pathans respectively). These are interspersed with peoples such as the Muhajirs, who migrated from India in 1947,[4] and numerous other caste-like and tribal factions. Each province has its own government and is relatively autonomous within a federated parliamentary system. Yet during the 1970s, for example, the struggle for independence from Pakistan by Baluchi separatists was met by fierce repression by then prime minister Zulfikar Ali Bhutto (Bradnock, 1992: 67), and divergent regional and cultural interests continue to be accompanied by power struggles between a variety of groups – the military and civilians, feudal landlords and technocrats, rich and poor, and a wide array of political parties.[5] These heterogeneities, alongside a weak democratic culture that has remained hostage to security considerations, have undoubtedly contributed to Pakistan's considerable political turbulence and numerous changes of government over the last 50 years.[6]

The president of Pakistan (currently Farooq Leghari of the Pakistan People's Party) is elected for five years by a joint sitting of the federal legislature. The latter is bicameral, with the lower house (the National Assembly) having 217 directly elected members who serve for five years, and the upper house (the Senate) having 87 members elected for six years, of which one-third retire every two years. Each of the four provinces elects 19 senators, with the remaining eleven elected from the Federal Capital Territory and the tribal areas (EIU, 1996e: 5).

Despite a mammoth drive to industrialise during the 1960s, largely with aid from the USA and Arab states, Pakistan still has to import most of its industrial machinery and manufactured goods, and remains a predominantly rural country. Its main exports are cotton yarn, raw cotton and textiles, which collectively generate nearly two-thirds of annual export income (EIU, 1996e: 17). Pakistan is self-sufficient in wheat, the national staple (Bradnock, 1992: 58). Only one-third of the population reside in urban areas (UNDP, 1995: Table 15). The annual rate of increase of the urban population is only 1.7 per cent, with most of the growth confined to the four major cities of Islamabad (the capital as from 1959), Lahore, Faisalabad and Karachi, the latter being the former capital and largest city, containing one-fifth of the urban population.

Pakistan's failure to industrialise is partly caused by power scarcity. While recent years have seen the construction of new thermal power plants, which have boosted the country's generating capacity by about 30 per cent, these run on costly imported oil. The fact that expenditure on oil looks set to double (to about US$4 billion) over the next three years (EIU, 1997: 17) will add strain to a deteriorating economic situation, part of which stems from the repatriation of Pakistani labour migrants from the Middle East after the Gulf War, and to the concomitant decline in overseas remittances. Indeed, although Pakistan's external debt is still relatively modest (US$32.3 billion in 1995 – EIU, 1996e: 6), the country found itself on the brink of a major repayment crisis in 1996, from which rescue was possible only by further borrowing (EIU, 1997: 13). Moreover, while growth in GNP per capita managed to hover at an annual mean of 3.1 per cent between 1980 and 1992, by this latter year, Pakistan had an average per capita GNP of only $US420, making it, in income terms, the poorest country in this book (UNDP, 1995: Table 20).

Income poverty is one factor contributing to Pakistan's classification by the UNDP as a country marked by 'low human development'. In 1992 it numbered 128 out of 174 nations on the HDI, with a score of only 0.483 (UNDP, 1995: Table 1). Contributing to Pakistan's low HDI position is limited achievement in social indicators such as education and health. In 1992, for example, only 36 per cent of the population could read and write (UNDP, 1995: Table 4), and among women, the proportion was a mere 22.3 per cent (only 67 women are literate for every 100 men) (ibid.: Table A2.1). These low levels of educational attainment undoubtedly reflect the fact that only a very small proportion of GNP is allotted to education (3.4 per cent) (Beall, 1997: Chapter 1). With the amount devoted to health expenditure being lower still (1.8 per cent of GNP), it is hardly surprising that life expectancy is shorter than in many other countries (61.5 years in 1992) (UNDP, 1995: Table 4). Although this represents quite a marked increase from 1960 (when it was 43.1), certain groups of people, such as poor women, continue to suffer excessive risks of premature death. For example, the maternal mortality rate per 100,000 live births between 1980 and 1992 was as high as 500 (UNDP, 1995: Table 7).[7] This contributes to the fact that although female life expectancy is often five to six years greater than men's, in Pakistan the gap is minimal (twelve months), with women having an average life expectancy of 62.5 years (ibid.: Table A2.2). These indicators provide important explanations for Pakistan's unusually high masculine sex ratio (1,078 men per 1,000 women according to 1981–82 figures). Given that, all things being equal, women have a biological advantage over men reflected in lower rates of mortality as infants and longer life expectancy, sex ratios in most parts of the world are feminine (see Harriss and Watson, 1987: 86, Table 5). The excess of males over females in Pakistan is explained as a socially induced process, reflecting, *inter alia*, less attention to the nutrition and health care needs of females (ibid.; see also Moghadam, 1996: 19; Smyke, 1991). More disturbing still, perhaps, is not only that the sex ratio in Pakistan is the most masculine in the whole of South Asia (which has the highest regional average in the world at 1,075 men per 1,000 women), but that between the mid-1960s and the mid-1980s, the gap between males and females in the population grew even wider (see Beall, 1997: Chapter 1).

The existence of such gender disparities makes it no surprise that Pakistan also ranks low on the UNDP's GDI. That Pakistan holds 103rd place out of 130 countries on this index means that it performs even less well on grounds of gender than it does in its overall achievements in human development (see UNDP, 1995: 74 ff.). An even bleaker scenario arises when considering the GEM, on which Pakistan ranks lower still, being third from bottom out of 116 countries (see UNDP, 1995: Table 3.5).

Embodied in these latter indices are women's employment, income and political participation, from which it is relatively easy to see why Pakistan scores poorly. For example, while in 1992 18.4 per cent of professional and technical workers were women, they formed only 2.9 per cent of administrators and managers (UNDP, 1995: Table 3.5), and women's share of earned income was only 10.2 per cent (UNDP, 1995: Table 3.5). Coupled with this, in 1994, only 14 per cent of women aged 15 or more were reported as economically active (UNDP, 1995: Table A2.3), such that they represented a mere 13 per cent of the national labour force (ibid.: Table 11). However, a number of studies have noted that women's involvement in income-generating activities is grossly under-reported, especially if home-based work is taken into account (see Beall, 1997). As for politics, despite the prominent profile of figures such as Benazir Bhutto,[8] women held only 2 per cent of parliamentary seats in 1994, and a mere 4 per cent of ministerial posts (UNDP, 1995: Table A2.4). An unprecedented number of women (55 in total) nevertheless contested seats for the elections for the National Assembly and four provincial legislatures in February 1997.[9]

In many respects the gender disparities described above indicate that although women were technically guaranteed fundamental rights and protection in the Constitution of 1973 (Bhutto, 1995), this has remained a rhetorical slogan rather than a practical reality. Although women stood to benefit from a more progressive state attitude to gender equality in the 1970s, their fledgling gains were largely eroded in the 1980s by renewed emphasis on female moral purity under the 'Islamisation' project of General Zia (Beall, 1997: Chapter 1). Indeed, a report commissioned by Zia in 1985 on the status of Pakistani women concluded that: 'The average woman is born into near slavery, leads a life of drudgery, and dies invariably in oblivion. This grim condition is the stark reality of half our population simply because they happen to be women' (cited in Moghadam, 1996: 20). That the report was suppressed is not surprising, since, as Valentine Moghadam (1996: 120) argues:

> It suggested the links among the treatment of women within the home, the legal status of women and the implications of Islamisation, the enforcement of universal education and the availability and quality of schooling for girls, and the willingness or lack thereof on the part of the state and the propertied class to develop the economy and modernise society.

The following sections explore how relevant these observations are to the lives, beliefs and socio-economic prospects of the survey participants.

Methodology

The survey was organised by a research consultancy firm between May and September 1995, and deployed ten male and ten female students from the University of the Punjab as interviewers. The students were mainly from the Social Work Department and came from both rural and urban areas, although three-quarters of them had been educated in towns and cities compared with only 15 per cent of their grandparents. Designated as the 'focus group', the 20 student participants were first interviewed by the project director from the consultancy firm, who introduced them to the aims of the study and gave training in basic interview techniques. In line with the methodology adopted by other countries in the volume, the students interviewed their parents and grandparents using a semi-structured interview guide. Given that four of the respondents were related to one another and had various kin in common, the total number of interviewees in the older age groups amounted to only 56. Conducted in Urdu, the interviews produced qualitative data that were analysed in aggregate by the consultancy firm and condensed and translated into English for the final report. Although such a small and localised sample cannot convey the wide-ranging ethnic and regional diversity of Pakistan, the Punjab (along with Sindh) is Pakistan's most populous province (containing between them around 80 per cent of the national population) (Bradnock, 1992: 67). In this way the research at least draws from an area with a substantial proportion of Pakistan's inhabitants.

Gender roles and relations

In general terms, differences in the lives and experiences of men and women are marked. For example, women's primary allegiance is to the home, and where employment threatens to undermine their childcare and household duties, it is generally disapproved of, especially among middle-income groups. Men do little domestic work but are expected to be the sole, if not primary, breadwinners in their households (Beall, 1997: Chapter 1). These divisions are firmly etched in the minds of the survey respondents. One of the middle-aged men, Rana, declared: 'Women bear children and bring them up while man is the economic source for women,'[10] and one of his female peers, Mishbah, said: 'Woman is queen of the house, and man is the king of the outside world.'

The assignation of men and women to different arenas of work is regarded as a major justification for men's dominance and authority within the household. Asif, a grandfather, maintained:

Family is for identity, and it has been written in the Qur'an. Man and woman are two wheels of a vehicle on which life's cart goes by, but males have got dominance because of their breadwinning role.

Men play such an important role in household decision-making that even when they migrate and leave women behind as *de facto* household heads, the latter still have to refer to their husbands before taking major decisions on production or expenditure (see Parnwell, 1993: 107; Rahat, 1986).

Gender differences in Pakistan are further reinforced by the institution of *purdah* or 'seclusion'. *Purdah* refers to segregation of men and women, but has come to symbolise a series of interrelated spatial, physical and social limitations on women that minimise their contact with men outside their immediate families and kin groups. This includes modesty in dress (veiling and so on), and may extend to separate living quarters for women, restrictions on their social interaction, and constraints upon their employment (Beall, 1997: Chapter 1). Principles of *purdah* are applied most rigidly to younger women, whose sexuality as single or young married females is deemed to require greater surveillance. This is one reason why economic activity rates are often skewed towards older women, with the latter frequently working as long as they can in order that their unmarried daughters, daughters-in-law and granddaughters do not need to seek employment outside the *basti* (settlement/neighbourhood) (Beall, 1996: 443).

Although seclusion tends to be more strictly observed among middle-than low-income groups, and some women do have a degree of freedom to interact at the neighbourhood (*mohalla*) level where they are known and familiar, the street and the marketplace (*bazar*) are places where men spend a considerable amount of their time in work and in social interaction. Where women enter these spaces, they are effectively made invisible by the veil (Beall, 1997; Chapter 1). Even at the neighbourhood level, women's use of open space is often restricted to courtyards sealed physically from public view, and symbolically from extra-familial social contact. In addition, male visitors to houses usually have to enter a men-only reception room (*bahtak*) (ibid.).

While gender divisions of labour, decision-making and spatial mobility are not always accompanied by inequality, in Pakistan gender has important impacts on the health and longevity of women, as noted earlier. These patterns were noted by the respondents in the survey. When people talked of illness, for example, and how health risks had increased with 'modern' gadgets such as air-conditioning systems, it was repeatedly mentioned that women's levels of well-being were lower than men's. One of the grand-mothers, Shamim, reported: 'People get ill accidentally, but sometimes due to negligence in getting treatment in time. Most people are ill, especially women.' Inadequate treatment of women's (and some children's) medical conditions was in part attributed to the fact that women did not have access to doctors (or more specifically, to 'lady doctors'), so went to 'quacks' instead. Beyond this, psychological problems were mentioned as being more likely to afflict women. As Sajjad, one of the males in the youngest generation, said:

> I think psychological problems and emotional deprivation should be matters for public discussion. People who get mentally disturbed fall ill. Women have got more health problems and they are different too, but nobody tries to understand their problems. Women have got more psychological needs.

Some went further to identify the really crucial factor affecting gender-differentiated morbidity and access to medical care as the undervaluation of women. For example, 20-year-old Rubina stated:

I don't think people are generally healthy in Pakistan. Health means you are capable of doing physical and mental work, but people here don't have sense how to be physically, mentally fit. Education counts a lot. Women are much more ignorant of their health. They accept the role of second citizen and take more care of their brothers and sons and ignore their own health.

Underlying these patterns, which are conceivably exacerbated by poor investment in health and education, are hierarchical notions of masculinity and femininity, with several eldest-generation males, in particular, believing that 'God has given an edge to men over women.' Men's advantage was usually linked explicitly with their physiology, which was felt to be accompanied by a range of superior psychological traits. Asif, one of the grandfathers, opined:

Difference is physiological, because in man there is sperm, while in women there are ova. The sperm is restless while ova are not that lively. However, women are careful, cunning and capable of quick learning.

Although one of the fathers, Zahid, also felt that women potentially had the same mental capacity as men, his opinion was broadly similar:

Men have got two halves and women have got one half of power. Women get irritated quickly and are less courageous.

Ideas about the 'natural' superiority of men were shared by a substantial number of female respondents, indicating a potent internalisation of gender stereotypes. Fehmida, a grandmother, noted that between men and women:

There is a hell of a difference in thought and practice and this will go on forever. Since God made men superior, important decisions to do with courage are always made by men ... This difference goes back to the beginning of time.

This was endorsed by Zareena, another grandmother:

Hell of a difference ... Man is man, woman is woman. Man is sturdy and better than woman. There is difference in learning and thinking. A woman is only for the household.

The notion that women are ill-equipped for more than motherhood and domesticity was a common justification for their exclusion from politics, and intermeshes with aspects of *purdah* discussed earlier. One of the grandfathers, Iftikhar, observed:

Politics is a man's job only. When women do politics they have to interact with men, which I don't think is good ... If man is fire, woman is *moam* [wax], so women melt in front of him. Hence they are unsuitable for politics.

This was echoed by another grandfather, Ishan:

> This is man's job only, if women take part in it, it is devastation all over. Women's involvement is illiterate, having little brainpower ... As the proverb goes, 'Man is wiser than woman and hence is better in charge of political affairs'.

Even the youngest generation of males felt similarly, as summed up by 22-year-old Hajji:

> I think both sexes should come into politics, provided the individual concerned has leadership qualities. But it is not fair that women be given the status of head of state straight away. Women are emotionally weak. While a man should also have qualities, however ... it has to be recognised that women use their brains less than their emotions. Even if a woman is intelligent, you can't give her too much power, since she won't make the correct decision.

Some women, such as Zahida from the youngest generation, agreed, feeling that unless women had exceptional abilities they should confine themselves to domestic and mothering activities:

> I personally dislike women's participation in politics because women's basic role is in the home, and it is told by religion that women should restrict themselves to the house.

Even women who resisted the construction of women as incapable of rising to the challenges of public life and making their own decisions often had recourse to gendered attributes in validating their opinions. One of the grandmothers, Sardar, declared:

> Politics is both men's and women's job. If a woman is given the chance, she is patient and far-sighted. Whereas men tend to be *joshelay* [excitable/ambitious].

Yet although 48 per cent of respondents in the survey as a whole regarded gender differences as 'natural', 50 per cent felt that upbringing was critical. Among the many women who felt that women's exclusion from public life was a result of gender-differentiated socialisation and marginalisation was Rukshanda, from the middle generation:

> The difference is physiological, but not psychological or of personality. God has made them equal even if people call men wiser. These days a woman can work as much as a man can.

Resentment about the ways in which custom and socialisation had contributed to women's secondary status was also voiced by elderly women. Kharshid, a grandmother, observed:

Inequality goes back a long way and who knows when it will end. Men consider women *joti* [footwear], and force them to obey all customs. Men take pleasure in doing sports, while women are forced to do household work.

Another grandmother, Kashash, was even more forthright: 'Girls are subjugated. As a reaction they strive for equal status and this is a positive thing in my view.' Such views are shared by the youngest generation of women, such as Zahida, who felt that women should be given as much opportunity as men in political careers: 'For politics, brainpower is required, and this is available to both genders.'

Socialisation and childhood The report concluded that male dominance in Pakistani society not only reflected gendered socialisation, but perpetuated itself through gender discrimination in the upbringing of children. Prescriptions for raising male and female offspring have retained a remarkable consistency over time and are often stated very explicitly. One father, Noor, declared: 'No equal chances should be given to each sex,' and one of his peers, Fazal, acknowledged: 'This is the new age. Now, more care and attention are given to children, although boys remain preferred in everything.'

Sajjad, a young man in his twenties who is still single and not yet a father, sees no reason to challenge these norms. In fact, he has already decided that when he has his own family, his daughters will be better off if he upholds tradition: 'I will discriminate in how my sons and daughters get brought up, because this is a sure way that girls don't get complexes.'

While similar views were stated by several male respondents, women felt much less comfortable about delineating between boys and girls. Yet recognising that the chances of overturning these customs were remote, it is no surprise that many women expressed the wish that they had been born male. One of the grandmothers, Kashash, who had grown up with her maternal grandmother and uncle during a period when her parents were abroad, said:

I never had communication with my father ... I was brought up in a such a strict home environment that they even thought it was bad for me to have an education. My brother ... had freedom while I had to do all the household chores ... It would have been better for me if I'd been a boy.

These kinds of differences persist today, with Hina, one of the young female respondents, declaring:

God has given an edge to man in protecting the woman and bearing her expenses. Although women are more sensitive, they are capable of learning similar things to men. But ... from a very early age, girls are neglected. For example, they do not get as many toys as their brothers. These experiences make it difficult for them to perform as well as boys.

Being a male child brings other pressures, and this is particularly noted by the youngest generation of women. Shazia, in her early twenties, conceded: 'In my opinion I'm OK with my girl status because boys are more tense. They have to do a lot to compete.' For all children, regardless of gender and generation, however, obedience to parents and other figures of authority during their childhood was regarded as an essential component of good behaviour. As one young man, Gulbaz, declared:

> Like parents, teachers try to see all their students as alike, but those who are most obedient will be favoured. Good students who study more and regularly are regarded more highly by the teacher.

The youngest generation also reported that boys were treated more harshly than girls in school, one of the reasons being that because young women are 'cared for' in Pakistani society, they are usually treated with more respect. Another reason why teachers (and parents) may be stricter with boys is that they are seen to need to be told what to do. As one of the grandmothers, Zareena, opined: 'It's easier to bring up girls than boys since girls do things on their own, while boys have to be asked.'

Parenthood Just as most respondents identified, rationalised and/or justified differences in the upbringing and socialisation of male and female children, mothers and fathers were often perceived in different ways. Mothers were frequently linked with nurturing, modesty and altruism, and words used included 'polite', 'sympathetic', 'self-sacrificing', 'caring' and 'sincere'. In the eldest generation in particular, maternal depictions were often heavily imbued with religious symbolism, with piety often cited as a favourable quality. Among the youngest generation, care and love were more frequently emphasised. Elements of both could be found in respondents' statements across the generational divides, with one middle-aged man declaring: 'Mother was an angel to us. She was our paradise,' and another saying: 'She has got heaven under her feet.'

Although fathers were frequently described as 'pleasant' in all generational groups, 'sturdy' was an adjective that came up frequently, as did 'harsh'. The latter was equated with strictness and the fact that fathers were often rather remote from their children's upbringing. As one young woman, Perveen, reported:

> There is a diffference in roles. The mother's role is loving, the father's is domineering, although you can still see 'dull men' and 'sharp women', it depends upon the person. The woman has to bring up the children, while the man

doesn't have to do anything ... Women are sensitive, and if they work, they do justice to everyone. Who says women are the frail gender? It is hard being a woman, bearing everybody's grief, shouldering responsibility and giving love.

While women continue to be closely involved in their children's lives emotionally and practically, however, they are just as reluctant as their husbands, if not more so, to communicate with their offspring on matters of sex and sexuality.

Sex and sexuality Sex is such a taboo subject that only 42 per cent of respondents answered questions on this topic. This is partly because promiscuity is considered a sin in Pakistani society, and is rarely discussed openly. People who engage in sex outside marriage do so clandestinely, not to mention criminally. Under the martial law regime of General Zia, for example, people found guilty of extra-marital relations were subject to Hudood Law, which prescribes extreme punishments such as stoning to death for adultery. The grounds for women's transgression of moral codes are even greater, as the concept of *izzat* (honour) places huge weight upon female chastity (Beall, 1997: Chapter 1). The emphasis on female purity is such that a rape victim who cannot provide proof of the attack becomes convicted of adultery (*zina*). The latter is a punishable offence and, according to the Committee for the Repeal of Hudood Ordinances, is often alleged by husbands whose wives apply for divorce (Tomasevski, 1993: 75). As for sex education, this is felt by some of the fathers, such as Noor, to be necessary only for boys. Within marriage, women also seem to bear a disproportionate burden of restraints. Notions about the polluting nature of menstruation and childbirth, for example, require wives to refrain from sexual relations until they have undergone a complete cleansing ritual. During these periods, women also usually have to suspend religious activities such as reading the Qur'an, fasting and praying (Jeffery, 1979: 111).

Only one-third of the respondents who answered questions on sexuality felt there was greater freedom to have relations outside marriage, and only one (a man from the middle generation) actually admitted to having had a premarital sexual relationship. In terms of guilt, shame and the risk of discovery, 'unfinished relationships' (partnerships that fail to culminate in marriage) were noted as extremely difficult to deal with.

Although some young people obtain basic sex education in schools, most of their information is acquired through friends, books and films. Satellite TV and video are also seen as encouraging eroticism among the young, with the increased availability of sexually explicit material in the media being equated by their elders with an undesirable Western influence. This was summed up by one of the mothers, Hamida:

> Now there is change due to technology. The satellite dish is common now. People watch English movies and try to copy them ... Now there are more means of spreading information about sex education, which I am against before marriage. I also disagree with the unnecessary intermingling of the sexes.

If older women are concerned about increased interaction and exposure to sexual information, declining standards of modesty are also perceptible to the youngest generation. One young woman, Asma, expressed anxiety at the sartorial habits of the headmistress at her former high school: ' ... the new principal used to wear a sari that left part of her body naked. Girls used to stare at her. In my opinion she should wear decent dresses.'

It was men of the oldest generation, however, who most lamented the perceived decline in moral propriety. One grandfather, Bashir, said: 'Earlier women were kept under the veil. Now they roam around uncovered,' and one of his peers, Abdul, observed: 'There is a change in sexual behaviour. Now people do sin as recreation.' These thoughts were echoed by Iftikhar:

> Some boys study earnestly, but others believe in staring at girls, and spending money on them. To tease a girl is not good for her parents' reputation, and it is also against the religious code. Boys and girls have the right to do anything they like after getting engaged (or rather, married). When young kids sit in such company where guys talk about girls ... they get influenced and do bad things. I suggest to them that they should see every girl as a daughter or sister, and that girls should take every boy they meet as brothers.

Although many of the younger males welcomed freer availability of sexual knowledge and increased opportunities to mix with girls, some were concerned about the increased contact. As Farooq noted: 'Sexual relations are rampant – phone calls are common.' Marriage remains the only arena in which physical interaction between men and women is tolerated, which is possibly why many people continue to enter wedlock at a young age.

Marriage, family and fertility

Courtship and marriage Women's average age at marriage in Pakistan in 1990 was 21.7, a slight increase on 1970 (19.7). This is partly because of the raising of the legal age of marriage for women from 14 to 16 by the Family Law Ordinance of 1961. Although the same piece of legislation raised the legal age of marriage among males from 18 to 21 (Beall, 1997: Chapter 1), the age gap between spouses has also fallen slightly. In 1970 women's average age at marriage was 77 per cent of that of men's, but by 1990 it had climbed to 82 per cent (UNDP, 1995: Table A2.5).

Even if there is a slight rise in age at marriage for both sexes, courtships are still closely supervised through chaperoning, and parents continue to exercise major control. Although the survey did not cover this topic in any depth, it seems that parental involvement is not always welcomed. Moreover, public support for greater autonomy among the young is revealed in the fact that in March 1997, the High Court in Lahore ruled for the first time that a marriage based on love and contracted without parental permission is valid and in keeping with the teachings of Islam.[11]

Another change linked with the judicial interventions is that the 1961 Family Law Ordinance required men contracting polygamous marriages within the Shari'a (Islamic Law) to ask permission from their existing wife before marrying another (Beall, 1997: Chapter 1). However, whereas women did not express any views in the survey on polygamy, they did comment on what they perceived to be negative influences on modern marriage arising from Western mass media. One grandmother, Zareena, complained: 'I think in our country, relations between the sexes are deep as compared with America where they are loose. In America, one can marry and leave whenever one feels like it.' This was echoed by one of the mothers, Anwar, who declared: 'Eastern types of relations between men and women are better than Western.'

Family formation and kin relationships Given the importance attached to marriage, to restraint of sexuality, and to the guardianship of women's morality, it is perhaps no surprise that the proportion of households headed by women in Pakistan is very low – estimated at 2.4 per cent for the nation as whole, and 3.9 per cent for urban areas of the Punjab (Beall, 1997: Chapter 5). Female heads of household are usually widows who lack the support of extended households or deserted women who attach themselves to shrines (Beall, 1996: 437). Indeed, people in the survey whose fathers had died had often moved with their mothers into the house of a paternal uncle in the interests of respectability and retaining a 'male protector'.

While the latter undoubtedly contributes to the formation of extended households, another important factor is the significance people continue to attach to kinship and to the primacy of joint households as a cultural ideal. Although extended households now form less than half the total in Pakistan, nuclear households are in only a slight majority (52.5 per cent), the latter rising only to 55.2 per cent in urban areas (Beall, 1997: Chapter 5). Having said this, labour migration, within and beyond national bound-aries, is perceived by respondents to be leading to the break-up of extended units. As one of the fathers, Rana, declared:

Twenty years ago there was joint family system which is now disrupted due to economic oppression, unemployment, less availability of time. If the country becomes more stable and is able to generate employment, family structure will automatically get better.

Aside from the threat to 'traditional' family structures from increased unemployment and labour mobility, declining religiosity was also felt to be a factor, with one father, Zahid, saying: 'There is change in family life; it's getting weak and disturbed. The main reason is that we are moving away from religion.'

Lowering standards of discipline in educational establishments, the diminished obedience of youth to elders, and rising materialism were also mentioned as contributing to the break-up of extended families. Even more frequently noted was the issue of in-fighting among female in-laws. One grandfather, Muhammad, declared: 'No joint family system now. Wife comes and shatters the family,' and one of his contemporaries, Bashir, observed:

> Earlier people lived in peace and harmony. Now there is disruption, no consensus in the family. Quarrels have shattered the family system and women have played the greater part in this.

This was echoed by men in the middle generation, such as Shahzal:

> Women initiate family quarrels which separate family members from the joint family system. We don't have close cooperation in our caste. Our caste [washerman] is small. Neighbours are good, however, and help out in times of need.

Although none of the female respondents specified in-fighting with her female kin as provoking the fragmentation of joint households, other studies have shown that age can be a factor in household friction, with older women tending to have more status and decision-making power than their younger counterparts (Beall, 1996: 443). Nevertheless, and accepting that respondents did not clarify why intra-family quarrels may have increased over time, women are clearly regarded as critical in maintaining family coherence. As identified by one of the grandmothers, Munawa:

> In the past, people used to live together … people are increasingly living separately … Living in a joint family system there were no worries, which isn't the case for sure in the nuclear family. There are conflicts like broken homes, and only women can save these homes. I have got a big family, living jointly, with a lot of interaction with brothers and sisters. For me, home is everything.

Fertility and childbearing While family size may be subject to diminution as a result of trends in family structure, this is partially counteracted by the fact that most couples continue to have many children. Although the total fertility rate in Pakistan fell from 7 in 1980 to 5.4 in 1994 (World Bank, 1996: Table 6), this figure is the highest of all other countries in the book, and helps to account for the fact that the current annual population growth rate is 2.8 per cent, which is only marginally lower than the average annual rate of 3 per cent in the period 1960–92 (UNDP, 1995: Table 16).

Part of the reason for continued high fertility is that birth control and 'modern' contraception have not been widely accessible or encouraged. Between 1986 and 1993, for example, it was estimated that only 12 per cent of Pakistani women used contraception (UNDP, 1995: Table A2.3). However, people often have recourse to 'traditional' methods of controlling births. For example, between 1980 and 1992 an estimated 88 per cent of Pakistani women were still breastfeeding at six months in order to reduce fertility (UNDP, 1995: Table 7), and in the early part of the 1980s, as many as 50 per cent of women breastfed for one to two years (Page et al., 1982).

Another reason for the maintenance of high birth rates is that levels of infant mortality are among the highest in the world, averaging 127 per 1,000 live births in the 1990s (Moghadam, 1996: 37). This figure is even higher among low-income households (152 per 1,000), and among mothers with no education (134 per 1,000) (ibid.). One factor posing risks to the health of infants and child is poor nutrition. As of 1992, up to 42 per cent of children under five years of age were underweight, which is only a marginal improvement on 1975, when the figure was 47 per cent (UNDP, 1995: Table 4).

Gender is also critical in maintaining high fertility rates insofar as most women go on conceiving until they have at least two healthy sons. According to the United Nations World Fertility Survey conducted in 1983, son preference was registered as highest in Pakistan (out of 39 countries), with the ratio of mothers who would prefer their next child to be male being 4.9 to each one who wanted a girl (see Tomasevski, 1993: 88). This is generally regarded to result from the status of males as family breadwinners.

Perhaps the most important reason for high fertility from the viewpoint of the respondents is that aside from being 'natural', childbirth and motherhood give women recognition, social legitimacy and power within the family. As one young man, Hajji, declared:

> It is not just important for women to become mothers in Pakistan, but to bear at least seven or eight children. Straight after marriage, women's first desire is to have a child. She gets security from society after doing so, like someone gets confirmed after a probationary period in a job ... In fact, without children she might even have to have a divorce. A childless woman is considered a symbol

of bad luck in the home. They have not fulfilled themselves in any real sense, and remain frustrated, irritable and strict.

Reflecting this, around one-third of respondents felt that barrenness in women signified extremely poor fortune, not only generating difficulties with in-laws, but even placing their marriages at risk. As one grandmother, Munawa, said: 'Childless women are worried people, afraid of their husbands remarrying.' Barren women are also felt to be irritable, pessimistic, jealous, lonely, restless and prone to inferiority complexes. As one woman in the middle generation, Anwar, declared: 'It is children who make a woman's life important and complete; the life of an issueless woman becomes hell for her.' This was echoed by one of the grandmothers, Mahmuda, who had felt extremely vulnerable early on in her marriage:

> I myself feared that I might not become a mother and was more afraid because before my mother gave birth to me, she lost a son and a daughter. My in-laws were apprehensive that history might repeat itself. I wished to have both a boy and a girl, and thank God this happened.

It was the young, who were as yet ignorant of their potential fertility, who expressed most concern about childlessness. One young woman, Shazia, said that she could not imagine not becoming a mother because: 'Issueless women are lifeless. They consider themselves dead. A woman doesn't feel complete without a child.' This was echoed by most of her female peers, including Perveen, who recalled the proverb that a woman is only half woman without being a mother. It is not until she becomes a mother that she ascends to the status of *gharwali* (literally, 'full owner of the house').

While the consequences of sterility for women were perceived as catastrophic, around half the respondents thought that men would be similarly affected. Without progeny men would feel 'incomplete', 'gloomy' and 'deprived', and may even demonstrate 'abnormal behaviour'. However, it was the social implications linked with fear of destitution in old age that most concerned men. As explained by a middle-aged father, Noor:

> Children are the only support for parents in their old age. Every mother thinks about having children because in Pakistan it is the tradition that when parents get old, their offspring take care of them, and even men too, for this reason, wish to have offspring.

A final factor is women's low educational achievement. The links between fertility and education are complex, but as Lawrence Summers, the former US under-secretary of the treasury for international affairs, estimated, the cost of only one more year of schooling for 1,000 girls in Pakistan would be worth a saving of around US$30,000 in saved lives, reduced fertility and reduced maternal deaths (Summers, 1992, cited in Buvinic, 1995: 5–6). Summers suggested that these outcomes would derive from a net gain of 20 per cent in women's wage levels and agricultural productivity, which would for every 1,000 women help to avert 60 child deaths. In turn, more education was likely to limit births and maternal deaths and to increase the use of contraception (see also Buvinic, 1995: Figure 8). Others, such as Moghadam (1996: 36) have also suggested that one of the major impediments to poverty alleviation and human development in Pakistan is limited access to public education (along with health and family planning services) among poor rural women and girls.

Education and work

Education It is disturbing to note that the gender gap in education in Pakistan has not diminished substantially over time. Although the percentage of girls of primary school age enrolled in school rose from 27 per cent in 1980 to 49 per cent in 1993, the latter figure is still less than the equivalent rate for boys in 1980 (51 per cent), not to mention 1993 (80 per cent) (World Bank, 1996: Table 7). At secondary school level only 44 girls were enrolled per 100 boys in 1990, and in further and higher education (the 18–23 age group), there were only 38 females for every 100 males (UNDP, 1995: Table A2.1).

Accepting that the youngest generation in the sample are a 'non-representative' group given their selection from among university students, it is not surprising that their grandmothers had been most deprived of access to education. As women of the oldest generation, such as Fehmida, lamented: 'I was brought up well, but we had restrictions on we girls. We were not allowed to go to school.' Limited education was held accountable for many problems women had experienced, and most of all for their enforced dependence on others. One grandmother, Khurshid, who had been fortunate enough to attend primary school, felt privileged: 'I can read, write letters, I am not dependent on anyone for reading, writing.' This was echoed by one of the mothers, Nazir: 'If I be illiterate, I be dependent on others.' Education was also seen by women as a means of raising their children better. As one of the mothers said: 'Because of education I could be successful in giving proper training to my kids.'

The value attached by women to education reflects the more general opinion in the survey that schooling and qualifications are vital resources in finding jobs, securing upward mobility, and attaining social prestige and 'honour'. As one of the young male respondents said, education 'made me social, helped me move in society'. Thus, although women have not benefited from rising educational opportunities, the young are obviously much better off than the elderly. Recognising, again, that all the youngest generation were university students, positive trends are apparent in that only 20 per cent of their parents had received higher education, and a mere 10 per cent of their grandparents. Similarly, 45 per cent of the latter were illiterate, compared with 10 per cent of the parents. Having suggested that access to education has improved within the sample group, however, the quality of education is not all it might be. As many as 45 per cent of the youngest generation said that rote-learning techniques were in common use. This was considerably higher than reported by their parents (17 per cent) and even their grandparents (36 per cent), and was attributed to the rising pressures of examination performance in an increasingly competitive labour market.

It should also be noted that most parents are fully responsible for the costs of their children's education. As one of the youngest generation, Hina, reported: 'Expenditure only my mother knows, I never asked any money from mum. She used to send us with a lunch box and a little money and if we required books she always arranged.'

Employment and economic livelihood   Although the youngest generation of survey respondents have not yet entered the labour market (except on a part-time basis to fund their studies – see below), it will be interesting to see whether they find it easier than their elders to get jobs. Only 32 per cent of the latter were able to obtain jobs on finishing school or college. Part of the reason for this was undoubtedly lower levels of education, with a completed high school education (matric, or tenth grade) generally at that time being necessary to enter formal sector work such as teaching and civil service positions. As one of the fathers, Zahid, recalled:

> My father put me into a training school and just after finishing, I got a job, teaching small children. My salary was 50 rupees and my boss treated me well. I had no bother getting a job … So few people were literate that there was little competition.

Another father, Muhammad, reported:

> When I left school I got a government job. My salary was about 20 rupees and I was happy in it. At that time, middle grade or matric could get a job easily. Government employment is good, and apart from that, having your own business.

Among men, the army was also a source of jobs, especially those of the oldest generation whose young adulthood coincided with the Second World War. Those who actually fought in the war were reasonably well paid, especially in the higher-ranking positions. However, even those lower down the hierarchy were content to have stable work. One of the grandfathers, Iftikhar, recalled:

> I was a cadet on meagre wages – only 120 rupees a month. I got the job on my wits. The higher officers allotted my work to me but they behaved quite well. I thanked God after getting that job, and even today I still thank the Lord that I was able to get a job at that time.

Some men in the oldest generation also worked in more informal occupations, including domestic service. These jobs were not particularly well paid or satisfying but, again, people seemed grateful to have work, and work experience could lead to upward mobility. One of the grandfathers, Abdul, stated:

> First I worked as a servant in various houses where I used to earn 10–20 rupees a month. Then I worked in a mess in a college and for the last five years doing a government job. No good no bad time I had during my job.

The idea that government work is more privileged than other forms of employment, particularly in respect of pay, persists. One young male respondent, Farooq, declared:

> I do a government job along with doing my studies. I got this job on merit, and my salary of 3,000 rupees means I can live alone. I like my work environment. I am satisfied. The officers behave well towards me ... I feel that I am a self-made person and better than other people.

It is somewhat unlikely that public sector employment will be available to the majority of today's graduates, since economic restructuring has curbed expansion of the national and provincial bureaucracies. However, if the young in the survey do find employment, they are much more likely to enter urban work of some description than to engage in rural activities. This is not only because they are presently living in the city for the purposes of their education, and because professional employment tends to be urban-based, but because, relatively speaking, economic opportunities in rural areas are on the decline. For example, although agriculture remains the single largest employer of the Pakistani labour force, by 1990–92, only 47 per cent of the workforce were in agriculture compared with 60 per cent in 1965. While the share of the workforce in industry rose only slightly between 1965 and the early 1990s (from 18 per cent to 20 per cent), in services it expanded from 22 per cent to 33 per cent (UNDP, 1995: Table 11).

Women are perhaps even less likely than men to find formal sector employment, since men tend to dominate the urban as well as the rural workforce. For example, there are only 16 women per 100 men in the registered service sector, and a mere 3 women per 100 men among clerical and sales workers (UNDP, 1995: Table A2.3). In order to try to lessen some of the disparities between men and women in employment, affirmative action policies have been instituted by the government. For example, 5 per cent of jobs in government and parastatal organisations are now reserved for women, female judges have been appointed to the superior courts and there are also some women-only banks and police stations in the country (Bhutto, 1995). Although these allocations are low, it may be that young women in the sample will display higher rates of labour force participation than their mothers and grandmothers, among whom as many as 86 per cent dedicated themselves entirely to the home. Yet at the same time, for many women in Pakistan lack of education, sex segregation in the labour market, and the primacy attached to women's mothering and homemaking roles means that 'household-based production remains the main site of economic activity' (O'Connell, 1994: 62; see also Parnwell, 1993: 107; Rahat, 1986). Indeed, in urban areas, women in low-income households are usually in informal employment, either as domestic servants or home-based pieceworkers (Beall, 1996: 437; Moghadam, 1996: 37). In Lahore, for instance, piecework includes making paper bags out of recycled waste, cutting straps for rubber slippers, assembling garments, and making trinkets and tinsel garlands (APHD, 1985).

Whatever women might do, their earnings are likely to be increasingly critical to household survival in the wake of mounting levels of male unemployment. Yet this is not to suggest that their personal gains from economic activity are likely to proceed apace. As Jo Beall (1996: 443) has pointed out with reference to a cross-class study in the city of Faisalabad:

> the variables of gender and generation are closely intertwined. The necessity for women's labour force participation and income-generation is dramatically changing the gender division of labour in urban Pakistan, not always with positive effects at the household level. Women's increased income earning activities are not accompanied by reduced domestic burdens or increased decision-making within the household. Neither are high levels of male unemployment accompanied by a reduction in consumption of household resources by men.

Labour migration and overseas experiences The difficulties of getting employment in general means that throughout the generations, people have had to migrate abroad. This can often provide the funds necessary to establish a business back home. As one of the fathers, Fazal, reported:

> After matric my brother-in-law took me to Dubai, where I did cloth merchandise. After earning enough money I got back to Pakistan and here I started a

construction business, building houses and selling them. I am good at that now … I have no worries regarding finances.

Although there are some very positive reports of overseas labour migration, in certain countries, especially North Africa and the Middle East, racial discrimination had been a problem. One of the young men in the survey, Aziz, had spent time abroad with his father:

> I went to Libya and stayed there between 1980 and 1982. My father worked there. Later on we moved to Saudi Arabia before we came home. The places were good but the environment was strange. They don't like Asians. They don't even hesitate to hurl stones at Pakistanis and Indians. We people feel quite a solitude there. We went there because you earn according to your capability which I think is missing here, as here is a hell of social injustice.

Overseas travel is also undertaken for reasons of education, to visit relatives in other countries, or for religious pilgrimages, such as to Mecca. Altogether (including travel for labour migration), just under half the eldest generation, one-quarter of the middle generation, and one-fifth of the youngest generation had been abroad. The most common destinations included the UK, Libya and the Middle East. For the most part, people felt positively about the places they had visited and, echoing the thoughts of the previous respondent, many made unfavourable comparisons with Pakistan. These included women who had travelled with their husbands or fathers while the latter were studying or working. One of the grandmothers, Mahmuda, who had visited a range of sacred places in Iran, Saudi Arabia, Syria and Iraq, claimed: 'People there are good; in Pakistan people are selfish.' In addition to the perceived egoism of Pakistani society, corruption, dishonesty, nepotism, poor infrastructure, and lack of cleanliness were all seen as problems by people with overseas experience. Other important factors were poverty and social inequality, as one of the grandmothers, Sardar, reported:

> I went abroad twice, once to England and Scotland (to visit my daughter and son-in-law), then from there to America and second time to America. There is a huge difference between the standard of living here and abroad. The major difference is that there was no discrimination on the basis of wealth and poverty. No difference between a minister and a gardener.

Some women also felt there was more respect shown to women in other countries, including the Middle East. As one of the grandmothers, Kashash, declared: 'My husband served in Saudi Arabia from 1985 until 1987. It was a very good experience, and I especially appreciated their civilised attitudes towards women.'

Conclusion

Considering that so many of the respondents in the sample have ex-perienced other cultures, it is perhaps surprising that there is so little evidence in the Pakistan survey of changing attitudes or practices surround-ing gender. In many ways, continuities in most aspects of gender roles and relations are also surprising given that at various junctures the Pakistani state has introduced legislation that has attempted to improve the status of women, particularly in employment and the judiciary. Beyond this, the rising political profile of women in the last ten to fifteen years has undoubtedly helped to create an image of women that encompasses more than homemaking, motherhood and private domesticity. Indeed, in her role as prime minister in the early 1990s, Benazir Bhutto declared:

> I believe that, slowly but surely, the women of Pakistan will soon attain a position of honour and dignity in our society. The trend we have set in gender equality through the emancipation of women is now irreversible (Bhutto, 1995).

While the survey conducted in Pakistan may not have picked up on changes that might be occurring in other sectors of society, or outside the Punjab, it is interesting that even in the few arenas in which changes are discernible (for example, education and female employment), progress towards equality with men is slow. In addition, to date these do not seem to have had much effect on women's personal freedom or autonomy, whether as single or as married women. If the gradual decline of extended households has something to do with what men describe as increased friction between female in-laws, this might imply that women are attempting to negotiate greater power for themselves in the home. This could presage other changes, such as greater equality in men's and women's shares of household labour and childcare, and less hierarchy in household decision-making. At present such scenarios do not appear to be on the horizon, especially as men in all generations seem unwilling to accede to any change. What is also clear, however, is that not all women are ready to accept the restric-tions imposed by existing inequalities, and these women may well forge a path towards greater social justice in time, and generations, to come.

Recommendations

Unlike most other countries in this volume, the respondents in the Pakistan survey did not express clear opinions about the changes they might like to see in respect of gender. Nevertheless, reading between the lines of the informants' opinions, the following suggestions might be welcomed among the youngest generation, especially by women:

- Programmes for parents encouraging them to address gender discrimination in the upbringing of children, and to give greater attention to the health and education needs of daughters.
- Provision of careers advice in schools and community centres to encourage more young women to pursue medicine (and to encourage parents to let them do medical degrees) as a means of increasing the number of female doctors available to treat female patients.
- Shift more of the costs of education on to the state in order that parents on lower incomes might be encouraged to keep daughters in education as long as sons.
- Extend existing initiatives for the recruitment of women into jobs in the public and parastatal sector.
- Encourage parents and children to communicate with each other over relationships and marriages by means of community programmes aimed at fostering greater inter-generational understanding and tolerance.
- Foster support of the appointment of more female candidates by political parties, and encourage political parties to establish pro-women agendas aimed at extending equality of status and opportunity between the sexes.

Notes

1. Compiled from a report prepared by Probe Research and Development Services, Lahore, Pakistan under the directorship of Raghib Hasan Majed and Atif Hasan.

2. Pakistan originally comprised the territories of East Pakistan and West Pakistan, divided by a 2,000-kilometre corridor extending across the Ganges Plain in Northern India. East Pakistan was the homeland of predominantly Bengali Muslims, who perceived themselves as disadvantaged by union with West Pakistan. Although the former had a healthy export trade in raw materials such as jute and generated a lot of wealth for the country in the immediate aftermath of partition, little of this was reinvested in the East. The progressive enrichment of the West and subsequent political developments provoked a mammoth Bengali campaign for self-government, which culminated in the secession of East Pakistan to the separate state of Bangladesh in 1971.

3. Religious minorities in Pakistan include Hindus, Christians, Sikhs, Buddhists, Parsees and Bahais (Beall, 1997: Chapter 6).

4. Given that the partition of India in 1947 represented a crude cut through existing social, cultural and economic groupings, it is hardly surprising that it was followed by mass migration into both East and West Pakistan. The entrepreneurial Muhajirs went mainly to the cities of the Sindh and Punjab provinces in the West, and as Robert Bradnock (1992: 52) notes: 'brought a new foreign element to the cities of Pakistan, changing their social character and creating a source of competition for space and for work which has fostered divisive tensions in Pakistan's urban communities'.

5. Pakistan's main political parties are the Pakistan People's Party (PPP) and

the Pakistan Muslim League (Nawaz) (PML [N]). Others include the Pakistan Muslim League (Chattha) (PML [C]); the hardline Islamic Jamaat-i-Islami (JI), Muhajir Quami Movement (MQM), Awami National Party (ANP), Jamiat-e-Ulema-e-Islam (JUI) and the Tehrik-i-Insaaf (Movement for Justice), led by Pakistan's former cricket captain, Imran Khan (EIU, 1996e: 5).

6. Power in Pakistan has repeatedly changed hands between civilian governments and the military. The military was in power between 1958 and 1971 (under President Ayub Khan until 1969), and again seized power in 1977 when the democratically elected government of Zulfikar Ali Bhutto was overturned in a military coup led by General Mohammad Zia-ul-Haq. This period of non-democratic military rule lasted until the assassination of Zia in July 1988 (Bradnock, 1992: 67). During the 1990s continued political turbulence has been marked by serial dismissals of the government by Pakistan's presidents. For example, Nawaz Sharif of the PML (N), who was prime minister between 1990 and 1993, was dismissed by then president Ghulam Ishaq Khan on charges of corruption and incompetence. Benazir Bhutto, who was voted in as prime minister of Pakistan in 1993 and who appointed Farooq Leghari (a one-time loyal supporter) as president, was forced to resign by Leghari (who is backed by the army and the judiciary) in October 1996. Ostensibly, the grounds for Ms Bhutto's dismissal were incompetence, but there were also fears about her mounting authoritarianism. Between Bhutto's resignation and the elections of February 1997 an interim government was led by Meinar Khalid, who, in addition to being prime minister, was also minister of finance (EIU, 1996e). Nawaz Sharif was reinstated as prime minister in February, with his party, the PML(N), winning 137 out of 204 contested seats in the National Assembly. Sharif's election makes him the seventeenth prime minister Pakistan has sworn in since 1947 (EIU, 1997: 9).

7. It is also estimated that over half of all maternal deaths each year worldwide occur in South Asia (predominantly Pakistan, India and Bangladesh) (Smyke, 1991: 13).

8. It has been often argued that Benazir Bhutto owed her political prestige to the fact that her late father, President Zulfikar Ali Bhutto, was immensely popular, especially in the family's home province of Sindh. However, resistance to Ms Bhutto has been mounting in recent months, mainly due to corruption and her alleged involvement (with her husband, Asif Ali Zardari), in the killing of her brother, Murtaza Bhutto, in September 1996. This was reflected in the failure of Ms Bhutto's party (the Pakistan People's Party), to retain more than 19 out of its 89 national assembly seats in the February 1997 elections, and even in the elections for the provincial assembly of Sindh the PPP won a mere 34 out of 97 seats (EIU, 1997: 10).

9. Apart from Benazir Bhutto, this included her widowed sister-in-law, Lebanese-born Ghinwa Bhutto, Jemima Khan (the wife of Imran Khan), Abida Hussain (former ambassador to Washington and stalwart of the Pakistan Muslim League), and Musarrat Shaheen, a former star of Urdu and Pushtu cinema (see Suzanne Goldenburg, 'Pakistan's women of power', *Guardian*, 28 January 1997).

10. In the interests of clarity, minor amendments have been made to some of the original translations of interview extracts from Urdu into English.

11. The case was that of Saima Waheed, a woman who married a college lecturer, Arshad Ahmad, without her father's permission. As a result of this 'transgression', she was locked in a room by her father in the parental home. Saima escaped to a women's shelter in Lahore. This was run by Asma Jehangir, Pakistan's leading

campaigning lawyer and head of the Human Rights Commission, who took up Saima's case. Saima's father, in the meantime, tried to get her marriage declared void, gaining the support of hardline religious groups such as the Islamic Human Rights Forum, who tried to rally support against the couple. In March 1997, after eleven months of legal battle, Saima won her case with the High Court ruling that the wedding had been valid and that the couple could live together. Yet although the court was two to one in favour of women having the right to choose their husbands without having to get the permission of a *wali* (guardian), Islamic groups have vowed to fight the decision and maintain that the issue can only be settled by the Supreme Court. The dissenting lawyer in the case, Ishan-ul-Haq, maintained that: 'Parents have a right to be obeyed by their children, and the obedience is judicially enforceable.' Although hundreds of women have filed cases in Pakistan's civil courts to defend the right to choose their husbands, many give up because of the harrowing and lengthy legal process. Saima's case is thus a victory, although her lawyer, Ms Jengahir, cautioned: 'This is not a landmark judgment. The floodgates of emancipation have not been opened but it may encourage women to approach the courts' (see Phil Goodwin, 'True love defeats a father's holy fiat', *Guardian*, 11 March 1997).

CHAPTER 7

CYPRUS[1]

Although all the countries in this book can be considered as divided by a number of criteria over and above gender and generation, Cyprus' political, ethnic and religious differences find physical expression in a ceasefire line that separates the southern territory, inhabited by its majority Greek Cypriot population, from the northern sector occupied by Turkish Cypriots. The Commonwealth-affiliated Republic of Cyprus refers to the area due south of the 'Attila Line', and it is from interviews with this population that the analysis draws.

Although war and civil strife have undoubtedly stood in the way of gains that may otherwise have been made in Cyprus, upward socio-economic mobility has been notable in the twentieth century. Between the early 1900s and the 1990s, Cyprus has undergone a transition from a predominantly rural, broadly impoverished agricultural economy to a society that is increasingly urban and industrial and earns a large part of its revenue from international tourism. Many economic, demographic and social changes have contributed to improvements in the status of women and to narrowing gaps between the sexes. Significantly, these accomplishments seem to have been accepted by men and women in all generations. Yet despite the fact that some shifts, especially in parental intervention in marriage, in attitudes towards female sexuality, and in educational attainment, have been dramatic within a relatively short space of time, most young women in the survey feel that steps towards equality have not gone far enough.

Country profile

Cyprus is an island of just under 10,000 km^2 lying in the eastern Mediterranean. Its population is around 700,000, excluding some 40,000–50,000 settlers from mainland Turkey (EIU, 1996f: 4). The average annual growth rate of GNP per capita between 1985 and 1994 was 4.6 per cent, and in this latter year per capita GNP stood at US$10,260 (World Bank, 1996: Table 1a). Although tourism and manufactured products (including clothing and foodstuffs) currently provide the bulk of the country's foreign ex-change, the island is also rich in metal deposits and as far back as 3000 BC had copper mines that supplied the rest of the region. It is from the Greek 'Kypros', the word for metal, that Cyprus' name is derived.

Cyprus is situated at the nexus of maritime routes between Europe, Asia and Africa and its history is one of successive invasions and annexa-tions, extending from the establishment of city kingdoms by Mycenaean Greeks in 1500 BC to its transfer from Turkish to British hands in 1878. The Turks had governed Cyprus since the sixteenth century and cession to Britain took the form of a leasing arrangement until 1925, when the status of British Crown Colony was conferred upon the island. Yet Greek Cypriots had been mobilising for unification with mainland Greece from 1900 onwards. During the 1950s intensification of this movement was marked by the formation of a terrorist organisation, Ethniki Organosis Kypriakou Agonos (National Organisation of Cypriot Struggle). This group mounted a campaign of assassinations against both Turkish Cypriots and Britons and was a major factor in the island's conversion to an independent republic in 1960. However, with nearly one-fifth of the population being of Turkish origin (mainly from the Anatolian peninsula), the situation proved fragile and within three years civil war broke out. Despite the deployment of United Nations forces, Turkey launched a full-scale invasion of Cyprus in 1974 and gained control of the northern part of the country extending from the coastal town of Karavostasi in the west to Famagusta in the east. More than 200,000 Greek Cypriots were expelled and/or killed during the manoeuvre, which culminated a year later with the declaration of Turkish Cypriot sovereignty. The sector was then proclaimed by the victors as the Turkish Republic of Northern Cyprus, although it remains unrecognised as such by Greek Cypriots and the rest of the international community, who refer to it as the 'Turkish Cypriot Zone' (EIU, 1995f: 15).

Flare-ups in inter-communal violence in 1996 testify to the continued vehemence of popular sentiment on both sides of the Attila Line and to the remote prospects of an easy solution to Cyprus' territorial crisis (EIU, 1996f: 5). Whereas the Greek Cypriots wish to see the renunciation of Turkish Cypriot claims to the northern sector and the substitution of an international peacekeeping force for Turkish troops (which have num-bered about 30,000 since 1974), the Turkish Cypriots are keen to develop closer ties with Turkey and to protect themselves from minority status within a single island administration. The importance of finding a mutually agreeable solution is arguably more marked than ever in the light of both Cyprus' and Turkey's desire for membership of the European Union, and the fact that violence is a major factor diverting a critical source of hard currency – foreign tourists – to other destinations from both parts of the island.

Despite the economic and social problems accompanying Cyprus' long-running geo-political crisis, and the fact that it is a small nation, both physically and in respect of population size, Cyprus ranks twenty-third in the world in its score on the UNDP HDI (0.906 in 1992). Average adult life expectancy in 1992 was 77 (marginally higher than some richer economies such as Austria, Germany, Denmark and the UK), and women's was higher still, at 79.2 (UNDP: Tables 1 and A2.2). Although adult literacy is lower than most other European countries (at 94 per cent in 1992) (ibid.: Table 1), this figure is impressive given that in the early 1900s an estimated three-quarters of the population could not read or write. Notwithstanding that education consumes only a relatively modest proportion of total government expenditure (11.3 per cent in 1990) (ibid.: Table 10), both the coverage and quality of educational provision for men and women have risen dramatically over the course of the twentieth century.

Other important changes include the rising presence of women in the workforce. Although women on the island have always worked in and outside the home, the economic activity rate of those aged 15 or more was 56 per cent of their male counterparts in 1994, compared with 47 per cent in 1970 (UNDP, 1995: Table A2.6). The modernisation of the Cypriot economy also seems to have created space for women among the ranks of professional technical and related workers (where they make up 40.8 per cent of the labour force). However, a crucial gap remains among the ranks of administrative and managerial employees, where only 10.2 per cent are women (ibid.: Table 3.5). While this latter figure is on a par with other southern Mediterranean countries such as Spain and Greece, it is lower than many northern European countries, and Commonwealth nations outside the region such as Australia, St Vincent, Barbados, New Zealand, Canada and Zimbabwe (ibid.). It is also significant that while women form 36 per cent of the overall labour force (UNDP, 1995: Table 11), their share of earned income is only 25.8 per cent (ibid.: Table 3.5). Indeed, given that income and employment status are two of the key variables incorporated within the UNDP's GEM, it is perhaps no surprise that Cyprus' rank in the GEM order is lower than its HDI position – forty-eighth out of the 116 countries for which relevant data (for 1994) are available (see above; also UNDP, 1995: 84–6).

Another variable used in the GEM is the share of parliamentary seats held by women, which is low in Cyprus. In 1994, women held only three out of a total of 56 directly elected seats occupied by Greek Cypriots in the House of Representatives (24 seats were reserved in the 1960 Constitution for Turkish Cypriots but these have remained empty since 1963).

The last parliamentary elections were held in 1996 and produced a coalition government between the conservative Democratic Rally (DISY) and the Democratic Party (DIKO).[2] The presidency also runs for five years and Glafkos Clerides, former leader of DISY, has been in power since the last elections in February 1993. The president is responsible for appointing the country's Council of Ministers, who are not allowed to sit in the House of Representatives nor to hold any party allegiance after ascending to the cabinet (EIU, 1996f: 3). At present, only 7 per cent of government ministers in Cyprus are women (UNDP, 1995: Table A2.4).

Methodology

The fieldwork was carried out between 1993 and 1995 and involved the participation of 211 students from the Education Department of the University of Cyprus based in the capital, Nicosia. Reflecting the predominance of women in the teaching profession, most of these were female. Within the general themes specified by WYAD (see Chapter 1), the students themselves formulated interview guidelines and used these to gather information from a total of 1,266 parents and grandparents. The first stage of the fieldwork in 1993–94 comprised 138 students collecting life history data relating to changing patterns of education across time, and identifying key questions for the second stage scheduled to take place during 1994–95. A total of 73 students participated in the second phase, which expanded to include a wider range of topics and led to 34 reports adopting the form of narratives recounted by family members and incorporating the comments and opinions of male and female student interviewers.

The experience of conducting the fieldwork was viewed almost without exception as positive and personally enriching by the students. Among the reasons given was the fact that the research was interesting, original and unlike other work students had done in the course of their education degrees. Other factors included the opportunity for their parents and grandparents to become involved in their children's and grandchildren's university work and to gain greater insights into how access to education had changed over their families' life courses. The students, in turn, felt that this not only opened up communication with their kin, but improved their knowledge and perceptions of the past, and their understanding of the views and behaviour of their predecessors. One female student, Katina, declared that the research provided 'an occasion to discover the secret world of the past and also [to make] new ties with my family', and one of her male counterparts, Yiannis, claimed that: 'I have come to better know my own family, my peers, myself.' In addition, the fact that the vast majority of the students enjoy a level of material comfort and privileges unknown by their forebears meant that many began to appreciate more fully the sacrifices their families had made over the years. The young also saw it as their duty to uphold the achievements of previous generations to fight for an independent Cyprus, free of domination, division and conflict. These sentiments tended to overshadow difficulties such as uneasiness about interviewing for the first time, the problems of contacting family members who had become refugees or moved abroad, and, in some cases, relatives' reluctance to talk about painful memories. Indeed, the students seemed profoundly grateful at having been able to share what they could with their elders. As one young woman, Eleni, said: 'Precious material has been collected. I'll keep these records because they are now relics of my family.'

Profile of informants Informants in the oldest (grandparent) generation were aged from their late sixties to their early nineties. Most had been born and raised in villages where they and their families depended on agriculture. Although some had sizeable landholdings boasting large numbers of crops and livestock, the majority were poor and had started their married lives with virtually no assets. The middle generation were mainly in their forties and fifties and while many had been born in rural areas, they had had more education than their parents. Many had also moved to towns in their early adulthood, some as a result of forced removal from the north during the Turkish invasion of 1974. Although poverty had coloured many of their childhoods, from independence onwards, expanding opportunities for accumulating wealth, coupled with general improvements in living standards and service provision, meant that they were generally able to give their own children a more secure start. The youngest generation, with an average age of twenty years, had access to opportunities largely unknown to their predecessors – a university education, greater time for leisure activities, and greater choice of career paths. Since all the youngest generation in the survey, who acted as interviewers, were still studying for their degrees, however, there is little way of knowing whether they will actually attain higher professional status than their parents, and interpretations of changing employment across the generations must be read with this in mind.

Gender roles and relations

As indicated above, reviewing changes in gender roles and relations across three generations in Cyprus involves taking into account considerable economic and demographic, as well as political, shifts during the twentieth century. Most of the grandparents had grown up in small villages, where livelihoods were rooted in agriculture, living standards were low, and wealth was determined by family property. Although women worked hard along-side men in the fields, their status was not equal, and families tended to be highly patriarchal (see Pantelidou, 1992). Men had almost exclusive access to education, and ruled in the home. This replicated a pattern passed down from their own parents. As one of the grandfathers, Koulis, recalled, his mother had stood in the shadow of his father, the 'master and judge' in the household, 'swallowing her own opinion, her own point of view, every day'; he even speculated that this might have been one of the reasons for her early death. Yet adhering to tradition was perhaps one way of maintaining a sense of psychological security and cultural integrity during the uncertain years of the Second World War, and the subsequent struggle against British rule. In the independence period, during the 1960s, when most of the middle generation were in their youth or raising their families, people perhaps became less fearful of change.

It certainly seems that divisions of labour, power and authority between men and women in the home, which in the earlier part of this century were extremely marked, have tended to diminish over the last sixty to seventy years. Among the oldest generation, wives tended to do all the domestic chores and to have little say in household affairs. Odyssia, now in her early forties, remembers that even if her mother was eating and her father wanted a glass of water, her mother would have to get up and bring it to him. Her father 'would never get up and bring water to my mother, and she would never ask him such a thing either'. Nina, aged 20, describes her paternal grandfather as 'the typical married man of the time. He worked to provide for his family but did not participate in the caring of the children.' Another young woman, Anita, reported that in her grandparents' generation, the 'chief in the family was always the father ... the woman was subordinate', even if women had some rights to express their opinions. Broadly similar views were articulated by a middle-aged man, Spyros, who recalled his mother having been treated by his father as a 'second-class citizen'. Although his father paid little attention to how the children were raised, within the house 'the father was everything: the alpha and the omega'. These opinions were echoed (and not without some pride), by some of the oldest male respondents, and indicate how authoritative household headship was undoubtedly a key marker of masculine identity. Yiorgos, in his late seventies, recalled:

> The woman had to obey the man. Obedience is the best. Many men, whenever their wives talked back to them, hit them. Some men liked to drink all day and then go home and beat up their wives so that the next day people would say:

'Last night he was drunk and he beat up his wife.' He was considered to be a 'tough guy'.

It is also interesting that the interpretations of younger generations of their elders' activities and relationships sometimes contradicted those given by the latter. An elderly widow, Andrulla, declared that she had had a good life with her husband and that they had jointly made decisions, whereas her son, Costas, felt that his father had grossly underestimated his mother's worth, often saying to her: 'Don't talk. You don't know a single thing. You are illiterate.' While refusing to speak ill of her husband may, in Andrulla's case, have owed something to respect for the dead, such unequal relations were something people tended to accept as a norm in the first half of the twentieth century.

As for the middle generation, boundaries between the sexes in various aspects of household life began to blur, even if these remained somewhat tempered by the legacies of the past. As 21-year-old Anita summed up:

> Mother and father share in the work, the benefits, and the authority in our family ... Surely sometimes my mother's contribution in the house is bigger than my father's. The remains of an old-fashioned mentality still exists; even though the past's influence appears weaker, it is still alive.

Women's increased presence in the paid economy may well have been one reason for their rising share of decision-making in the home. One of the fathers, Spyros, admitted to having denied his wife much say in financial matters because she did not earn an income. Yet some young women felt that household life was still weighted in men's favour, regardless of the tasks women performed. As 21-year-old Arianna commented:

> In the majority of families, as in previous times, decisions are taken mainly by men. Even in cases where women are working, it is the men who have responsibility for financial matters. Women, whether working outside the home or not, have the responsibility of household chores and raising the children. In these areas, it is vitally important to change the mentality. Cypriot men ... expect everything to be prepared for them at home.

These patterns may have proved hard to erase due to their roots in the childhood socialisation of previous generations.

Socialisation and childhood Among the oldest informants, childhood was recalled as a happy state, but also as one in which children were obliged to help their parents. The chores of one of the fathers, Manolis, began with carrying water in buckets from the village fountain to the house, and, as he grew older, helping his father in the fields and in the family butcher's shop. Other boys would help tend the animals or assist their fathers in repairing farm tools and machinery.

Part of the reason for boys helping their fathers was the fact that this groomed them for their roles in later life, namely household heads and breadwinners. Spyros, a man who grew up in the 1960s, was forbidden to fraternise with unemployed people: 'Labour was everything in a man's life. You lived to work. This was your purpose and destiny.'

Girls, whose idealised (and virtually inescapable) destiny was wife- and motherhood, helped their mothers. Vasoulla, a 77-year-old grandmother who grew up in a village near Nicosia, reported having spent her childhood doing a multitude of tasks:

> I kneaded, washed, wove. We had to do a lot of chores, not just one or two. I was weaving trousers, making socks, making clothes … looking after the children.

While these responsibilities had been a major factor in forcing Vasoulla to give up school, in the middle generation they could sometimes be accommodated around school timetables. As 42-year-old Odyssia commented:

> When I was in primary school, since my mother was working, I was responsible for feeding the chickens, tidying up the house, and helping with food preparation. Later when I grew up a little bit, I had to prepare the food entirely by myself so that it would be ready when my mother came home so that she could use her time doing the wash and kneading bread.

Over time the burdens imposed on children of both sexes seem to have decreased, with 21-year-old Anita reporting:

> Today a child does his homework, and this is enough to keep his parents happy. Today the child has the right to voice his opinion, to deny, to argue, to suggest. These are situations unprecedented in the past.

Changes in work patterns are caused by a variety of factors, one being the decline in agriculture and along with it the need to engage children in production, another being the spread of consumer goods and reduced domestic toil. The fact that education is now free and compulsory for all children until the age of 15 is also significant, with other changes in the educational system being relevant to the nature of discipline in the lives of the young, as explored below.

Parenthood and parenting roles Mothers in all generations were often identified as spiritual and moral guides, whereas fathers were more concerned with their children's material futures and career status. One young man, Petrides, claimed:

Mother played a significant role in our upbringing. She taught us how to live in love and away from hatred. At the same time, my father is the one who helped us at school from the beginning and I can say that he implants in us the wish for further studies. No matter how much I try to convince myself that my decision to study to become a teacher was my own decision, I hear my father's voice when I was a child and he caught me 'giving lessons' to the children of the neighbourhood: 'You will become a teacher one day.' I also believe my brother, who studies today in the military school, is acting on the suggestions of my father's (shattered) dream. As for my third brother, he is probably also going to follow the path to become an army officer. Is it his choice? Who knows?

In the middle and oldest generations parenting appears to have been quite strict. Children were rarely allowed to question their parents' decisions and, since many issues were taboo within the family, the usual refuge for teenage boys and girls was to discuss personal matters and problems with friends. Although most young Greek Cypriots continue to show considerable respect towards their parents, communication within families seems to have opened up. As a female student, Anita, declared:

Today we discuss a lot of things with our family, even sentimental problems, even sex, which would have been considered something unbelievable decades before. Of course, discussions today are somewhat reserved and have their limits. My parents, for example, did not take the initiative, they did not find it important to inform me about sex. I took the risk and asked, so they talked to me about it ... The past may have weakened, but everything shouts that it is still here.

While the efforts of parents in providing their children with 'training for life' are appreciated by the youngest generation, they wish to move towards a more flexible model of parenting when they have their own families, including tolerance of greater autonomy among young people. As articulated by Petrides, for example:

I want my children to grow up in a democratic environment, which I was probably deprived of, making their own choices and decisions. I want to make sure, in advance, that they acquire the required maturity, away from dogmatic models. I will try to avoid implanting in them religious fanaticism, and at the same time, I will make them aware of the particularities of religion. Their free will and love will bring them close to the church, and not my insistence and imposition.

Religion and 'institutional parenting' Religion *per se* is worth discussing here, since in previous decades it constituted an important adjunct to moral and spiritual aspects of parenting and has continued to play a major part in the lives and values of the eldest generation. One of the grandfathers, Nicholas, now 80, and like the vast majority of respondents an observer of the Greek Orthodox faith, stated:

> I used to go to church every Sunday. It was the only thing we loved, it is the sweetest thing there is … Religion is to do the things that you are asked to do like loving your fellow man, being regular at church, doing something good whenever you can, and being merciful.

Many of the oldest generation were also involved in the struggle for independence and wove their enduring religious beliefs into their political activities. Paraskevas, aged 78, belonged to one of several 'Christian clubs', which were crucial in mobilising support for union with Greece during the 1940s.[3]

By the middle generation, church-going continued among the young although it tended to dwindle in their later years. Strict religious observance in childhood partly resulted from the fact that many of the middle generation were raised in rural areas where communities were disapproving of those who did not conform. As one of the mothers, Soulla, noted: 'If someone didn't go often to church, he would be the target of gossip and comments at that time.'

The importance of religion was stressed by schoolteachers as well as parents, and in village primary schools was often underscored by the prominence of religious education. One grandmother, Christalla, who attended elementary school in a mountain village near Limassol in the 1930s, remembers little other than religion in her formal instruction:

> Our teachers taught us the biographies of the saints; in order to become teachers they were required to study at the seminary. They made us love the church by frequently taking us to attend the services. I am still very devout. The first priority in my life is religion.

Even in the subsequent generation, teachers would also take it upon themselves to police attendance at church services in village communities. A middle-aged man, Christopher, claimed:

> It was mandatory that we went to church … the school punished the children who were absent, no matter what the reason, from Sunday's congregation.

Although most of the young generation profess fidelity to the edicts of Greek Orthodoxy, there is now far less pressure exerted upon children to attend church. This is partly because of declining sanctions on the part of educational establishments, which, at the time of the oldest generation, would sometimes employ 'overseers' to punish children who 'violated the law'. In addition to non-attendance at church, 'violations' included failing to comply with regulation school uniform, hanging around on the streets, and frequenting billiard halls and coffee-houses. Even without overseers, discipline in schools was such that people were often in considerable awe of their teachers. Corporal punishment was common, and frequently brutal (kneeling on sharp rocks, for example), with a graphic illustration provided by one of the grandfathers, Michaelides:

> We used to be beaten with a pomegranate tree stick. There were thorns on it. They used to send us out to cut and bring the sticks to the teacher ... One time the teacher was beating my cousin so much that the stick stuck to his leg.

Support for such discipline seemed scant among the informants, and the decline in the use of physical force was particularly celebrated by members of the youngest generation, such as Elisa:

> In my school life I have only met with authority a few times, and even fewer times have I seen hitting. And surely, there is not today the tension and level of discipline that there was in the past.

Elisa's view was endorsed by one of her colleagues, Nina, whose mother still bears a scar on her forehead from not learning her spelling: 'Nowadays, if a teacher dares to lay a finger on a pupil he will be taken to court.' In short, while access to education has expanded, its disciplinary element has softened, complementing a growing democratisation of parenting within the home.

Sex and sexuality Attitudes towards sexuality have also relaxed. Although past mores continue to weigh rather more heavily on the behaviour of young women than men, the loss of female virginity outside marriage is no longer the crime it was considered to be half a century ago. As Christalla, a 64-year-old grandmother, declared, in her day it was better for a young lady to 'have her eye pulled out than her name', or in other words to lose an eye rather than her honour. In order to ensure chaste conduct and an unsullied reputation, young women were regaled with 'dos and don'ts' by their parents and relatives. Christalla continued:

> We kept men at a distance. When somebody talked to a man she was considered a whore. We were ashamed in front of men and afraid of them. Our parents taught us to be that way, from the time we were babies. I hated men. We confronted them as though they were wild animals. Old men were drunk and they didn't behave themselves. They were teasing, even their cousins.

Control of young women persisted into the middle generation, with adolescent girls rarely allowed to go out, except to attend weddings and other family celebrations. Conservative rules of clothing such as the

avoidance of revealing garments and garish colours were also strictly
observed so as to avoid malicious gossip.

Virginity was a virtual *sine qua non* for marriage among women in the
older generations, and one of the grandmothers, Ellou, now 68, had a
dog constantly by her side to fend off would-be attackers. This is significant since even in cases where women had fallen victim to rape and loss
of virginity was patently not their 'fault', their lives thereafter would be
'in ruins'. A tarnished reputation meant that a violated woman would stay
single, unless, in the words of one elderly man, Sotiris, she 'could find
someone who was not one hundred per cent (mentally), so that he could
marry her'. This also applied to divorced women who, though few in
number, had much greater difficulty than their ex-husbands in finding
new spouses. However, the penalties for single women who became
pregnant out of wedlock were arguably the gravest, including loss of
respect and/or social isolation within their communities. As Toula, one of
the mothers, remembered, when this happened to someone in her home
area: 'the whole village turned against her, and whenever she was out in
public she was insulted by disgraceful comments'.

Over and above these forms of control, new brides in the oldest
generation were subject to having their wedding bed-sheets inspected by
their mothers-in-law. If they bore *korasata* (blood stains from the breaking
of the hymen), this verified the 'purity' of a new wife. In the case of
Ellou, a grandmother, the inspection was carried out by her husband's
sisters:

> My sisters-in-law came on the Monday and wanted to see the *korasata*. They
> thought that I was not only poor, but also dishonourable.

Men of the oldest generation also tended to feel that virginity or 'purity'
was a prized virtue in a bride-to-be, with one of the grandfathers, Sotiris,
declaring that it was: 'the most important thing that has to do with the
woman … Why should I take a used thing? I don't want it.'

Although sexual activity among men seems always to have been accorded greater tolerance, if not positive endorsement, it was still difficult
for men in small villages to have relationships without it becoming known
and/or a subject of scandal. As a result, men's licence to pursue sexual
experiences (at least in their immediate localities) was rather limited. This
is evident in the description one young man, Stavros, gave of his grandfather's youth:

> The situation at that time was difficult enough for a teenager aged 15 to 19. At
> the same time that their first erotic stirrings were awakening and their first
> sexual instincts were surfacing, the young men of that age had to stay as far

away as possible from the girls. The only groups of friends that could be seen were solely male or solely female.

Spontaneous or informal associations between the sexes could meet with harsh punishment. A grandmother, Stavroula, declared that keeping company with boys was something girls did not dare to do for fear of social exile, and similar sanctions seemed to apply even to men from the subsequent generation. As one middle-aged man, Georgiou, recalled: 'When they saw you talking to a girl they could expel you from school.'

Some of these practices now seem to have relaxed. The inspection of sheets seems to have disappeared during the time of the middle generation, and one of the fathers, Nicos, maintained that even though nearly all women were virgins when he got married, he would just as readily have married a non-virgin. While Nicos' view is the exception rather than the rule for his age group, such shifts are strongly welcomed and supported by male and female members of the youngest generation. Petrides, a 22-year-old man, for example, claimed:

> I see myself in the distant future, creating my own family. With my choices, all mine, away from the mistakes of past generations, away from ridiculous decrees like those of matchmaking and dowry and the myths of virginity.

However, the situation remains difficult for girls, and in the words of one young woman, Koulla:

> In our days, to a certain degree, the matter of virginity still exists and unfortunately only regarding that of the woman. There is a certain taboo about this subject and many people, including young people as well, are ready to judge a girl who chooses to have full relationships with a boy because they fell in love.

Marriage, family and fertility

Courtship and marriage While courtship and marriage are by no means one and the same, in the past they were much more closely intertwined. In the older and middle generations, where people (especially women) tended to become engaged at a young age, marriage would generally be preceded by one courtship only, and a long one at that. Among contemporary youth, there are more opportunities to mix freely with the opposite sex and to have a greater number of relationships before 'settling down'. Indeed, while in rural areas of Cyprus it is still by no means unknown for women to get married in their early teens, some of the female respondents suggested that they might not get married at all. Given the regimented nature of unions between men and women in previous decades, this shift is one of the most remarkable in respect of changes in gender.

Courtships in the oldest and even in the middle generation were usually initiated formally by a 'matchmaker', often a relative of the husband's family, who would approach the bride's father and ask for her hand. While attraction or infatuation may have been the basis of the match, there was far less freedom to 'marry out of love' and important factors included the material circumstances of the couple's families. Dowry was expected from the bride's family and could be a major burden on those with little property and many daughters. Dowry notionally included land, a house, furniture and household goods, the latter often consisting of silk items that women wove themselves. In accordance with the Cypriot proverb: 'I promise my vineyards so that I can engage my children', women from wealthy households could usually expect to find a match much more easily.

Family histories and reputation were also important in determining whether courtships would be formally endorsed. One of the grandmothers, Ellou, recalled how her father's womanising, reputed criminality and mysterious absences from their home village did not help her prospective husband, Koulis, to convince his family that she would be a good match, especially since her own family was so much poorer than his. Koulis also had five sisters whom he was obliged, as a dutiful son and brother, to help marry off before he could think of matrimony for himself. Although Koulis gave his sisters the best pieces of the relatively sizeable family estate, and left himself with only a small property, no dowry was asked of Ellou, and the marriage took place to a woman whose physical beauty had inspired a virtually immediate decision on his part: 'I saw her, she was nice. She was beautiful, like the sun. I said, "I will marry her".'

Saving for marriage, or winning parental approval, both constituted major reasons why courtships were often long drawn out. One middle-aged couple, Pavlos and Chrysanthi, were engaged in the 1960s for three years. They first met when Pavlos drove the buses that took Chrysanthi between her home village and the town where she was studying hairdressing. From the moment they caught sight of one another in the driver's mirror, romance blossomed. Yet because Chrysanthi came from a poor family, Pavlos' wealthy relatives were unwilling to let them marry. Ultimately, the only way to get Pavlos' family to accept the marriage was for Chrysanthi to get pregnant – the social shame that this would have brought upon the family was deemed greater than that attached to their son marrying 'beneath his station'.

Another women of humble origins, a grandmother, Roula, had to wait until the age of 33 before she had enough dowry to please her husband's family, and in the case of the nonagenarian, Andrulla, both she and her husband had parents with limited resources and endured a five-year engagement before they had enough money to set up home together.

The long engagements of many people from the older generations, particularly grandparents, would often be heavily policed by relatives. In their weekend meetings, couples would be chaperoned and/or on no account be allowed to touch one another. This tight control meant that some couples found it difficult to get used to one another when they finally married. One grandfather, Paraskevas, who was married at the age of 23, described the early years of his marriage as difficult because he did not know his wife's 'character, her peculiarities, or the way she conceived the world. I was overreacting because I didn't understand her behaviour. When we got used to each other, we were doing fine.' Another factor is that age gaps between husbands and wives were often significant. For example, Anita's maternal grandfather was 15 years older than his wife, whereas her own parents are the same age.

An important reason for closing age gaps between marriage partners is women's rising access to education and the labour market and the concomitant decline of the idealised notion of men as principal or sole breadwinners. In the past, men were usually expected to be established before taking on the responsibility of a wife who was likely to bear children soon after the marriage and thus be unable to work on a full-time basis. Marrying a younger woman therefore tended to be widespread. Another related, and crucial, influence on closing age differences at marriage has been exerted by the decline of arranged marriages where women were often betrothed from a young age to guard against potential spinsterhood. Stavroula, aged 77, whose own mother had been engaged at the age of 10, when she was still 'playing with dolls under her bed', recalls bitterly how, without her consent, she was forced into her engagement as an adolescent:

> I was 15. I was screaming, and I was saying that I was going to fall into the pit … They gave me that man without me wanting him … Until I was 15 I was happy, until I was 15 years old, until I was engaged. Then I suffered martyrdom … They gave you a husband without knowing him. Like that. Like a dog.

Narrowing age gaps in marriage are also the result of urbanisation and increased access to education, with young people in their teens and early twenties having greater opportunity to meet people of their own age in high school and university. Another important factor is the increase of tourism, which has facilitated contact with other cultures and led to a diversity of social environments over and above fairs and weddings in which the sexes can interact away from the watchful eyes of their parents and relatives. Andreas, a father who spent his youth in Limassol, described how his social horizons had widened with the building of cafés, arcades, recreation areas and clubs. By the same token, there is little evidence that young people today have many more relationships than in the past, or are particularly ready to engage in premarital sex. Indeed, although mixing between male and female peers is decidedly easier, dowry and matchmaking are increasingly 'out of fashion', and courtship and marriage are much more a matter of individual choice, most of the young continue to desire their parents' approval. For young women it could also be said that the shadow of parental intervention is never far away. Twenty-one-year-old Arianna, for example, complained that: 'The father and the brother believe that the girl is a person who needs to be watched and protected, and they think it is their right to interfere.' She added:

> Relationships between the sexes are more easy to hold, even though the previous generations do not approve of them. As a result, they are often held in secrecy, and many of us still feel that those involved in these relationships are doing something wrong.

In some cases, parents try to restrict the possibilities of relationships developing by giving their daughters limited scope to socialise outside the educational environment. As one of Arianna's contemporaries, Nina, remembered, during her adolescent years at the *lyceum* (senior high school):

> My afternoons were packed with extra lessons, any friends I had were within the school, and my social life consisted of the odd coffee at a cafeteria and an occasional visit to the cinema at weekends … my mother was rather strict about outings.

Although constraints on courtship and marriage have undoubtedly weakened, therefore, there seems to have been less readiness to concede to changes for women.

Family formation and links with kin In the light of the above, it is perhaps no surprise that the family as an institution remains fairly strong in Greek Cypriot society. Ties between family members living far apart (even in different countries) are usually kept alive by regular communication, although demographic mobility has clearly played a part in weakening more peripheral links over the past few decades. The gradually rising incidence of divorce, which at one time was vehemently disapproved of, and in which declining religious observance may be significant, has also contributed to some degree of fragmentation. As one one young woman, Anita, declared:

> The family in my parents' and grandparents' time was a stronger and holier

institution, an institution which was inviolate and unshaken. The divorces, the
dissolution of the families, were not accepted.

Family cohesion in the earlier years of the twentieth century was reinforced
by the close proximity of relatives in village communities, and by customs
such as shared meals. One woman in her forties, Rita, recalled: 'At noon,
everyone had to be at the table ... and at night, at dinner, everyone had
to be there too.'

Contemporary pressures of employment, higher education and so on
have meant that people find it harder to observe these practices. Nevertheless, even if relatives are also more dispersed, they almost invariably
get together on special occasions such as festival days.

Fertility and childbearing A trend towards the nuclearisation of family
units may be one reason for a slight rise in fertility in recent years.
Although Cyprus does not have a particularly high rate of population
growth, averaging only 1 per cent per annum in the 1990s (UNDP, 1995:
Table 16), in contrast to most countries in this volume the growth rate is
greater than it was in previous decades (0.7 per cent between 1960 and
1992). This is partly due to a drop in infant mortality from 30 per 1,000
live births in 1960 to 9 in 1992 (ibid.: Table 4). Indeed, back in the time
of the oldest generation, mortality rates were even higher, with four out
of grandmother Ellou's twelve pregnancies culminating in miscarriage,
and only two out of thirteen children surviving in the family of the
grandparents of 21-year-old Anita.

However, rising fertility also has a part to play. The fertility rate among
women aged 15–19 reached 27 per 1,000 in 1990 compared with only 21.2
in 1970 (UNDP, 1995: Tables A2.2 and A2.5). The total fertility rate (the
mean number of births likely to accrue to women surviving throughout
their childbearing years) is currently 2.5. While this may be higher than in
recent decades, it is substantially lower than in previous times.

The oldest generation, especially the wealthier among them, valued
children highly. Ellou, for example, claimed: 'Children are a blessing. And
since we were rich we wanted many children.' This is not to suggest that
other people, particularly poorer individuals, did not wish to restrict births.
For example, Andrulla, a grandmother who had married at 20, delivered
a total of twelve children, and although only seven survived, she was so
upset at getting pregnant at 47 and having grandchildren who would be
older than her own offspring that she put rocks on her belly and worked
herself into the ground in a vain attempt to induce a miscarriage.

The fact that young women such as Anita are only children is not just
a result of increased access to contraception, but, as her father explained,

results from a conscious decision to adjust to better survival rates and to the rising costs of children in modern society by having fewer offspring: 'The mentality is changing. You have to look at society, its demands, the conditions, you see the expenses.'

Education and work

Education   Among the oldest generation, it was relatively rare for people to have more than an elementary education, and only those from wealthy families were able to proceed to high school. Women, however, tended to be disadvantaged on all counts, especially when their parents were poor. This was due partly to lack of funds to buy school materials, partly to parents' need for help in the home, and partly to the fact that resources tended to be channelled to sons, as investment in men was deemed necessary given their primary role as household providers.

One grandmother, Andrulla, now 90 years old, never went to school and according to her granddaughter, Maria, never wondered why: 'In fact, my questioning her about education seemed odd to her.' Another grandmother in her seventies, Vasoulla, however, had been distraught when, as an 11-year-old child, she had been withdrawn from primary school:

> I went to school up to the fourth grade and they took me away, because they had to buy me books. I was bursting into tears, I was going to school with no books ... There were three sons older than me, and they bought books for those three sons and didn't for me. I was taking care of the children and weaving and doing everything. I was crying to go back to school.

Things began changing by the time of the middle generation, although even then women were rarely given the opportunity to go beyond primary education. This is partly because although primary education was made free and compulsory for all just after independence in 1960, secondary education remained optional and still had to be paid for. Further education also carried a high price. One father, Zinon, who passed his entrance exams to the Technical School in Limassol in the late 1960s, had to follow a vocational course in metalwork instead of an academic preparation for a university degree in a field such as architecture, engineering or chemistry, since the former lasted only four years as opposed to six. In the summer holidays, Zinon had to work hard to earn money for his tuition fees and school materials. Nowadays, however, most men and women not only finish their compulsory three years of secondary school (*gymnasium*), but proceed to senior high school (*lyceum*) and thence to higher education. This is remarkable given one young woman, Eugenia's, comment that as recently as 30 years ago: 'It was unthinkable that Cyprus would offer a university education.' Indeed, until 1989, when the University of Cyprus was established, people wishing to pursue degrees were forced to go to institutions in the UK or other countries.

Despite the fact that gaps between the sexes are closing, one 20-year-old woman, Nina, recalled that during her years in elementary school girls had to wear a uniform, whereas boys could wear what they liked. Although much of the curriculum was shared, sports and instruction in practical subjects were often gender specific:

> We had lessons in housekeeping while the boys had lessons in woodwork or gardening. The boys played football in physical education class, while we played other games more 'suitable' for girls. We used to take our revenge out on them during recess, by making fun of them and calling them names.

Women are still a minority in higher education establishments (both within Cyprus and in foreign universities) and tend to be channelled into courses that prepare them for jobs that have become increasingly feminised, such as teaching.[4] Yet a university education is increasingly a necessity for both men and women in a country where entry to most professions is barred to those lacking tertiary-level qualifications.

Employment and economic livelihood As of 1990–92, only 15 per cent of Cyprus' labour force was engaged in agriculture, compared with 21 per cent in industry and 64 per cent in services (UNDP, 1995: Table 11). This marks a radical contrast with the early years of the twentieth century, when around 80 per cent depended on agriculture and most were extremely poor (see Pantelidou, 1992). The growth and diversification of Cyprus' economy partly reflects the steady growth of urbanisation on the island in the last few decades (averaging 1.2 per cent per annum 1960–92). Over half the population (53 per cent) now live in urban areas, compared with just over one-third (36 per cent) in 1960 (ibid.: Table 15). Accompanying the shift from rural to urban employment and the removal of British rule, working days have shrunk from an average of 16 hours per day in the early part of this century (from sunrise to sunset in accordance with the rhythms of agricultural production) to a legislated 8 hours in formal urban employment together with entitlement to join trade unions.

As noted earlier, women's economic activity rate has risen over the last 20 years, perhaps as a result of urbanisation, although women have traditionally played an important role in agriculture. One of the grandfathers, Koulis, who became a wealthy landowner, butcher and bus company operator, employed a majority female population among his agricultural workers. His wife, Ellou, was also fully engaged in production, opening and running a grocery store and a shop in which she sold clothes and silverware: 'I wasn't a housewife. My mind was in business.' Being wealthy, of course, also allowed Ellou to circumvent the main problem faced by women working in all generations: reproductive labour. Ellou was able to hire a woman to help in the house, and by having her widowed mother-in-law come to live with her in later years, was also able to delegate the cooking. Poorer women of this generation, however, who had little choice but to work, either as maids or picking olives and potatoes, were forced to neglect their household duties. In fact, 90-year-old Andrulla had worked so hard alongside her husband in crop-growing and cattle-raising that she saw looking after children at home as a luxury: 'The children grew up on their own in the village and in the fields.'

By the middle generation, poorly educated women in urban areas began to enter factory jobs and laundry work as well as domestic service, while their male counterparts pursued trades such as painting, decorating, metal-working and construction. Given that women's overall rate of labour force participation today remains lower than that of men (who form 74 per cent of the workforce), it is clear that female workers face something of an entrenchment in traditional female sectors such as clerical work and sales (where they form half the workforce), and services (where they constitute 45.3 per cent of workers) (UNDP, 1995: Table A2.7). This is not to suggest, however, that men have fared much better. Compulsory military service (lasting 26 months) has often interrupted their education and careers, and several men over successive decades have emigrated to other parts of the world such as the UK, Australia and the Middle East in order to better their lot, especially with the decline in mine-working from the 1960s onwards. Nevertheless, men form around 90 per cent of administrative and managerial employees within Cyprus, and their average wages in the non-agricultural sector are at least one-third higher than those of women (UNDP, 1995: Table 2.5), testifying to women's continued disadvantage. This reflects not only a lag in women's educational achievements, but gender discrimination on the part of employers. As one 21-year-old, Nina, commented wrily: 'Let us refrain from discussing the lower wages offered to women for the same qualifications and jobs.'

Conclusion

In the eyes of informants, the most positive features in the evolution of gender roles and relations across three generations include rising educational opportunities for women, declining parental control over marriage, and greater opportunities for contact and communication between the sexes. Less progress has been made in reducing gender discrimination in the labour market, in lifting constraints on female sexuality, in devolving divisions of labour in the home, and in increasing the political visibility of women. While many of these problems are felt deeply by young female respondents, they require major attitudinal shifts and could be elusive in the short term, especially given that adherence to tradition may fulfil an important cultural need in the face of continued uncertainty over the island's future. While changes could well be hastened by policy initiatives, and Cyprus' prospective entry to the European Union could provide a stepping-stone, breaking the long-standing deadlock with Turkey is likely to remain the key priority for the population as a whole. Given the complexities of this situation, resolving territorial conflict may well slow the process of giving women's strategic interests the helping hand they so urgently need.

Recommendations

In the short and medium terms, recommendations that might be made to alleviate women's continued disadvantage include:

- Programmes aimed at encouraging greater sharing of household duties between spouses. These could be instituted in schools and at the community level. Additional assistance could be provided by community-based childcare facilities.
- Educational and community-level consciousness-raising programmes concerning sexual rights and with the aim of encouraging tolerance of premarital sexuality, especially among young women. This could include information on birth control and access to contraception.
- Elimination of gender-stereotyping in subjects at all levels of the educational curriculum: in elementary schools by giving all schoolchildren instruction in a wide range of practical subjects such as domestic science, woodworking and so on, and at university level by encouraging women to pursue 'masculine' subjects such as engineering and the natural sciences, and stimulating men's interest in the arts, humanities and education.
- Policies for affirmative action in respect of the appointment of women to managerial positions within firms, and, in the political domain, for the support of female candidates for parliamentary seats and cabinet positions.

Notes

1. Compiled from a report prepared by Michele Kefala, Education Department, University of Cyprus, Nicosia.
2. Other opposition parties include the Progressive Party of the Working People

(AKEL: communist), the Socialist Party (EDEK), the Liberal Party, and the Democratic Socialist Renewal Movement (ADISOK).

3. A plebiscite held in Cyprus in 1950 showed that 95.7 per cent of Greek Cypriots desired union with Greece (Pantelidou, 1992).

4. In the past teaching posts tended to be restricted to men, because of their better education and the fact that they were often required to move from village to village and to live alone.

CHAPTER 8

NEW ZEALAND[1]

This chapter deals with a relatively affluent nation, known for its socially progressive attitudes and policies. Although recent economic recession has undermined many achievements, the legacy of a commitment to social equality remains. This is particularly evident in the arena of gender roles and relations, which have undergone significant transformation over the past three generations. New Zealand was one of the first countries in the world to grant female suffrage (in 1893), and the promotion of gender equality has been institutionalised since the end of the nineteenth century. Despite this, it is only among the younger generation where parity between the sexes has been realised to any great extent. With marked gender inequalities characterising the lives of older informants, those from the middle generation began to challenge prevailing patterns, and the youth of the country now seem to be enjoying the fruits of their parents' efforts. Perhaps because of the early commitment to gender equality, there has been little resistance to many changes, although fears were expressed among informants about the decline in 'family values', the fragmentation of the family and the lack of parenting skills among the young. With contemporary society oriented towards 'attaining a lifestyle' rather than 'making a living', many lamented the loss of traditional values revolving around close community and family networks. This has been exacerbated by increased urbanisation, international mobility and the recent economic crisis.

Country profile

New Zealand, otherwise known by its Maori name of Aotearoa, is located to the east of Australia and south of Melanesia in the South Pacific.[2] With a surface area of 268,000 square kilometres, New Zealand comprises two main islands (North Island and South Island), as well as a number of smaller islands. Although New Zealand was named by the Dutch explorer, Abel van Tasman, who arrived in 1642, the (re)discovery of the country is most commonly associated with the Englishman James Cook, who arrived in 1769. Prior to Tasman's arrival New Zealand was inhabited by people of Polynesian origin, known collectively as Maoris. Early interaction between the Maoris and Europeans (the latter known by the Maori name of 'Pakeha'),[3] rested primarily on trading agricultural goods to new settlers, as well as negotiating land transactions. While most early land was bought for small sums from Maori tribal chiefs, conflict between Maoris and Pakeha also led to large tracts being confiscated during the nineteenth century. Although the Maoris were ostensibly guaranteed land rights through the Treaty of Waitangi, conflicts ensued when they refused to sell their land to the new settlers (Murton, 1987).[4] Although New Zealand became a self-governing British colony in 1856 and a dominion in 1907, it was not until 1947 that it became fully independent.

The demographic composition of New Zealand is currently a complex mixture of Maoris and Pakeha in what is now considered a multicultural society (Bedford and Heenan, 1987). Out of a total population of 3.58 million in 1995 (EIU, 1996h: 3), Maoris represent around 13 per cent, compared with 48.6 per cent in 1858. The bulk of the Pakeha population are descendants of immigrants (78.3 per cent), mainly from Great Britain, and other countries such as Greece, Italy, the Netherlands, France and Germany, as well as some from Eastern European nations. Closer to home, Pacific Island Polynesian migrants from Western Samoa, Tonga and the Cook Islands have been migrating since the 1950s, with the largest intakes in the early 1970s (currently representing around 5 per cent of the total population). Despite a reversal in patterns of population movement from immigration to emigration in the 1980s (prompted largely by economic recession), the 1990s saw another upsurge in new arrivals to New Zealand. These flows mainly comprised Asians, who made up 60 per cent of the 55,000 immigrants who arrived in 1995 (EIU, 1996h: 10). This reflected the government's relaxation of entry requirements for wealthy and skilled immigrants in the belief that this would stimulate economic growth and foreign investment. Despite the apparent benefits of such a policy, it has also given rise to an anti-immigration lobby, led primarily by the New Zealand First political party. Indeed, this party won a considerable percentage of the vote in the national election in October 1996, allowing them to form a coalition with the incumbent National Party, with Winston Peters, the leader of New Zealand First, taking up the post of deputy prime minister and treasurer. New Zealand's political system is based on a parliamentary monarchy, with Queen Elizabeth II as the head of state, represented by a governor-general. The national legislature comprises a House of Representatives, elected for the first time in 1996 by a mixed-member proportional representation system, replacing the 'first-past-the post' method.

Since 1984 New Zealand has undergone economic reforms based on liberalisation and free-market principles, marking a shift from a welfare state towards an open-market economy. While this initially brought some economic growth, in 1987 the country fell into deep recession, following low GDP growth rates since the 1970s (1.9 per cent between 1970 and 1980, and 1.5 per cent between 1980 and 1993) (World Bank, 1995: Table 2). Despite negative growth rates in the early 1990s (−4.2 per cent in 1991), real GDP growth increased to 2.5 per cent by 1995 (EIU, 1996h). In 1993, real GDP per capita stood at US$14,990, and GNP at US$12,660 (UNDP, 1995: Table 21). Alongside these fluctuations in growth rates, New Zealand's economy has also diversified. While it is still a primary producer country, with dairy products being the most important export in 1995, followed by forest products (timber), and meat (lamb and beef), manufacturing, trade and financial services are now the largest contributors to GDP (EIU, 1996h: 3).

Although New Zealand is renowned for its progressive social reforms and far-sighted legislation dating back to the late nineteenth century (including old-age pensions and minimum wage structures), the recent shift towards a free-market system has led to a drastic erosion of state welfare. Many programmes have been cut, such as the state-funded health insurance system, and others have been privatised. These changes, together with deregulation of the labour market and the weakening power of trade unions, mean that the nature of New Zealand society has been transformed in the last decade and a half. Although the changes have brought increased income disparities, basic social indicators remain high, with widespread literacy, 78 per cent educational enrolment, a life expectancy at birth of 75.7, and a fertility rate of 2.2 (UNDP, 1995: Tables 21 and 33).

Social progress in New Zealand has been accompanied by high levels of gender awareness, at least in the formal political realm. As early as 1876, women had the right to be elected to local government, although they could not stand for the national parliament until 1919. However, channels for voicing women's concerns were available from 1896 onwards through the National Council for Women, established by Kate Sheppard as a non-party organisation, which was widely viewed as a 'Women's Parliament'. This early commitment to women's representation in New Zealand society stems partly from the role of women in pioneer settlement. Although the relatively egalitarian nature of gender relations among the indigenous Maoris was undermined by the British and their patriarchal notions of gender roles, colonisation served to temper the more extreme manifestations of male dominance. Through a physically and emotionally demanding life for both sexes during early settlement, the distinction between home and work was broken down and women played a crucial role in maintaining their families' well-being both socially and economically (Olssen, 1980; Pearson and Thorn, 1983). However, although British Victorian gender ideologies were reinterpreted in the New Zealand context, women were still perceived as socially inferior, and were denied many basic legal rights. Indeed, until the mid-twentieth century the so-called 'cult of domesticity' was very much in evidence and women's domestic roles were exalted, and often institutionalised, through the Mothers' Union, the League of Mothers and the Country Women's Institute (ibid.).

The early commitment to gender equality in the formal realm has not always translated into high levels of political participation in contemporary New Zealand. Although 35 per cent of local council members were female between 1990 and 1994, only 21 per cent of seats in the upper and lower chambers were held by women, and a mere 8 per cent of ministerial posts (UNDP, 1995: 60).[5] This is still substantially greater than most other countries in this volume, and women's voices have increasingly been heard through the Ministry of Women's Affairs, established in the mid-1980s, which has provided a forum for women to contribute to government policy (Harrison, 1994). In the economic sphere, women's presence in the paid workforce has increased with activity rates of 41 per cent in 1994 (although this was only 53 per cent of male activity rates) (UNDP, 1995: Table A2.3). Women also tend to be concentrated in white-collar and service jobs, and are still largely excluded from upper-level managerial positions. Moreover, women still earn less than 80 per cent of men's income, despite fifteen years of lobbying to achieve 'pay equity' and better working conditions for women. Nevertheless, much progress has been made over the last 20 years in bringing women's issues to the fore through the establishment of national level groups such as Rape Crisis, Women Against Pornography (WAP), and Right to Life (pro-abortion) (Harrison, 1994). Legislation has also been passed, such as the Domestic Protection Act of 1982, which provides for non-molestation and non-violence orders, as well as emergency shelter for women wishing to escape violent domestic situations.

Methodology

The methodology employed in the New Zealand case was based on in-depth analysis of the lives of three generations. The study was conducted by the Department of Anthropology at Victoria University in Wellington, the capital of New Zealand. The researchers were drawn from final-year anthropology students taking a course in anthropological methods. Twelve students participated in the research. These came from a range of rural and urban backgrounds, with one student from a part-Pakeha, part-Maori family, another with Maori family ties, and one with a Polynesian back-ground. The project was carried out between March and June 1995, during which time the twelve students conducted interviews with three family members, one from each generation: grandparents, parents and siblings. Most of the interviews were carried out in Wellington itself, although some students had to travel beyond the city at weekends. A total of 36 interviews were conducted using a semi-structured format covering the range of issues included in the other country studies. Although focus group discussions were not held with informants (see Chapter 2), the interviews were discussed with other students on the course, providing important insights and perspectives.

While in general the interviewing process was straightforward, there were a number of problems. The informants were often reluctant to discuss politics due to lack of interest. The topic of sex and sexuality proved a difficult one, especially among the older generation, and this was exacerbated by the fact that all researchers were related to their informants. Interviewing family members also created problems in terms of a few informants not taking the project seriously enough – siblings would say, for example: 'You know that, why are you asking me?' The younger generation was also the most impatient, with discussions being more disjointed than with other generations. Indeed, each generation and gender tended to focus on different issues, with fathers being most expansive on issues such as work and education, but less informative on topics relating to spirituality, health and sexuality. Mothers had the most to say on each topic. The researchers themselves were also anxious to stress that they were only able to provide insights into a small window of New Zealand society, given the small sample size. The informants were drawn from a range of rural and urban backgrounds, with the grandparent generation originating mainly from rural areas, and the middle and younger groups from urban settings. Their ages ranged from one grandmother who was 92 years old to a sister who was 15. Given that all the informants were relatives of university students, the majority were from relatively well-off backgrounds.

Before discussing gender roles and relations, it is important to outline how the informants perceived the broad changes in New Zealand society. Although the country is still deemed to be relatively affluent and egalitarian, all generations voiced concern over the decline of the welfare state and recent economic recession. These factors, encompassed in the notion of a 'user pays' climate, were seen as contributing to the creation of deep divisions in society, particularly between rich and poor. Indeed, poverty is a relatively new phenomenon in New Zealand, given its comparative rarity until the 1960s. Other changes included the increasingly urbanised culture;

although the image of New Zealand is one of a 'clean green' country, the majority of the population now live in urban areas.[6] As a result, rural living has become denigrated in the national consciousness, with one young man going as far as to say that: 'Rural kids are pretty stupid, dumb.' In part, urbanisation has been blamed for the decrease in community spirit and a so-called 'breakdown in family values', as people have become more mobile both within New Zealand and internationally. On a more positive note, there was a general feeling that a 'Kiwi culture'[7] has emerged over the last three generations. This was partly related to the greater prominence given to Maori concerns, but also linked with increased international mobility, which encouraged people to appreciate the distinctive features of New Zealand. It was also felt that the youth of the country were offered more opportunities today, in terms of freedom, mobility, and the ability to attain an 'advanced lifestyle'. It was in the area of gender roles and relations that the majority, especially women, felt that many important changes for the better had occurred, a view that cut across all generations.

Gender roles and relations

The nature of gender roles and relations in New Zealand is broadly egalitarian, although the reality has often been very different. There have been marked changes and improvements over time, as most informants agreed. Despite a commitment to gender equality since the end of the nineteenth century, the experiences of the older generation in particular reflected widespread inequalities. Informants from this generation discussed how women were expected to be domesticated and to 'keep the tins full' (ensuring that enough baking had been done to meet the needs of hospitality). Men were expected to be the main economic providers, bringing in a single cash income on which women depended. There was little questioning of these roles, with grandmothers noting how their own mothers had encouraged them to become 'good wives and mothers', and how there were peer expectations for young women to marry shortly after finishing secondary school. The only woman from the older generation who had not married or had children remembered how she was treated differently from her peers, of whom she said: 'Friends had such traditional values instilled in them.' Although grandfathers discussed how they had grown up expecting to have a family and to work to support a wife, all felt they had been considerate to their wives' wishes. This might suggest that gender divisions of labour were not as strict as they may have appeared, and/or that men themselves were not rigorously enforcing these divisions.

Therefore, while both men and women of this generation generally accepted this gender division of labour as 'natural', women from the parents' generation began to question normative gender roles. One mother, Nancy, felt that she was treated as a second-class citizen in the past, and even today described her role as 'chief bottle-washer and cook'. However, many parents felt that there was a greater balance of commitments between men and women in their generation, fuelled largely by women's incorporation into the labour market. It is among the younger generation where disparities have been challenged by both women and men. As a result, awareness of gender differences and the need for shared domestic and economic responsibilities is now fairly well established. One mother, Geraldine, who considered herself to be 'gender-aware', noted how her two sons ensured that she was up to date on gender issues: 'But they, in actual fact through their schooling, sometimes fill me up on gender-related issues, about this sexist remark, or you shouldn't say it like that.' Despite these changes, however, almost all the informants across the generations believed that there were 'natural' differences between the sexes based on biological factors, although most conceded that socialisation was also critical. Although some legacies of traditional patterns remain, resistance to change has been muted, with even grandfathers accepting the re-constitution of gender ideologies.

Socialisation and childhood   Patterns of socialisation were felt to have undergone dramatic changes, especially in relation to the devolution of socialisation functions to sectors of society beyond the family, such as schools, churches, the legal system and the media. One grandmother, Emily, felt that these shifts were negative: 'In our day, you just got on and did things.' Another grandmother, Mary, shared these sentiments: 'Whereas family business was family business to be clear of gossip, today family business seems to be everybody's business, whether it is neighbours, community, or the welfare agencies.'

In line with these changes has been the questioning of gender roles, especially among the middle and youngest generations. This has been the result, first, of the feminist movement in the 1960s and 1970s, and second, of peer group pressure among youth in particular. Indeed, the youngest generation noted how gender-related issues are brought up in everyday conversation and negotiated, an opportunity not available to their grand-parents. Reflecting this, the oldest and middle generations made most distinction between boys and girls in the way they were raised. One parent, Helen, felt that boys tended to monopolise or dominate their families, attracting more attention, while girls just got on with their tasks. Others from this generation felt that even when attempts were made to treat boys and girls in the same manner, differences were inevitable when they became teenagers. Harold, for example, thought that: 'Boys and girls may not be raised differently, but as teenagers different concerns arise, such as safety of girls, and the emphasis on girls and boys having the same opportunities in sports and education.' Several parents also thought that it was difficult to escape stereotyping; as Hilda pointed out: 'Some people gloat on traditional values, particularly for a man to be a real masculine man.' Despite a general consensus that boys and girls should be treated equally, all informants remembered girls' tasks around the home being different from boys'. Barry, a father, recounted how boys did more chores outside the home, such as mowing the lawn, while girls helped with the cooking, cleaning and washing. However, divisions were not clear-cut, with one mother, Mary, remembering how she and her sisters were expected to help on the farm in the busy season. Furthermore, it was noted that many differences in the treatment of boys and girls will remain as long as safety for women remains an issue. Jenine, a mother, recalled her bitterness at the fact that when she was growing up her brothers had been allowed to stay out late with their friends, whereas her own movements were strictly curtailed. However, she now does the same with her own children because she fears for her daughters' safety. In general, however, all generations felt that parents have become more liberal, with less difference in the socialisation of boys and girls.

Another aspect of changing socialisation patterns was in the field of child discipline. Several grandparents felt that they had been raised very strictly. Many lived under the threat of corporal punishment, in the form of the cane or slipper. In contrast, parents today dare not touch children for fear of retribution. Certainly, for anyone outside the family to punish a child, especially physically, is absolutely forbidden. While these notions are incorporated in the Children and Young Persons' Protection Act, and the New Zealand Children and Young Persons' Service, there was some resistance to the the idea that children have rights that should be protected at all times. Louise, a parent and schoolteacher, reported how difficult it was to impress the gravity of a wrongdoing on a young person nowadays. It was also felt, especially among the older and middle generations, that children have many more privileges today, both economically and in terms of opportunities. One grandfather, Wesley, recounted the hardships he suffered when he had to take a job as a grocer's assistant at the age of twelve, in order to earn a few extra shillings for his mother. In contrast, parents today give children pocket-money, although there was little consensus as to whether this should be a right, or in exchange for doing tasks around the home. Moreover, parents now provide 'the best' for their children, which involves costly activities such as music, dancing or elocution lessons. While in the past these activities were seen as privileges, children now feel that they have a right to them. Louise, a middle-aged schoolteacher, pointed out how low-income families found it difficult to fund such activities, both in school and outside. Therefore, while children are encouraged to engage in a wide range of extra-curricular activities, this is often only possible for those in better-off families.

Parental roles and parenthood In the past parenting fell heavily on mothers, while fathers were committed to generating income. Many women from the older generation said that there were strong social pressures on them to be 'good mothers'. Motherhood was seen as a self-sacrificing role for which women were naturally equipped. Among grandfathers, their responsibilities lay in economic support, as well as holding the family together and presenting a face of unity to the outside world. While the older respondents generally accepted this situation, informants from the middle generation expressed their disquiet at these inequalities. Geordie, a middle-aged man, remembered: 'Dad took us fishing, hunting and into the bush, while mother had to wash all the dirty clothes and make sure there was food on the table to feed us.' Indeed, many from the middle generation felt they were at a turning point in terms of attitudes. In particular, women felt that they were increasingly asserting their individual rather than family interests, reflected in their move into the labour market. The younger generation were all of the opinion that parenting must be a shared activity. The vast majority thought that it should be integrated with careers for both males and females. Contradictions arose, however, in that respondents of both sexes across all generations still believed that women were better suited to bringing up children.

In spite of this shift towards sharing responsibilities concerns about parenting were voiced by most respondents. These were related to the perceived difficulties of modern living, with parents juggling time commitments, which in some cases involved parents moving abroad to find work. The implications of this included children going unsupervised at home, homework being neglected, and child truancy.[8] On the other hand, many informants felt that social disorder was emerging through the dissolution of families as people neglected their responsibilities to their children. This debate was intertwined with worries over the increase in single-parent families and irresponsibility on the part of fathers. Strategies to deal with these difficulties were discussed, with a number of people from the middle generation believing that the lack of role models could be remedied by introducing some form of teaching on what parenting involves. On a more pragmatic level, Susan, a divorced mother, reported how she had asked a non-family member to come and live with her and her children as a designated care giver in order to overcome problems of balancing her commitments. In another two cases where mothers had become sick or injured, the eldest daughters had taken over domestic responsibilities and cared for the younger children. While this put great strain on intra-household relationships, in later life the two women involved felt they were better people as a result.

Sex and sexuality The issue of sex and sexuality was the most difficult and sensitive, especially among the older generation. At the same time, it is in this sphere that most changes have occurred over the past three generations. The topic was widely considered taboo until the 1960s, but contemporary New Zealand has a much more tolerant and open attitude. While two grandparents declined to discuss sexuality, preferring to 'skip that one', the others recounted how sexual matters were not discussed with parents, at school or even between spouses. Sexual activity was generally confined to marriage, although two grandmothers admitted how they had become pregnant before they married. Interestingly, this was the first time that this had been discussed openly in the family.

For the middle generation, there was a move towards greater openness. Although discussion of sex was still forbidden with parents, information was gleaned from friends, with some experimentation with partners before marriage. In the words of one mother, Marlene:

> In the 1960s couples were sleeping around, but there was still a taboo on sex as an open topic of discussion ... people are more honest and talk about it now whereas the parents' generation tried to pretend it did not happen. Mother and I had a little talk, which we both found embarrassing.

While the middle generation were more sexually active, some felt that this also led to unwanted pregnancy and high divorce rates. Phil, a father, noted: 'Our peer group were sexually active with no precautions. So people got married, and now there are many divorces.' Indeed, the topic of sexuality was banned for discussion openly in schools to those under 16 until 1988. Until then, schools faced the problem of teenage pregnancies with no way of counteracting this through a formal teaching programme. The views among the younger generation were considerably more tolerant, with information on sex and sexuality garnered from a range of sources such as parents, peers, books and the media. Sexual experience outside marriage is now considered 'normal', although elements of social opprob-rium remain as far as women are concerned. A young respondent, Jill, pointed out that: 'Women don't have to be a virgin, but still you get that society pressure ... you know that women can't act like a guy. If she does they'll think gosh, slut.' Therefore, while most young people thought that discussing sexuality was 'natural', women are still constrained by the legacy of past attitudes.

Marriage, family and fertility

Partnerships and marriage Marriage as an institution has undergone a significant reconstitution over the past three generations. While for many, marriage remains the main accepted entry point to the creation of new families, for others, mostly from the younger generation, strong partnerships based on shared responsibilities are often considered as being of equal worth. Moreover, while the church retains the notion of the sanctity of marriage, the state now recognises other forms of partnerships such as cohabiting couples.[9] The significance of these changes is clear in the views of respondents from different generations. While grandparents tended to view marriage as an unbreakable bond sanctified by the church, the middle and younger generations realised that this bond was becoming increasingly fragile. While one young man, Jason, noted how: 'Marriage is the fusion of all families and children are the symbol of marriage,' he also recognised that the reality was very different. Marriage for life is no longer considered to be as likely for the younger generation as it was for their grandparents. While the majority of the young were still in favour of the notion of marriage, it was not seen as a prerequisite for establishing a partnership and having children. Furthermore, they were also aware of the fairly high likelihood that marriages and partnerships would fail in the long run, reflected in the fact that one in three marriages in New Zealand now ends in divorce. At the same time, they felt that their generation were better equipped to deal with marriage break-up because many had experienced the divorce/separation of their own parents. Divorce was also seen as more acceptable for both sexes. Whereas men have always tended to escape stigma, some parents commented on how divorced or separated women in the 1960s were treated as social outcasts. Nowadays, as women have acquired greater economic and social autonomy, the status of divorcée is not the burden it once was.

The causes of contemporary marital discord and break-ups were perceived differently across the generations. Members of the older generation thought the reasons lay in a lack of willingness among couples to work at their relationships, and to give up too easily. Young people cited the fact that there are more pressures on couples to perform tasks in different, often incompatible, spheres of life, and thought that as people live longer and their interests diverge, couples 'drift apart'. It is interesting that differences between Pakeha and Maori cultures were mentioned by a few informants. One grandparent, Jim, discussed how the Pakeha ideal of marriage was based on British Victorian principles advocated by Christian missionaries and supported by colonial government edicts. On the other hand, he noted how Maori culture puts less weight on marriage, with the sibling tie and the *whakapapa* (ancestral line) being at the core of family life. Along with many of the younger generation, Jim felt that this Maori ideal (which is much closer to contemporary reality) should be given greater importance in wider society. Marriage, therefore, was the cornerstone of New Zealand society until the 1960s, but has since become less of a social necessity. In turn, while marriage may give women some social status, economic success and striving for one's children are now deemed equally important.

Fertility and childbearing While there was little in-depth discussion of the informants' experiences of childbirth, it was widely accepted that there has been a dramatic decline in fertility. Among the oldest generation, it was common for women to have between five and eight children, while the norm among the middle generation was two or three. While most of the younger generation expected to have one or two children, some declared that they did not want to have children at all. This is reflected in national figures: between 1970 and 1993, the total fertility rate declined from 3.0 per cent to 2.2 per cent (World Bank, 1995: Table 26). While the availability of contraception was seen as important, other factors were also involved. Many of the grandparents who came from large families were raised in rural areas where they were expected to help on the family farm. In addition, as their parents got older, at least one, but sometimes two or three children, remained living close by to care for them and ultimately take over the landholding. However, with the expansion of the education system and employment opportunities, sons and daughters often moved elsewhere, the importance of farming declined, and along with it the need to have large numbers of children. This reduction in fertility has also been accompanied by changes in family structures and relations.

Family and community relations Despite changes, and in the eyes of some, fragmentation, the majority of informants still considered a strong notion of the family as the ideological core of New Zealand society.[10] Some informants identified ethnicity as an important factor differentiating family structure. The Pakeha notion of family was broadly seen to correspond with a nuclear residential unit based on the marriage tie. The Maori concept of family, known as *whanau*, was seen to be based on extended structures revolving around the *whakapapa* (genealogy) or *aiga* connections. The *whanau* holds its members together by virtue of their knowledge of kin ties, and includes all siblings and their children, as well as more distant relatives such as aunts, uncles and cousins. The social core of the *whanau* is the *hui* or family gathering (mainly weddings and funerals) rather than the residential unit. While the oldest generation of respondents still held expectations that the Maori would adopt Pakeha family structures, the youngest embraced diversity, noting an ever widening range of options of family forms and less pressure to marry.

Beyond recognition of ethnic differences, discussion centred mainly around perceptions of the meaning of family and its changing composition from personal and societal perspectives. Accepting that the majority of respondents were Pakeha, most considered family as parents, siblings, and offspring, as well as nieces and nephews. However, there was also a broad consensus that the family had undergone considerable 'down-sizing' over time, with a perceived decline in the existence of extended units. In turn, the importance of nuclear families was also seen to have diminished given the increase in single-parent units and households comprising non-related members. The other key idea was the recognition of friends as family members on the basis of emotional closeness. One informant from the middle generation, Helen, noted that she had 'two layers of family', one being her parents, siblings, children and husband, the other her aunts and uncles. However, she also included some close friends in her inner circle as more important than the latter. Indeed, this identification of friends as quasi-family members was particularly common among the younger genera-tion, reflecting a broadening of the concept of family in recent times, and, in some cases perhaps, the decision not to have children.

Yet the weakening of blood ties, or what many from the older and middle generations termed 'family breakdown', was a concern to many. One father, Harry, claimed that the old view of the family unit as a secure environment had disappeared, and like many respondents he attributed this to geographical mobility, both nationally and internationally. Dorothy, a mother, remembered how her own mother's close kin had all married within her home area around Auckland and settled around the family homestead. Dorothy, however, moved away to Wellington along with her sister, in order to improve her employment opportunities and to provide a 'better life' for her children. This led to some emotional distancing from her natal family, which has not since been resolved. Among the middle and younger generations, overseas travel for extended periods has also contributed to a breakdown in family cohesion. Nina, a mother, re-membered how returning from New Zealand from a visit overseas initially strengthened family ties, yet ultimately, her new experiences have set her apart from other family members. One manifestation of the dispersal of families was the decline in the importance of Christmas. While in the past, gatherings at the home of grandparents at Christmas were central to family life, they have now lost their social significance due to the difficulties of drawing together family members from many locations.

One aspect of family transformation frequently raised was the issue of 'dysfunctional' families. While, in general, this referred to tensions in contemporary family relationships, more specifically, it alluded to the increase in single-parent households and the rising divorce rate. Indeed, a mother bringing up small children without the presence of a husband/ father was perceived by many as the biggest cause for concern.[11] While lone parents were largely accepted by middle and younger generations, the older generation held negative views, blaming such structures for the 'distintegration' of the family in a broader sense. From a more pragmatic perspective, Kelly, a student, saw her own family as dysfunctional after her parents split up. Her sense of loss was compounded by the fact that she was living in a different city at the time. In this light, it is no surprise that her relationships with friends strengthened and effectively took the place of immediate family.

Summing up the picture of the views we have from the respondents, it is clear that nowadays family support is seen as less important. While family loyalty is still apparent, there is diminishing responsibility among relatives to help out in times of crisis. Furthermore, community support networks, which are common among the oldest generation, no longer play a role in the lives of the middle and youngest generations. Instead, the individualism associated with urban living is perceived as the preponderant societal principle.

Time management The breakdown in family and community relations was also blamed on increased pressures on time, particularly among the middle generation. It was thought that family members spend little time together as they have too many commitments and their careers interfere with socialising. People rarely make time for leisure pursuits or talking. Peter, a father, pointed out: 'The problem with family life at the moment is time ... being able to commit sufficient time to the family and dividing your time satisfactorily.' One major change has been the loss of mealtimes as a forum for communication. Vera, a mother, remembered the roast dinner on Sundays and the big gatherings at Christmas as the 'idyllic days of the family', blaming their demise on television, leisure activities and membership of clubs. Conflicting interests were also seen to have taken their toll on marriages, and on relationships between parents and children. One mother spoke of the time devoted to taking children to various activities, and to attending school meetings. She felt that this was a major change from her mother's day when there were fewer activities for children, and they just worked or played around the farm or neighbourhood.

Education and work

Underlying many of the changes in the areas discussed so far has been increased access to education and employment. These have opened up over time, with a particularly marked shift in the opportunities for women. This has had important ramifications for gender roles and relations. While education is mandatory and free for children between the ages of 5 and 15, there has been a recent increase in the proportion of people entering higher education, either in one of the seven universities, or the numerous polytechnics.

Education The importance of education has increased substantially in the last 50 years. Although grandparents recognised the need for formal education in their day, the highest level of educational aspiration in the 1940s and 1950s was secondary school. This was mainly because girls needed to be able to care for children and the home, whereas boys needed to learn a trade in order to support their families. As a result, boys' education was considered more important. Judith, a mother, recounted how her grandfather discouraged her own mother from furthering her academic career: 'He happily paid for her to attend a dressmaking course, although there was little emphasis on her pursuing a long-term career.' By the time Judith herself was at school, she remembered greater encouragement for girls to do well, particularly from mothers. She also pointed out how there was little discrimination among the younger generation on grounds of gender: 'My daughter and my sister's daughter are both being encouraged to complete tertiary education with the aim of entering the paid workforce.' She went on to offer an explanation: 'Such a trend may well reflect a greater influx into the paid workforce of women pursuing long-term careers and climbing the employment ladders in competition with their male counterparts.' Today, it is therefore just as important for women to pursue education as for men, and if possible to gain some form of tertiary education, preferably a university degree.[12]

The nature and role of education in New Zealand has also altered over time. Discipline was mentioned by many informants as the hallmark of schooling in previous decades. Stuart, a middle-aged father, remembered how caning was a regular part of his schooldays, whether for not having polished his shoes or being late for class. However, he also thought that these measures were positive in that they 'brought respect for authority and developed the "right" attitudes'. Manley, a grandfather, shared these views, on the grounds that strict discipline taught young people to respect one another and to follow social mores. While the oldest and middle generations criticised the lax discipline in the contemporary education system, youth generally condoned it. Moreover, the younger generation stressed how education taught them self-worth, or, as Jenny pointed out, how it 'schooled your self-esteem'. It was suggested that education has evolved from a means to acquire basic qualifications to a way of improving life chances. Aspirations have increased as higher education has become attainable for a wider number. Jack, a father, claimed that education has allowed young people to seek more options in their careers, and in broadening their horizons through travel overseas, or what is known as 'OE' (overseas experience). Indeed, OE has been an integral part of the educational experiences of youth since the 1950s onwards, prompted by the desire to learn about other countries. A central element of Kiwi culture, OE initially involved working in London, but now includes a wide range of countries, with South East Asian countries becoming popular in the 1980s and 1990s. Interestingly, while OE is confined primarily to young, single people, and is often deemed an important pre-marriage experience, informants reported that more women travel abroad than men. Indeed this, more than any other factor in contemporary New Zealand society, is testimony to the freedoms experienced by young women today.

Work and economic livelihood While there was no information on the specific occupations held by informants, many expressed their views on wider issues relating to employment and careers. One important issue to emerge was that people have shifted from aspiring to a certain job or type of employment, towards aspiring to a lifestyle. This was summed up by one of the fathers, Steve: 'Now lifestyle is more important than work,' reflecting the widening diversity of occupations available to people, and the all-encompassing nature of work today. Underlying this was the fact that the work/leisure distinction has become more blurred as individuals and companies choose to work in many different places and with varying schedules. For example, many more leisure activities are offered as part of the workplace, such as 'fitness clinics'. Work for the oldest generation, especially on the farm, was time-consuming but involved no pursuit of leisure. Indeed, many grandfathers recounted the immensely arduous nature of their work, and commented on the contrast between this and the 'office jobs' held by the middle and younger generations today. Samuel, for example, described how he had started work at the age of 13, and continued to work throughout his teenage years while still at school, to provide money for the household. He worked during the day and went to polytechnic at night to study English and bookkeeping. He eventually got a carpentry job through the post-Second World War Rehabilitation scheme, and earned £3 6s for a 40-hour week.

In line with the expansion of educational opportunities for women, the major change in employment patterns has been the increased participation of women. Women in New Zealand have always worked in some capacity, beginning with the colonisation process. During the 1880s the manufacturing sector developed, providing jobs for women in factories and giving them an alternative to teaching and dressmaking. Moreover, in the early twentieth century, domestic service and clerical work were particularly important for young single women before they married (Olssen, 1980). The most rapid expansion of female employment, however, came between 1936 and 1976, when the female workforce increased overall by 192 per cent (Pearson and Thorns, 1983: 177). Among the informants, this 'revolution' was prompted by economic necessity. While few women from the older generation were involved in paid work beyond the homestead, women from the middle generation began to enter the labour market in the 1960s. Although three mothers and a single woman had developed their own careers, all had started working because of economic need and/ or separation from a spouse. While Mary, a teacher, felt she had enriched her life through her career, she also recognised that it set her apart from the mothers of her children's schoolfriends. By the 1970s, however, this stigma had largely disappeared, with many women working out of choice as well as necessity. With the foundations set in place by their mothers, women from the younger generation all expected to be able to pursue their careers along with marriage and raising a family. While wage rates between men and women have not yet achieved parity, the differential is not as large as in other countries in the volume: women's average in non-agricultural employment is 80.6 per cent of men's (UNDP, 1995: Table 2.5).

A more recent characteristic of employment patterns in New Zealand is the impact of rising unemployment and economic recession during the 1980s. While previously unemployment was practically unheard of, redundancies began to affect many families, regardless of their socio-economic status. Unemployment rates were particularly high among men, with a number of fathers recounting how damaging this was to their self-esteem. Some blamed the state and politicians for job losses, although it was widely recognised that economic restructuring was greatly to blame. As Gerry, a father, pointed out: 'Unemployment is a sign of the times which makes people suffer; it will never be solved because there are less jobs now due to industrialisation.' A few, however, especially from the oldest generation, held the view that some people were just lazy and needed to look for work. Overall, there was concern over increased levels of poverty in society, which most blamed on the distintegration of the welfare state. For some, the affluence of New Zealand society, originally founded on a strong economy, is now under threat.

Conclusion

New Zealand has shifted from a largely rural society based on a foundation of conservative, traditional values revolving around family and community, towards a highly urbanised culture based on individualism and materialism. Concomitant with this have been changes in the social and economic structure of the country, manifested in the transformation of family forms, and increased opportunities in education and employment. The youth of New Zealand are presented with many more opportunities than their grandparents. Partly as a result of OE, there has been an increasing awareness of New Zealand's place in the wider world from the 1960s onwards. While the oldest generation viewed Britain as the mother country from which models of legal and social systems emanated, ties with the UK are currently considered less important. With a renewed focus on Kiwi culture as distinct from British, there has also been an increasing recognition of Maori society and values over the last 20 years. Many of the Pakeha youth are now turning to Maori values and social mores as a source of inspiration for modern living.

While the emergence of a Kiwi culture and the opening up of opportunities have been largely welcomed, concerns were also expressed about the negative corollaries of change, especially from the older generation. In particular, the fragmentation of the family and the emergence of 'dysfunctional' families were seen as potential threats to the stability of society. Many perceived the rise in divorce rates and in single-parent families, as well as the declining importance of marriage, as undermining the social fabric. Fears were also expressed about divisions among the population related to recent economic recession. Previously unknown phenomena such as poverty and unemployment are creating new forms of tension.

Nevertheless, in the sphere of gender roles and relations, shifts towards gender equality have met little resistance. While the oldest generation accepted a fairly strict gender division of labour, women from the middle generation began to question their confinement to the home and the narrow expectations accorded to them. Gradually, women began to aspire beyond their association with the reproductive domain, and asserted themselves through educational attainment and participation in higher-status jobs. Over time, women placed their individual interests on a par with family interests and gained a degree of autonomy. Although women today have still not achieved parity with men, especially equal pay, significant strides have been made. These have been made easier by the general acquiescence of men to changing gender norms. Both women and men from the youngest generation now tend to share the view that women are equal citizens, and that commitments in both productive and reproductive spheres are the responsibility of both sexes. The androcentric image of New Zealand as the land of 'rugby, racing and beer' no longer appears to be engrained in national consciousness.

Recommendations

• Parent education programmes comprising courses on parenting skills, aimed primarily at the youth.
• Ethnic awareness programmes aimed at raising awareness and high-lighting the beneficial moral and cultural influences of ethnic minority and indigenous groups (especially Pacific Islanders and Asians) for wider societal progress.
• Consciousness-raising programmes to encourage the acceptance of multiple family forms.

Notes

1. Compiled from a report prepared by Nancy Pollack, Department of Anthropology, Victoria University, Wellington, New Zealand.
2. Aotearoa literally means 'Long White Cloud'. This has been increasingly adopted since the Maori Language Act was passed in 1987, making Maori an official language. Government ministries and departments, as well as official documentation, now use Maori terms in conjunction with English.
3. Nowadays, the term 'Pakeha' refers to people born in New Zealand of European descent. Although it remains a contested term, it is a standard classification of ethnicity used in the New Zealand census (Longhurst, 1996: 148).
4. The Treaty of Waitangi involved Maori chiefs ceding their sovereignty to the British crown in exchange for full rights and citizenship of England. Maoris were guaranteed possession of their land, with the Crown agreeing to act as an agent when they wanted to sell it. Although the rationale for the treaty was an attempt to prevent the illegal appropriation of Maori land by colonisers, it remains disputed, with the state still negotiating claims from Maoris against the Treaty Settlement through the Waitangi Claims Tribunal.
5. The absence of women at ministerial level has continued in the new government of the National Party and New Zealand First coalition sworn in in December 1996, with only one woman, Jenny Shipley, in a cabinet comprising 20 ministers. Beyond this, two other women hold ministerial positions: Christine Fletcher, the country's most popular MP with a majority of more than 20,000, and Debbie Morris, who at 26 is the youngest MP in history to have reached ministerial status. 'Cabinet sworn in', *New Zealand News UK*, 18/12/96.
6. In 1960, 76 per cent of the total population lived in urban areas. By 1993, this had risen to 86 per cent, reflecting an annual growth rate of 1.5 per cent (UNDP, 1996: Table 40).
7. The term 'Kiwi' to describe people and/or culture from New Zealand is derived from an indigenous, flightless bird of the same name, which is also the main symbol of the country.

8. Recently, various 'home-alone' cases have come to the attention of the national media, placing the issue of parenting under the national spotlight.

9. Christianity is the most common religion, dominated by Anglicanism (Church of England), practised by 25 per cent of the population, followed by Presbyterianism, practised by 18 per cent, and Roman Catholicism, accounting for around 16 per cent.

10. 'Family' has taken on a broader connotation insofar as it is increasingly accepted that families may take different forms (Harrison, 1994: 64).

11. In 1980, 23.9 per cent of households in New Zealand were headed by women (UNDP, 1995: Table A2.5), and while some of these are likely to be widows, many are undoubtedly lone parents.

12. The enrolment ratio among tertiary school age (18–23 years) in 1970 was 65 women for every 100 men, while in 1990 this had increased to 104 women for every 100 men (UNDP, 1995: Table A2.6).

CHAPTER 9

CANADA[1]

The wealthiest nation included in this book, Canada is an industrialised nation with high levels of economic and social development. While dominated by both British and French influence from its colonial past, the population is also a rich mosaic of indigenous groups, and a range of immigrant groups who have been drawn to the country's many different physical environments and economic opportunities. As a result, Canada is a country in continual renegotiation of its identity, in terms of both nationality and constructions of gender. This is reflected here through the discussion of the life histories of 75 women included in the country survey. Given the richness of the initial case studies, the chapter can, at best, provide only a brief insight into the lives of the women, with regrettably little or no discussion of a male perspective. Moreover, the stories have a strong regional and ethnic character rather than national emphasis (covering the provinces of British Columbia, Alberta, Manitoba and the Northwest Territories, Ontario, Quebec and Nova Scotia).

Although regional variations are marked, a number of common themes emerged from the life histories. Throughout the provinces, women reported significant shifts towards equality between men and women, both in the private sphere of the household and in the public realm of the workplace, with the widening of educational opportunities being cited as particularly important. While women of the oldest generation often reported being constrained by ideology and society into the 'traditional' lifestyle of homemaker, the strength and independence of women of this age group shone through forcefully. Although some argued for the maintenance of 'old-fashioned' values, the majority recounted ways in which they had tried to subvert tradition. With the path already broken, their daughters and granddaughters were able to forge ahead, albeit slowly in many instances. While the youngest generation have certainly not reached any state of parity with men, they all expressed how their lives were easier, and how they had more freedom. At the same time, many refrained from laying the blame at the feet of individual men, recognising the importance of individuality and complementarity between the genders.

Country profile

At the outset it is important to emphasise the complexity and diversity of both landscape and people of Canada. The second largest country in the world, it covers 9,970,000 km², although only around one-eighth of the territory is effectively occupied. Indeed, the population of almost 30 million (EIU, 1996h: 3) is concentrated in a narrow strip 150 to 300 kilometres wide across the southern part of the country. The nation is made up of ten provinces and two northern territories.[2] While it can be divided into a range of different regions, such as the English- and French-speaking areas, or the 'heartland and hinterland' (with southern Ontario and Quebec as the heartland and the rest of Canada as the hinterland – see McCann, 1982), most commonly, the four eastern provinces are known as the Atlantic or Maritime Provinces, the mid-western provinces as the prairies, and Ontario and Quebec as Central Canada.

Canada was first populated by Native Indian groups who migrated from Asia across the Bering Strait at the end of the last Ice Age 6,000 to 10,000 years ago. By the beginning of the sixteenth century there were around six different Indian tribal groups, as well as the Inuit (meaning 'people' and originally called Eskimo) who had migrated from the Arctic to southern Greenland. With the arrival of European settlers, known as the charter groups (Fleras and Elliot, 1992), the Native population was reduced from around 350,00 to 100,000 through wars, disease and settlement of their lands. Despite some Viking settlement around AD 1000, it was the French who first laid claim to Canada at the beginning of the sixteenth century, with Jacques Cartier asserting rights to the area around the St Lawrence river, which came to be known as New France.[3] However, it was not until the seventeenth century that the French took particular interest in Canada, which until then had served merely as a source of fish and furs. The country then became a province of France in 1663 after Samuel de Champlain set up missionary posts in Quebec and Montreal. Throughout the seventeenth century, the fur trade dominated the economy, which led to continuous disputes with the Native Indian population and the building of a series of forts as far as Louisiana in the south and Saskatchewan in the west. By the beginning of the eighteenth century the British had started to assert rights over the east coast, and after a series of battles culminating in the British defeat of the French at Quebec City in 1759, the French then handed over the country to the British at the Treaty of Paris in 1763. Although the British gave French Canadians entitlement to practise their religion (Roman Catholic), the use of French civil law and the right to political office, they maintained positions of power in business and politics. This period therefore laid the groundwork for the Quebec separatist movement. The nineteenth century saw the arrival of settlers from the United States and the pushing back of the Canadian frontier, although this also led to tensions between the British and the United States and the war of 1812. After various rebellions and calls for independence, the British North America Act was passed in 1867 by the British government, making the colony a confederation and establishing the Dominion of Canada. Not until 1982, however, did Canada gain full independence from Britain with the Charter of Rights and Freedoms under the premiership of Pierre Trudeau.[4]

Canada remains a constitutional monarchy, ruled by a parliamentary system. The national legislature comprises a bicameral federal parliament, a House of Commons of elected members, and a Senate appointed by the prime minister (currently Jean Chrétien of the ruling Liberal Party) (EIU, 1996g). The ten provinces are largely self-governing, each with a premier who is elected provincially, as well as a lieutenant-governor appointed by the federal government, with the two northern territories remaining under federal government control. Political developments in the 1990s have been characterised by considerable upheaval. After the Progressive prime minister, Brian Mulroney, stepped down in 1993, followed by the short-lived Kim Campbell, Canadians then voted in the Liberals led by Quebecker Jean Chrétien. By 1997 the traditional opposition parties, the Conservatives and New Democrats, were virtually absent from parliament, with the separatist Bloc Québecois party forming the second largest party and the official opposition.

The demographic composition of Canada reflects what is often referred to as a 'mosaic' (rather than 'melting pot' as is commonly used to describe the USA) (Fleras and Elliot, 1992).[5] The largest single population group are Canadians of British descent (40 per cent), with a further 27 per cent French descendants of the first pioneers, concentrated in the province of Quebec. The rest of the population of European origin includes Germans (the largest group), Italians, East Europeans, Dutch and Scandinavians. More recently Asians, and particularly Chinese from Hong Kong, have settled, along with Latin Americans and Caribbeans (ibid.). Also important in Canada are aboriginal or 'First Nations' people, who make up around 4 per cent of the total population with around 330,000 Native Indians, 27,000 Inuits, and approximately 400,000 Métis (which refers to those of mixed aboriginal and European blood). Around 72 per cent of Native Indians reside in 2,250 reserves and 600 registered 'bands', with the majority living in poverty and often dependent on government assistance. More recently, the profile of First Nations peoples has been raised, often through violent confrontations with federal and provincial governments, although the issues of Native Indian rights and claims remain to be resolved. One of the most important is the Inuit Land Claim, which brings with it the promise of the federal government to create a new territory in Canada in 1999, called Nunavut (our land). Significantly, the Nunavut Implementation Committee is considering gender equality in the New Legislative Assembly, with each riding (district) having one male and one female representative to reflect the gender composition of the population.

With the coming to power of the Progressive Conservative Party in 1984, Canada has witnessed dramatic economic reforms along neo-liberal, free market lines. As with such measures elsewhere in the world, this has involved trade liberalisation, the promotion of export-led growth, and widespread deficit reduction. Recent years have seen cutbacks in public expenditure involving the shift of the burden of social welfare from the federal government to provincial governments, the elimination of social programmes such as mothers' allowances and federal social housing projects, a reduction in old age pensions, and reduced spending on education, health and welfare payments (Griffin Cohen, 1994). The delivery of other services has been affected by privatisation, and deregulation of transportation, postal and communication systems. Laying the groundwork for Canada's push for 'international competitiveness' and economic reform was the North American Free Trade Agreement (NAFTA) and the General Agreement on Tariffs and Trade (GATT) (ibid.). The reforms were accompanied by a slump in average annual GDP growth rates from 4.6 per cent for the period 1970 to 1980, to only 2.6 per cent between 1980 and 1993 (World Bank, 1995: Table 2). While real GDP growth stood at 4.6 per cent in 1994, it had fallen again to 2.2 per cent by 1995 (EIU, 1996h: 3). In 1993, GNP per capita was US$19,970, showing a decline from 21,070 in 1992 (UNDP, 1996: Table 26; UNDP, 1995: Table 21). While Canada is often associated with agriculture, forestry and fishing, this represented only 2.9 per cent of GDP in 1995, with services accounting for the largest share (40.6 per cent) (EIU, 1996h: 3). The dependence of the Canadian economy on the United States, facilitated further by the NAFTA, is illustrated by the fact that almost 80 per cent of exports and 75 per cent of imports in 1995 were to the United States (ibid.).

While economically Canada has lower average per capita growth rates than many industrialised nations such as the United States and Japan (although higher than New Zealand), levels of social development are among the highest in the world. Recent economic reforms are threatening to undermine progress in this area, but in 1993 Canada had the highest HDI of all countries included in the UNDP ranking (UNDP, 1996: Table 1). This is reflected in an average life expectancy of 77.5, an adult literacy rate of 99 per cent, and a combined education enrolment ratio of 100 per cent (ibid.). Interestingly, however, when the GDI is considered, Canada drops to ninth place, although it is ranked fifth in the GEM (UNDP, 1995: Tables 3.1 and 3.5). Furthermore, gender inequalities in terms of income, life expectancy, literacy and educational enrolment have deteriorated over time, in that 1970 GDI figures rank Canada in second place (ibid.: 79). Overall, women have high levels of participation in Canadian public life, even if it is somewhat lower than would be expected from a country with such high levels of human development. Politically, women's representation is highest at the local level, where 18 per cent of council members are female. Although at a parliamentary level women hold 17 per cent of seats in the upper and lower chambers, they occupy only 14 per cent of ministerial posts (UNDP, 1995: Table A2.4). In the economic arena, women's position is contradictory. Economic activity rates are high with 43 per cent of women aged 15 and over being active in the labour force (ibid.: Table A2.3). Women are also well represented in administrative and managerial posts (40.7 per cent of employees), and professional and technical positions (56 per cent), despite a concentration in clerical and sales work (67.6 per cent) and services (57.1 per cent) (ibid.: Table A2.7). However, it has been noted that women's move into the higher echelons of the labour market has led to a substantial under-valuing of these jobs, which were previously held by men (Griffin Cohen, 1994). At lower levels of the economy, recent recession and economic restructuring has contributed to an increase in temporary and part-time work among women, although full-time rates have remained fairly static (ibid.).[6] Recession has also done little to improve the wide wage gap between men and women. For example, women in Canada earn only 63 per cent of men's non-agricultural wages, which is lower than all other industrialised countries, and significantly lower than many less-developed countries, such as Vietnam, Tanzania and Bolivia (ibid.: Table 2.5; see also Griffin Cohen, 1994). Overall, however, women's position has improved since the Second World War, with more women moving into the labour force (largely into service occupations), a decline in fertility through increased access to family planning, and improved educational attainment (Truelove, 1996). However, it is important to guard against generalisations in this large country.

Methodology

Coordinated by Greta Hofmann Nemiroff of Carleton University and the University of Ottawa, in conjunction with five women's studies academics from the University of Victoria, University of Calgary, University of Winnipeg, Laval University, and St Mary's University in Halifax, the methodology employed was a country-wide effort. Based on in-depth interviewing techniques similar to those used in the other chapters, the methodology was constructed through discussion of a basic plan through tele-conferencing and consultation with students from various disciplines within the women's studies programmes in each university (including English literature, history, philosophy of education, anthropology and sociology). In each university, five to seven female students were identified who would each interview three female generations of their family, including themselves. These students represented the diversity of Canadian population in terms of social class, sexual orientation, race, ethnicity and occupation. Although there was little emphasis on uniformity, with each region developing its own questionnaire, a 'tip sheet' on interviewing techniques was devised after consultation, along with a 'release form' as a basic guide for the interviewees. Despite drop-outs, 24 students finally participated, along with six teachers. In total, 75 people participated in the survey in 1995. Each interviewee was required to write a short account of her interview together with an introduction on the situation of women in her region. These were then collated in the final report, discussed on a region-by-region basis. In all but one locality (Quebec), students worked as a group, which was an important part of the interviewing experience.

Overall, a great deal was learned. Linda Christiansen-Ruffman from St Mary's University, for example, said she learned about the importance of feminist pedagogy by understanding that the researcher is in a constant state of discovery. Huguette Dagenais from Laval University found that students needed to learn the flexibility of qualitative interview methodologies, and how people often reinterpret their lives through being interviewed. Keith Louise Fulton from the University of Winnipeg was interested in how women processed their accounts and why some women dropped out of the project. Eliane Silverman from the University of Calgary learned about the conventions involved in telling life stories, and gender differences in the narration of accounts rather than the events *per se*. For example, she wondered if women followed 'male' conventions, and that if left to their own devices, they would perhaps tell different life stories from those elicited in the project. Furthermore, she noted how difficult it was for some students to bring the 'voices' of their mothers and grandmothers to life, being struck by the inadequacy of written and spoken languages and how much it takes to express the uniqueness of each person's life. Finally, Christine St Peter from the University of Victoria stressed how eager students were to publish their family stories, with one Guatemalan contributor, Ana, from British Columbia stating: 'You have no idea what this means to my grandmother to be part of a Canadian story.'

While numerous difficulties were encountered, particularly in relation to confidentiality and 'family secrets', as well as problems in editing such

CANADA   183

a richness of personal accounts, the overall process was seen as rewarding.
As Christine St Peter of the University of Victoria pointed out: 'My
students are so in love with the words of their mothers.' Overall, the
students were surprised by stories they had not heard before, or by attitudes
and values they had not realised their mothers and grandmothers held. In
one case, a mother and daughter from British Columbia managed to
rediscover their 'intimate ties': 'Getting to interview my mother broke
down those barriers, reforged a connection between us as adult women.'
As a group, the students were proud of the accomplishments and strengths
of their forebears, and felt the experience of being able to interview them
as stimulating and validating. In the words of Greta Hofmann Nemiroff:
'The lives women lead are central to the well-being of society, and the
skills and wisdom we have developed in this process merit recognition as
true knowledge and true art.'

All 75 informants are female, ranging from a 13-year-old teenager from
Alberta, to a 96-year-old Native Indian woman whose life is interpreted
through her granddaughter and sister. Around half the women are widowed,
divorced or separated and they live in a variety of domestic arrangements:
nuclear families, single-parent households, and female-only units comprising
lesbian couples and their children from previous heterosexual partnerships.
Education levels vary, increasing from the older to the younger generation,
although many women from all groups have some form of higher education. The employment profiles of the women are skewed towards the
caring professions, especially teaching, nursing and community work. As
noted earlier, the ethnic origins of the informants is varied, on account of
not only the inclusion of First Nations people (Native Indian and Inuit),
but also the wide range of immigrant groups.[7] It is also worth pointing out
that there have been changes over the generations with respect to how
people discuss their lives. Alice, a grandmother from Nova Scotia, did not
want to use her real name because she felt that her family's 'good name'
should be protected.[8] In contrast, her daughter Yvonne and granddaughter,
Valerie, were unconcerned with safeguarding family privacy. As Yvonne
notes: 'I'm sure this is a reflection of the changes in society toward more
openness and frank discussions about matters which were once "taboo".'

Gender roles and relations

Gender roles and relations in Canada have undergone major transformations. It was generally agreed that women have gained more recognition
over time, and that they have been able to fulfil many more roles. The
asymmetry between women and men has gradually lessened with time.
The stories of the older generation were dominated by accounts of

inequality, especially with respect to men's power over women. In one extreme case, Kwei-Yun (Precious Cloud), a Chinese-Indonesian grandmother from British Columbia, noted: 'The females were treated as slaves and the males were the slave drivers.' Another grandmother, Barbara, also from British Columbia, reiterated this: 'In my day, women were more chattels than they are now. Men thought they could rule the roost.' Most also agreed that the prevailing ideology at the time was that 'women's place was in the home', and that men were the breadwinners, with both roles imbued with a strong sense of duty. As Madge, an elderly woman from Alberta, pointed out: 'In my generation, you knew where your place was. You were the wife.' Despite this rigid role assignation, many grandmothers were far from submissive. As Adrienne, from Ontario, stated: 'Be your own person and be independent. I wouldn't want my daughters and granddaughters taking orders from a man, 'cause I never did.' While most grandmothers welcomed the greater equality, some were nostalgic. Alice, a grandmother from Nova Scotia, believes that women are less respected nowadays: 'We had freedom and respect. Men tipped their hats when they met a woman in the street, and removed their hats when they entered a restaurant.' Madge shared similar sentiments: 'I am just now beginning not to expect a man to hold the door open for me, and I think that women are missing something when we let that go.'

Although more 'traditional' notions were adhered to among women of this generation, they also inspired their daughters. Julie, a mother from British Columbia, stated: 'Older women have such a marvellous perspective of what life is and should be, whereas younger women are so challenged and so "fast lane" that they haven't got time to have their philosophies.' In many cases, the middle generation took a lead from their mothers, either deciding to be different from them, or continuing their moves towards the goal of greater equality. This generation saw themselves as redefining their place in society. While most embraced change, this was not without stress, as Jackie, from Nova Scotia, remembers. She felt that so many changes were 'scary', and that sometimes it was 'difficult to keep up'. This is echoed by Yvonne, also from Nova Scotia: 'My generation seems like an in-between generation, where lots of things changed.' The youngest generation expressed more security and were more at ease with their roles and relations with men. Indeed, much of the antagonism expressed by their forebears had disappeared among this group. Shelley, from Manitoba, stressed the importance of treating men and women as individuals, noting: 'Sometimes men surprise me … some say the nicest things, some say the most horrible things, some say human things. They're not just women, they're not just men, they're people.'

Changes in gender roles and relations were linked in many cases with

feminism and the women's movement. Although some of the older generation were unsure as to the precise meaning of feminism, when prompted
they all expressed strong views. Lillian, a grandmother from Nova Scotia,
was not sure of its meaning until voting rights were mentioned. She then
went on to say that in the past, voting was a 'man's thing', but that since
then: 'Men have learned that there's more in the women's brains than in
theirs a lot of the time.' Dorothy, a grandmother from Ontario, thought
that feminism had changed women, who are now:

> more into their own these days, they are not under a man's thumb as they used
> to be. I believe women are smart, most women are morally superior to men. I
> think they should be put into parliament. I think men are crooked and women
> should run everything.

While a number of grandmothers considered the feminist movement to
have caused considerable damage as well as bringing progress, most still
believed it had benefited women. Jenny, a grandmother from Alberta of
Ukrainian origin, thought women had become more 'aggressive', and
'sometimes get carried away', also noting that: 'If women want to play
ball, they should form their own teams and not play on men's.' In one
definition of feminism, Margaret, from Nova Scotia, thought it meant: 'a
woman using her own name, not her married one. She keeps her own
identity.' The middle generation were also in broad agreement over feminist
principles, although many disagreed with feminism and the women's
movement *per se*. Elizabeth, a mother from Alberta, does not 'agree with
feminism. It is much broader than that, standing up for women's rights
and everybody's rights. I wouldn't exclude men. I don't have to go and be
militant about it.' The youngest generation was most clear about feminism
and its value, as Christine from Alberta, states: 'Feminism is everything.
It is a lifestyle, it is political affiliation, it means that women are trying to
gain the respect they deserve.' In turn, Valerie, from Nova Scotia, stressed:
'I prefer the word equalist to feminist. We don't need to emphasise on
one sex or the other. We don't have to do what men have done to us in
order to make us equal.'

Socialisation and childhood Although patterns of socialisation have
changed somewhat, children still tend to be brought up along broadly
'traditional' lines. This is particularly evident in the allocation of domestic
chores, which has remained fairly constant over the three generations. Just
as Jenny, a grandmother from Alberta, remembers cooking, cleaning and
looking after the younger children while her brother looked on, Leita, a
daughter, also from Alberta, recalls how: 'Girls had baths and boys had
showers ... Mom knitted and sewed; Dad built things.' Similarly, Donna,

a mother from Ontario and the eldest of twelve children, reminisces with some bitterness how she was brought up in 'a male-dominated home [where] the girls did the bulk of the chores'. Indeed, it was the eldest daughters from all generations who seemed to bear a disproportionate burden of labour in the home compared with other siblings of both sexes. Rachelle, a young woman from Ontario, shares similar experiences with Donna: 'Everyone has some things to do but I feel that I have the largest share … make supper, do the dishes, pretty much everything … things that everyone else doesn't do.' In a slightly different context, Helen Thundercloud, a mother from Manitoba, remembers how she was withdrawn from her residential school in Ontario (Native Indians were required to go to such schools to learn the 'Canadian way of life') to take charge of her three siblings when her mother's alcoholism grew worse: 'I pretty well was playing mother, making meals, chopping the wood.'

While tasks within the home were shared unequally between boys and girls of all ages, parents also seemed to be more protective of daughters than of sons, who were given a much freer rein. Jennifer, a daughter from Ontario, noted the differences:

> My parents always seemed more over-protective and questioning with me than my older brother. Expectations concerning household responsibilities seemed to be placed more heavily on me as well. I often was at home baby-sitting while my brother was out socialising and I frequently cleaned up after dinner while the boys watched sports.

Variations in these patterns occurred only when parents were divorced or children were brought up in so-called 'non-conventional' families. Isabele, a grandmother from Nova Scotia, recalls how her parents were divorced when she was seven years old. Both she and her siblings (male as well as female; younger and older alike) were required to contribute substantial domestic labour to help their mother: 'There was work to be done, whether you were a boy or a girl, it did not matter.' Emily, a daughter from Winnipeg, grew up in a 'lesbian household' after her parents divorced when she was four years old. Her relationship with her mother, her mother's partner and her brothers is very harmonious. Rather than her brothers being a source of resentment, they are role models for Emily:

> My brothers are important for what it's like to be a kid growing up. They show not only what good things I should do, but also things that now I think I won't do.

While parents and family are the major arbiters in the socialisation process across all generations, children's peer groups are also important in shaping behaviour and attitudes even if the latter tend to reaffirm 'traditional' gender stereotypes. Jennifer, a daughter from Ontario, complained about the negative implications of this:

> Seeing girls unquestioningly lose their identity for the sake of 'popularity' made me cringe growing up. Stereotypes of women were reinforced as they acted dumber than, weaker than, or less than they were. I made the choice early on to be true to my convictions and conform for no-one.

Parental roles and parenthood Socialisation processes and childhood experiences of the informants were fundamentally influenced by their relationships with their parents. In some cases the roles presented by parents have served to perpetuate 'traditional' notions of men's and women's place in society, particularly among the elderly. Dorothy, a grandmother from Ontario, remembers a strict division of labour between her parents. Interestingly, however, she chose her father as her role model:

> My role model was mostly my father. He sort of ruled the roost, most men those days did. Mother was pretty hard-headed betimes, and pretty pushy too, but she went along with dad mostly. My mother worked in the house, she baked, cooked, milked cows and helped my father in the fields on the farm. She never worked [outside the home] until dad was older, after we lost the farm. My father was not a good manager [but] he wouldn't allow her to look after things. A man was the boss, he was the king of his little domain.

As gender roles have undergone renegotiation, the responsibilities of parents within the home have become more equal. Susan, a younger woman from Ontario, described how:

> My father does the grocery shopping, baking and vacuuming, and my mother does a lot of the cooking, cleaning and laundering. When either one of them needs support, the other is always willing to help out. This could be the result of the ever changing world and the realities of having two working parents.

Across all generations, women have looked to their parents for inspiration. While in a minority of cases, informants' negative experiences have given them the determination to change their own lives for the better, most drew on the characteristics they most admired in their parents. Donna, a mother from Ontario, recalls her father with bitterness, yet recognises how her experience made her stronger:

> I had an authoritarian father who is ... very self-centred and is also an alcoholic, which ... crippled the family. His behaviour was never challenged ... I was numb to my reality, but ... vowed at a very young age that no man would ever dominate me.

In general, however, women looked to their mothers and grandmothers as role models, as well as discussing them with deep affection. Xiao-fa, a mother of Chinese-Indonesian origin from British Columbia, said: 'As for my mother, she was my role model. And I would still choose the same role model now because she is a very stable person even though her life was a very unhappy one.' Similarly, for Sophie, a daughter from Quebec, her mother encompassed many roles: pedagogue, psychologist, teacher and nurse.

Beyond recognising the multiple duties their mothers had taken on, it was the strength and independence of their mothers and grandmothers that women found most admirable, especially when they subverted the norms of the day. Debbie, a mother from Nova Scotia, sees her own mother as 'a capable and empowered woman' and believes that if her mother had been 'born into politics, she would have been a leader in the forefront'. Kathy, a daughter from Alberta, admires her grandmother for similar reasons: 'She was active politically long before women were commonly in public roles and she didn't do much housework. I really admired her because she was the head of the household and because material possessions didn't mean much to her.' Sally, from the middle generation, who lives in Manitoba in a lesbian relationship, and whose mother refused to adhere to her gender-typed role (until she died from a self-induced abortion when she was only 29 years old) recalls:

My dad was a logger so my mom did all the chores. She was very athletic and strong, both fun and funny, an intimidating person. She dressed in dad's work shirts and pants and old hats and swung around that farm like she had everything in control. She chopped wood and dug ditches. She scythed the fields with a hand scythe. She could build just about anything with a hammer and a saw. She could do plumbing, electrical work and the mechanics of a car.

Motherhood, which is historically and ostensibly the rationale for women's domesticity, was important for most women. Many commented on the centrality of mothers to family cohesiveness, as well as the contradictions inherent in the role. Debbie, a mother from Nova Scotia, never aspired beyond her traditional role: 'I felt the need to be a wife and mother. Society and family expected me to be, and I didn't want to be a nurse or a secretary.' One of Debbie's peers, Julie from British Columbia, said: 'I knew that I would be a mother. I had to be a mother even if it meant adopting children.' As women took on other roles, especially in the labour force, motherhood became more of a secondary concern. Shelley, from Manitoba, asks:

'Will I be a good enough mother, will there be a nuclear war, will we all be living like a Third World country? ... I have so much yet to do ... when I'm ready, maybe too late for the other person ... I feel I have so much more to accomplish in today's society.

Over time, the boundaries between mothering and homemaking have become more distinct. While many grandmothers perceived the two as intertwined, the youngest generation differentiated between motherhood and domestic labour, considering the former to be more important. Chelsea, a daughter from Alberta, for example, wants to be a mother, but is not interested in cooking and cleaning.

Sex and sexuality Sex and sexuality rarely emerged in discussions with survey respondents, although among the older and middle generations this may have reflected reluctance to discuss such a sensitive subject, and perhaps the younger generation simply did not consider it significant. Indeed, the only context in which sexual matters arose were in relation first to lesbianism, and second to sexual abuse. A number of lesbians were included in the sample and they openly discussed their experiences and the effect of their lifestyles on their family and friends. Laura, a daughter from British Columbia, explained her difficulties:

> I also spent the first part of my life caught between my mother's standards of 'proper behaviour for girls' and what I see now as a need to prove my own hetereosexuality to myself. For the most part I felt very asexual and that didn't fit with what I saw around me ... Even the word 'lesbian' did not exist in my adolescent imagination. It was only as a result of my first contact with the gay community at university that I began to understand my earlier experiences.

Despite problems with homophobia among other family members, the experience of lesbianism was perceived as largely positive. Emily, a daughter from Manitoba who lives with her mother and her mother's partner, thinks her mother's sexual orientation has made her more broad-minded and politically motivated:

> [mother] really pushed politics into my face ... Life politics. It's always there. And I think it gave me an analysis of life that other people around my age didn't have ... It's also given me an opportunity to think in ways other people haven't had.

While not widespread, sexual abuse was discussed by a number of women. Emiline, an Inuit grandmother from Nova Scotia, recalled her own abuse in an indirect manner: 'And I remember men going around chasing women and the women were literally scared but nobody really helped them. If they raped somebody it wasn't considered rape. It was the man's right. Maybe it was different for others, but it was hard for me.' Although these types of experiences have been painful for the women involved, they have also learned from them. Jennifer, a daughter from Ontario, who was sexually assaulted by two 'friends' at the age of 14, now feels very strongly about fighting back: 'Being a fighter, my need to challenge others to work for change has never been stronger.' Similarly, Sally from Manitoba, who was abused as a child by a neighbour, and did not tell anyone at the time, now works as a counsellor for the battered women's movement and in the Manitoba Youth Centre.

Marriage, family and fertility

Courtship, partnerships and marriage Courtship prompted little attention in women's life histories, with marriage taking precedence in discussions. However, a number of women from the younger generation noted how formal courtship and dating has become less popular. This appears to be related to the move towards viewing men and women as individuals rather than as bearers of their gender. Emily, a daughter from Manitoba, noted how: 'I see people my age following less roles – actually very few people date. The prime requirement for going out with someone is being a really good friend.' At the same time, dating is seen to encompass notions of romanticism, which is treated with cynicism by youth. As Shelley, from Manitoba, put it: 'Fairy tales made me demented, in their depiction of a helpless damsel, when [I] knew [I] could handle anything. I was no helpless damsel and knew it.' Among certain ethnic minority populations, courtship also took on significance with respect to dating. Michelle, a Chinese-Canadian daughter from British Columbia, discusses the constraints imposed upon her by her parents:

> Compared with my mother's generation, I feel that women have more control in their relationships. My parents disagree with interracial relationships; they believe that their children should date and marry only Chinese-Canadians. I think to some extent their disapproval of interracial relationships has affected the way I perceive my relationships. There is a part of me that wants to please my parents, and a part of me that wants to make my own choices.

Part and parcel of the waning importance of courtship is that the institution of marriage has become increasingly unstable over time. While marriage was generally perceived as the bedrock of society among the older generation, the middle and young generations were much more circumspect. Among grandmothers, marriage was entered into largely as a result of social expectations, as Madge, from Alberta, illustrates: 'Besides being a nurse, I wanted to marry, have children, and have a nice home; and I wanted to have frilly curtains on every window ... You were supposed to stay at home and be a housewife.' Marital relationships among

CANADA

elderly women were mainly successful, although for different reasons. Lora, a grandmother from Manitoba, has been happily married for 50 years. The basis of her happiness, however, lay not in romantic love, but in the mutual respect she shared with her husband. In contrast, Adrienne, from Ontario, has been with her husband for 48 years and says: 'I think having a sexual life is fine, but finding love and compatibility in a person is everything, like what grandpa and I have.' Marital conflict was not entirely absent from this generation, as the case of Dorothy from Ontario shows. Dorothy was married young and raised four daughters. When she was 33 years old she left her husband, who had been physically and mentally abusive towards her, as well as consistently unfaithful. She later remarried and had a happy relationship with her second husband until he died after ten years of marriage. Dorothy notes: 'In my first marriage, my husband was the boss but in my second marriage, I was the boss.' For this generation, then, marriage defined women's identity, and more specifically, they were categorised by their husband's economic status, such as a minister's wife, or a farmer's wife. In Nova Scotia, several women in the project pointed out that they would have preferred to have been called Mrs John MacDonald, for example, rather than their Christian names, as this defined the way they conducted their lives and derived their status within the community.

Women from the middle generation also felt the need to conform to these ideals, although their marriages tended to be less successful. Indeed, marital breakdown was most common among this generation, largely because they bowed to societal pressures only to realise too late that they had made a mistake. In an increasingly liberal environment, they had greater freedom (both social and economic) to terminate unhappy partnerships. The experience of Donna, from the Mi'kmag Native Indian group from Nova Scotia, reflects this. Recalling her mother's words: 'She used to stress, "Marry a nice man and settle down." I married, but didn't settle down, and didn't live happily ever after.' While Donna is now divorced, and 'dead against marriage', she is now more interested in pursuing 'native' ideals of partnerships, which put greater emphasis on harmony. In a similar vein, Jane from Ontario discusses her disillusionment: 'With little faith in marriage or interest in raising children, I married despite an already dysfunctional relationship. I soon realised that 'happily-ever-afters' are figments of collective imaginations but seldom realised in real life.'

Commonly experiencing the break-up of their parents, the youngest generation of women were extremely wary of marriage. If anything, marriage in contemporary Canada was viewed as a sentence to enslavement for women and/or the stifling of individual expression. Irene, a daughter from Manitoba, pointed out:

In spite of my father's $10 bet with me that I would be married by twenty-one, I have never married. And I realise now that it is Marj [her surrogate grandmother] and my mother who empowered me, who have given me the right to choose 'not-marriage', who have instilled in me the belief that I could achieve anything I desired, because they did.

Young women were not eschewing conjugal relationships *per se*, but their institutionalisation. Rachelle, from Ontario (Jane's daughter), said: 'I don't want marriage or children but I would like to have a relationship, someone to talk to or do things with.' These attitudes have also been adopted by older women who during their youth held very different views of marriage. Sun Rose, a Native Indian grandmother from the Mi'kmag people in Nova Scotia, discussed her change in views: 'Men and women marry and live happily ever after. At the time I agreed, but today I do not agree, people do not need to live together for ever. Today they do not "live to death do you part" and that is OK.' Overall, therefore, the increase in divorce rates, the reluctance to commit to one person for a lifetime, and the desire to explore other avenues of life have meant that marriage is becoming an outmoded institution. It is no longer something to aspire to for the young as it brings with it connotations of traditional attitudes that no longer obtain in society at large. In its place, cohabitation is becoming the norm.

Family and community relations Family ties were central to all women's lives across the generations, although the nature of family forms has changed over time. Most grandmothers stressed the importance of the nuclear unit, reinforcing the notion of the patriarchal family of the male breadwinner and female nurturer. In Alberta in particular, the so-called 'frontier family' of the prairies was a male-dominated structure with the men in charge of finances and women attending to the emotional side of family life. While in reality this is no longer the norm in the province, it still pervades public rhetoric of what 'the Alberta family' should be. The importance of the nuclear family was also instilled in the minds of the middle generation, as Kathy, a mother from Alberta, realised only after her divorce: 'The whole media image of the heterosexual family with 2.2 children is the ideal to strive for.' Before she became a single parent herself, she had 'always thought that the government would never support a single parent with three children through university ... I suddenly realised that none of this was true and that it was just a myth to make sure that I stayed where I was.'[9] Indeed, one of the main differences between the eldest and middle generation throughout the provinces was that while many women embarked upon married life in nuclear units, they often chose to develop alternative or different family lifestyles later. By the time the youngest generation was growing up, alternative family forms were widely accepted and increasingly prevalent.

Among all generations, the extended family was an important source of support. Irene, a daughter from Manitoba, went as far as to suggest that: 'My extended family is the way I understand life and growth – not individually but in a common good.' Lora, a grandmother also from Manitoba, spoke of the assistance she received from her sister: 'Mae and I worked so closely together [that] her kids were my kids and my kids were her kids.' While these blood relationships were often critical to women's lives, the importance of female friends was usually emphasised even more strongly. This prevailed for all age groups, regardless of context. Jenny, a grandmother from Alberta, remembered how: 'Women would work together ... We used to get together and do big meals around Christmas and brandings ... We used to do pancake breakfasts.' Donna, a mother from Ontario, considers what she refers to as her 'female mentors' to be crucial to her personal development. She perceives these relationships to be very special: 'The affirmations women give to one another can't come from men. There's not that depth.' In many ways, female friends have taken the place of family members, especially for the younger generation who have moved away from home. Among the younger generation, the concept of the home, whether comprising family members or friends, seems to have replaced the notion of the family as a source of security and solace. As Rachelle, a daughter from Ontario, states: 'My home is where my hat is, it's important because there are people here [in Ottawa] that I like.'

Fertility and childbearing A decline in family size was noted throughout the provinces. In Nova Scotia, among the twenty-four women interviewed, the number of children per family dropped from eight to three in one generation. In Quebec, over three generations in one family, Irene, the grandmother, had nine children, Margot, the mother, had five, and Chantal, the daughter, had only one. Many grandmothers came from extremely large families, such as Lillian, from Nova Scotia, who was one of fourteen siblings, or Adrienne, from Ontario, who was one of eleven.[10] In the latter case, her mother's life was put at risk from such high fertility levels, and Adrienne was very critical of the ethos behind this:

> Well it's a good thing [her mother] stopped at eleven ... because she had ten miscarriages and 21 births. It's no wonder she died very young at 55 years of age. She was married at eighteen and was just a housewife. Those days women were treated like work-horses ... they stayed at home and had babies. Mother was very talented. No one ever really knew it though.

Many women learned from their mothers and made a conscious effort to limit the number of children they had. Lillian, for example, acted on the knowledge that her own family of 14 represented hard work and lots of self-sacrifice. She did not want to place on her daughter the kinds of demands her mother had imposed upon her with respect to assistance in childrearing. As a result, she had only one daughter. More generally, family planning, coupled with women's move into the labour market, has led to a rapid decline in fertility among the middle and youngest generations. Jane, a mother from Ontario, considers birth control as: 'the most important social change in my lifetime. I am sure that my mother and grandmother would have welcomed the option to control the number and spacing of their children.'

Decision-making and domestic labour As discussed with respect to socialisation patterns, the nature of domestic divisions of labour has become more equal over time. In the past, while women carried a disproportionate burden of reproductive labour, it was often men who were the main financial decision-makers. Jenny, a grandmother from Alberta, recalls how she did not know how to write a cheque until her husband died. By the time the middle generation had their own families, tasks within the home were more equally shared. Yvonne, a mother from Nova Scotia, discusses the evolution of shifting domestic responsibilities:

> As I was growing up my father was the breadwinner and my mother stayed at home, doing all the household work and most of the childrearing ... today my husband does as many or more chores than I do. My husband shared in child-raising much more than my father had done. In my daughter's house, she still does more household work, but her husband shares the cooking equally ... She expects her husband to share responsibility of raising their children equally.

Indeed, it was with respect to childcare that the younger generation felt men were more prepared to assist than they were in the past. Shelley, from Manitoba, notes: 'Men are getting better ... They're taking care of children, they push strollers, they aren't afraid to change diapers, they will let a woman work and they will be housekeepers.' Another daughter, Maggie, from Nova Scotia, made an interesting comment about the symbolic nature of domestic chores, reflecting how such tasks have become a choice for the younger generation whereas they were a necessity for their forebears as well as a source of exploitation. She does not feel the need to fulfil certain kinds of 'women's roles', yet likes to do laundry because it makes her feel grounded and is a 'tie to the women of the past'.

Education and work

Education   Education is viewed as a key to empowerment among women of all generations, as Jennifer, a daughter from Ontario, put it: 'Education plays a key role in attaining equality and freedom. It opens up the world and reveals all the possibilities, empowers you to be strong, and never allows you to limit your vision for the future.' While education was deemed important for all, it has really only been in the last 50 years that opportunities have opened up for women. Before this, schooling was deemed appropriate only for men. Marj, an elderly woman from Manitoba, recalls how when her father died she left school to go out to work 'because it was more important that boys finish school ... girls were judged by how many bales of hay you could move, not by your marks at school'. While these restrictions were imposed mainly by parents who did not consider daughters worthy of educating, girls themselves were also aware of the roles expected of them. Lillian, a grandmother from Nova Scotia, attended school only to grade six, and although she would have liked to have stayed on, stated: 'I felt guilty if I didn't stay home to help. Poor old mom was working herself to death ... She's your mother so you want to help her.' The other major reason for withdrawing children from school at this time was poverty, with many families able to afford to keep only their sons in education. Dorothy, a grandmother from Ontario, who grew up in the Great Depression of the 1930s, had to leave school at the eleventh grade (fourth year of secondary): 'There was me and my brother and sister. My mother couldn't afford to keep us [the girls] going or buy clothes for us, so we had to quit. I was 14 at the time and I went to work. There were no jobs then – all you could get was housework.'

High school education in particular tended to be sacrificed as this often entailed travelling far from home, which incurred additional cost. Lora, a grandmother from Manitoba, pointed out:

> I guess I should have finished high school, but I would have had to go [to the next town]. You had to board, buy your clothes and books ... I remember my mother taking apart old coats to make jumper [pinafore] dresses. There was very poor boots. I never wore boots all summer because that wears them out.

Although some grandmothers were able to attend high school and go on to university, this was the exception rather than the norm, and often involved substantial hardship. Joan, a grandmother from British Columbia, was encouraged by her mother to continue to high school after elementary, which was unusual: 'Many of the students from my elementary school didn't go to high school. They just went out to work.' Joan's school was 21 miles down lake and the only access was by paddle steamer once a day.

She therefore had to live in a room and work in the Pine Lodge boarding house in order to pay her way. She continued at the University of British Columbia and completed her teacher training in 1942. Unfortunately, she gave up her course on the birth of her first child in order to devote more time to her family.

For the middle generation, educational opportunities expanded, although many women's hopes of going to university were thwarted by lack of money. Donna, a mother from Ontario, stated: 'University was not an option for economic reasons ... It was always something I dreamed of but it didn't happen.' Instead, Donna married at the age of 22, and worked as a secretary for years. For the younger generation, educational attainment was both encouraged and sought after, particularly in the university sector. Nowadays, however, as Susan, a daughter from Ontario, points out: 'Today it is not gender that stunts students my age from getting a higher education; rather, it is the competition for spots within the universities.'

The desire for education is now so great among women that many of the informants entered university as mature students, particularly those from the middle generation who felt they had not fulfilled their potential because of mothering and domestic responsibilities. Helen Thundercloud, a Native Indian mother from Manitoba, had a very traditional marriage, but wanted to carry on her education once her children had grown up. She enrolled to do a part-time degree in sociology, but had to do so 'on the sly'. When her husband discovered what she was doing their marriage began to fall apart, and ended in divorce. Shelley, a daughter from Manitoba, dropped out of high school at the beginning of year ten because of peer pressure and because her parents were separating. However, she returned to complete her high school education at an adult learning centre and is now planning to go to university. In both cases student loans have given women the economic freedom to resume their education.

Throughout the generations, educational choices have been heavily gender-typed. This was most noticeable at the tertiary level, where women tended to choose the nurturing and administrative professions. Yvonne, a mother from Nova Scotia, recalls: 'I knew no women students in engineering or medicine. My friends and relatives who went to university in the sixties became teachers and nurses.' Susan, a daughter from Ontario, discusses how women of her mother's generation were often pressurised into particular 'traditional' educational paths:

> While my mother was growing up, the educational opportunities for girls were mainly directed towards ... teaching, nursing and administrative work. Women chose which route they wanted to take at high school, and took courses according to that choice.

Only among the younger generation have opportunities opened up, as Nancy, a daughter from Nova Scotia, points out: '... now you can do whatever you want to do ... The educational opportunities are there, whatever you want to make them.'

Angela, a mother from British Columbia, said of her hopes for her children, who are now grown up:

> I wanted my children to get an education and get out and see the world. I say it doesn't matter if you get a job or not; your outlook on life with every subject taken is widened ... Education is really important. Maybe not to get a job anymore, but it's an education just to go to university.

This latter point was reiterated by other women who felt they had difficulties in finding a job that matched their qualifications. Yvonne, a mother from Nova Scotia, had an honours degree in English and an MA in English, but her job expectations were still not fulfilled.

Work and economic livelihood Women's experiences in the labour market broadly mirrored patterns of educational attainment. Women's employment rates have increased because of a range of factors including the expansion of the service industry, smaller families, the women's movement, and more liberal societal attitudes. Not only have greater numbers of women entered the labour market, but work has become engrained in women's identity. The life histories show how women from the oldest generation derived their identity from their husbands and families, but many working-class women were economically active. However, the rationale for employment in those days was usually economic necessity rather than the pursuit of independence. Adrienne, a grandmother from Ontario, remembers:

> Oh Dear God in Heavens, I worked at everything I could get my hands on. In 1939 the war came so I went to work at a manufacturing company making tents [for the army]. Then I went to the government in 1944. In 1947 Joe, my husband, was able to keep me at home to have my four children.

Adrienne returned to work in 1960 after her children grew up: 'I was young and knew I couldn't spend the rest of my life as a homemaker. I wanted to see what was going on in the world. A lot of other women looked down on me though.' Despite the economic rationale for entering the labour force, a number of grandmothers also discovered satisfaction and self-respect through their work. Dorothy, from Ontario, discusses the process:

> When I was married to my first husband, I never thought I was worth a penny. It wasn't until I left him that I really found myself. It wasn't until I got into the plants [factory work] that I found I could do things, make money, save money.

Increasingly, however, satisfaction has become as a crucial reason for women working, rather than a by-product. Jill, a mother from British Columbia, who works as a teacher, says: 'My job is very important, not at a social level, but at a respect level, it's very, very important to me.'

Although women consider their employment a fundamental part of their identity, gender-typing of occupations is still very marked in Canada. Just as women were encouraged to follow traditional educational paths, so the jobs available to them were predominantly in the caring professions. The most common occupations among the women interviewed were teaching, nursing, counselling and secretarial work. While this obtains across the board, there have been some improvements over time. A number of grandmothers could find work only in domestic service, whereas younger women now frequently become teachers and nurses. However, many from the middle generation complained that they had little choice in their career paths – Linda, from Alberta, recounts how she was channelled into nursing: 'I honestly don't know what else I could have been. I was never encouraged to think about it.' As Fiona, also from Alberta, said: 'When I was looking for a career, women were either a nurse or secretary or a teacher.' This stereotyping has lessened over time, with some of the youngest generation denying its existence. Michele, a hairdresser from Nova Scotia, said: 'I don't feel there are any jobs exclusively for men or women; they can do anything they want to.'

In general, it appears that there has been a shift in Canada from women defining their place in society through family responsibilities to one where their achievements in the public sphere are central to their identity. However, women still appear to be restricted by gender-typing of occupations and gender-differentiated wage rates. The latter problem has been exacerbated by the recent economic recession, which has reduced labour demand and caused a proliferation of part-time casual work. More importantly, perhaps, women are still constrained by their domestic roles, despite improvements in childcare facilities.

Female employment and domestic responsibilities Women from all generations discussed their concern over balancing various roles. Although there was a marked shift towards sharing of tasks within the home, many women still complained of the problems involved in working and caring for their families. Kathy, a mother from Alberta, pointed out: 'Sometimes I feel like I am swinging back and forth. I am putting too much energy in at home and then I have to put more energy in at work and then there isn't enough left for home and so on and so on.' Such are the pressures, that some women even decided not to enter the labour market. Donna, from Ontario, made this choice, saying: 'The quality of life deteriorates ... when both parents work. I personally don't think you can effectively balance the two without a great deal of sacrifice.' Despite this, the youngest generation felt much more optimistic, although they were also dependent on the co-operation of their partners. Kelly, a daughter from Alberta, who is about to get married and is thinking about having children, said:

> I want to have a family but I also want the fulfilment of succeeding in something of my own. It is going to be difficult but I expect help [from my future husband] to make it happen.

Conclusion

Gender roles and relations in Canada have changed quite dramatically over time, with the inner strength of women being turned outwards since the beginning of the century. The dichotomous nature of relations between the sexes seems to have been broken down and equality is currently being striven for through greater complementarity. This is not to say that anger is absent from many perceptions of male–female relationships. As Tagalik Katheleen, a half-Inuit daughter from Nunavut in the Northwest Territories, puts it:

> I wouldn't want to be a woman before. Now, they're not scared to say what they think, most of the time. My dreams for my children – do what you want to do without worrying about other people, be the best you can be, and for my daughters – never let any man walk all over you.

At the same time, it is important to stress that many women of the oldest generation were content with their roles as nurturers of both their own families and the wider community. It was really the middle generation of women who began to challenge their position in society as they realised other options were open to them beyond wife- and motherhood. Further-more, this transition has not always been smooth, with casualties often taking the form of broken marriages. Nevertheless, the young seem to be coming to terms with their new-found independence, with Madge, a grandmother from Alberta, noticing that women and men are closer, and that boys and girls communicate more easily with one another. In Madge's view, heterosexual relations, rather than autonomy, are enhanced by con-temporary feminism. Indeed, the testimonies of young women displayed a sense of optimism about their lives. They have benefited from enhanced educational and employment opportunities and seem better able to define their place in society in a holistic manner, rather than in the confined terms of their role within the family. However, while women have re-negotiated their position at a personal level and secured greater freedom, wider societal and economic structures still appear to be lagging behind, particularly in respect of the gender-typing of occupations and the male–female wage gap. However, most women are optimistic about their own and their daughters' futures, as summed up by Yvonne, a mother from Nova Scotia:

> My mother had hoped I would have a respectable husband. I hoped that my daughter would have a career that would allow her to live a comfortable life if she chose to live independently. My daughter hopes that her daughter will have a happy life.[11]

Recommendations

While the survey did not include any specific policy recommendations, a number of issues may be pertinent in the case of Canada. These include:

- Federal legislation aimed at reducing the wage gap between men and women.
- Ethnic awareness programmes aimed at recognising the contribution of First Nations peoples and ethnic minority groups to the development of the nation.
- Consciousness-raising programmes to encourage shared parenting and domestic responsibilities.

Notes

1. Compiled from a report by the Women's Changing Landscape Project Coordinating Committee entitled 'Changing Landscapes: Three Generations of Canadian Women Tell Their Stories'. The committee director was Greta Hofmann Nemiroff, Carleton University and University of Ottawa, Ontario. The remaining committee members were Linda Christiansen-Ruffman, Huguette Dagenais, Keith Louise Fulton, Christine St Peter, and Eliane Silverman.

2. From east to west, the provinces include Newfoundland, Nova Scotia, Prince Edward Island, New Brunswick, Quebec, Ontario, Manitoba, Saskatchewan, Alberta and British Columbia, and the two territories are Northwest Territories and the Yukon.

3. The name Canada is said to come from *Kanata*, a Huron–Iroquois word for village or community, and a term mentioned in Cartier's journal.

4. This charter is the equivalent of a formal constitution, although Quebec has still not ratified it.

5. The term 'mosaic' is used to describe the ideal of Canadian multiculturalism, where the interconnections between various groups are stressed while recognising the distinctiveness of individual cultures. This is in stark contrast to the metaphor of the 'melting pot', used to describe the United States, where minority groups are expected to blend with the dominant culture and disregard their own identity. The

use of the term 'mosaic', however, has been widely criticised on the grounds that the commitment to diversity by state and society has been overstated, particularly with respect to legislation (Fleras and Elliot, 1992: 64–5).

6. Griffin Cohen (1994) notes that there has not been a 'feminisation of the labour force' in Canada during restructuring in the manner commonly found elsewhere. She relates this to the fact that men's jobs are not changing in a way to allow women to move into them, and when men are made redundant, their jobs disappear altogether.

7. Countries from which immigrants originated included England, France, Germany, the Ukraine, Russia, Egypt, Japan, Indonesia and Guatemala.

8. Real names are referred to when women explicitly gave their consent, otherwise, pseudonyms are used.

9. In 1980, 25.4 per cent of all households in Canada were headed by women (UNDP, 1995: Table A2.5).

10. This is reflected in national patterns, with a decline in the total fertility rate from 2.2 in 1970 to 1.9 in 1990 (World Bank, 1995: Table 26).

11. It is important to stress other changes that were raised in the project report but are excluded here. These include the importance of religion and spirituality, which often served as a central source of support for women of all ages. Racism was also discussed, particularly by the First Nations people and immigrant groups. Many of the eldest generation recounted their negative experiences of belonging to ethnic minority groups. This was evident at a personal level in terms of being the brunt of abuse at school for being 'different' or being discriminated against in the labour market, as well as at the institutional level – many, for example, were unable to secure the vote for many years after white Canadians.

CHAPTER 10

ZIMBABWE[1]

This chapter deals with changes in gender roles and relations in a country that spent most of the twentieth century under British rule and where sovereignty is less than two decades old. The recency of post-colonial restructuring and nation-building in Zimbabwe may have sidelined gender policy initiatives to a greater extent than in countries that have had longer to establish their independence. In some respects, however, the lives of young women bear such scant resemblance to those of their grandmothers that shifts in gender roles and relations seem to have formed an integral component of the transition from a white-dominated British colony to a democratic black republic.

The chapter attempts to provide a synopsis of some of the major changes that have taken place in the arena of gender across three generations of black Zimbabwean women. The focus on women derives from the fact that the survey on which the bulk of the discussion is based included data only on female informants. It should also be noted that the Zimbabwe report was less wide-ranging than those for most other countries in the book and dwelt mainly on changes in marriage, education and employment. In order to bring the chapter more in line with those of the other case study countries, complementary information is taken from a broader range of additional sources.

Country profile

The Republic of Zimbabwe gained its independence as a black African state in 1980, following around sixty years as the British colony of Southern Rhodesia, and a decade-and-a-half under the white minority government of Ian Smith of the Rhodesian Front.[2] Although a large number of the country's white population left in the aftermath of independence, around 150,000 remain. Despite the fact that whites form only about 1 per cent of Zimbabwe's 11 million inhabitants, they continue to enjoy better standards of living than the majority black population. Around 80 per cent of the latter are Shona, who have inhabited Zimbabwe for between eight and nine centuries. The remainder are Ndebele (also known as Matabele), who descended from a tribe of warriors led by Mzilikazi that broke away from the Zulu nation in the 1830s. Since independence, Zimbabwe has been governed by the Zimbabwe African National Union – Patriotic Front (ZANU [PF]), under the leadership of Robert Mugabe (prime minister between 1980 and 1987, and president from 1987 onwards).[3] The ZANU (PF) was brought to power by an overwhelming majority in the first democratic elections held in the country and proclaimed itself as committed to building socialism (Kanji and Jazdowska, 1995: 133). The main opposition party, spearheaded by Reverend Ndanbaningi Sithole, is the Zimbabwe African National Union (ZANU [Ndonga]).[4]

Women were a significant presence in the guerrilla war for liberation in Zimbabwe, providing food, shelter, clothing and paramedical and intelligence services. Their participation in the struggle was such that the new independence government could do little else but give gender a place on the post-colonial agenda:

The principle of equality between men and women is basic to the political philosophy of our government. It is the objective of our government to create such an environment to make these objectives possible (cited in Lapchick and Urdang, 1982: 108).

The first pragmatic step towards gender equality came in 1981 with the setting up of a Ministry for Community Development and Women's Affairs (MCDWA). This year also saw the passing of the Customary Law and Primary Courts Act, which gave women greater opportunity to escape the constraints of customary law and to obtain cheaper and easier access to the courts. Another significant piece of legislation passed in the immediate aftermath of independence was the Legal Age of Majority Act of 1982, which gave all men and women automatic legal majority at the age of 18 (including, as a matter of course, women's freedom to marry without parental consent and to administer property). Further legal landmarks included the Immovable Property Act of 1982, which outlawed gender discrimination in the ownership of immovable property (such as land and housing), the Matrimonial Causes Act of 1983, which stipulated egalitarian shares of property in the event of divorce under customary law, and also changed the procedure whereby fathers had automatic rights over their children (see Kanji, 1994: 56), and the Labour Relations Act of 1985, which prohibited gender discrimination in employment and gave working women entitlement to maternity leave.

Despite this legislation, gender inequalities persist in many spheres. As Nazneen Kanji (1994: 55) observes: 'Just as a government's proclaimed commitment to socialism does not make a country socialist, such commitment to women's emancipation is not sufficient to achieve equality in gender relations.' Kanji goes on to point out not only how the MCDWA has been marginalised within government policy-making, but that 'although the ZANU government has facilitated incremental gains in basic civil rights for women, it has been unwilling to challenge the fundamental structures of gender relations within the family' (ibid.: 57). Given President Mugabe's re-election in March 1996, it is difficult to foresee radical changes for women in the near future.

Although dissatisfaction with the government's handling of the economy has increased in the light of its concerted adoption of structural adjustment measures (see below), Mugabe has enjoyed an uninterrupted spell in office since 1980 and for the moment his position appears stable (EIU, 1996i: 6). While the presidency is elected every six years by universal suffrage, the legislature consists of a 150-strong House of Assembly where 120 of the seats are elected on the basis of geographical constituencies every five years (the most recent elections were held in April 1995). A further eight seats are occupied by provincial governors, ten by customary chiefs, and the remaining twelve are appointed by the president (EIU, 1996i: 5).

Zimbabwe is still a predominantly rural country, with only 30 per cent of its population residing in urban areas in 1992 (UNDP, 1995: Table 6). Nevertheless, the proportion of Zimbabweans in towns and cities is over twice the level of 1960 (when it was 13 per cent) (ibid.: Table 15). Most urban growth (which has averaged 2.7 per cent per annum between 1960 and 1992) has been concentrated in the capital, Harare, and the second biggest city, Bulawayo. According to census figures for 1988/9, these two cities generate over 75 per cent of all manufactured output in the country and 80 per cent of employment (Kanji and Jazdowska, 1995: 135).

Tobacco is the biggest crop in Zimbabwe and remains its largest single export, generating $US425 million in 1994, about one-fifth of the total by value (EIU, 1996i: 5). Other important exports are gold, ferro-alloys and nickel (ibid.). Maize is the biggest food product but is grown mainly for internal consumption. Under the first major structural adjustment programme initiated in 1991 (see below), large commercial farmers were encouraged to grown more tobacco and other export crops such as tea and coffee (McDonald, 1996: 3). Despite drought during the early 1990s, agriculture managed to maintain positive annual growth rates (averaging 1.6 per cent between 1990 and 1994). Industry, conversely, registered negative growth during the same period, with a mean annual rate of -3.6 per cent (World Bank, 1996: Table 11). Nevertheless, because export industrialisation has been strongly encouraged by recent structural adjustment measures, manufactured items made up as much as 38 per cent of Zimbabwe's exports by value in 1994 (World Bank, 1996: Table 15).

With several national parks, wildlife reserves, natural attractions such as the Victoria Falls and the Zambezi River, and stone relics from the pre-colonial Shona civilisation, tourism is also a major source of foreign revenue. Having generated US$115 million in 1995, profits forecast for 1996 were US$150 million (EIU, 1996i: 22). However, although Zimbabwe has traditionally attracted international tourists because of its relative safety, rising outbreaks of crime may undermine the confidence of overseas visitors.[5] The growing incidence of violence and robbery has proceeded alongside increased unemployment, which in 1995 amounted to 50 per cent of the workforce (EIU, 1996i: 12). The latter is widely held to be a consequence of structural adjustment in Zimbabwe, which even the World Bank concedes has been largely detrimental to the poor (Moghadam, 1996: 34).

The first economic structural adjustment programme (ESAP I) was implemented in early 1991 for a duration of five years. It had two major aims: to sustain higher medium- and long-term economic growth, and to reduce poverty (Kanji, 1994: 61). Critical components of the programme included the scaling down of consumer subsidies and public expenditure, the liberalisation of price and import controls, and the promotion of exports (ibid.). To date, these measures seem to have benefited only large entrepreneurs, white expatriates and/or multinational interests who have most to gain from export expansion and least to lose from government social sector cutbacks. Low- and middle-income households have had to contend with deteriorating social and economic circumstances, which have intensified downward economic trends inherited from the previous decade. For example, average annual growth in per capita GNP was negative (-0.9 per cent) between 1980 and 1992 (UNDP, 1995: Table 20), and in this latter year GNP per capita stood at only $US580 (ibid.: Table 2). Total external debt in 1992 was only $US4 billion, although debt service as a percentage of exports of goods and services was as much as 32 per cent (compared with 4 per cent in 1980) (ibid.: Table 13). Beyond this, there have been steep rises in the costs of living. Between mid-1991 and mid-1992, for instance, low-income urban households faced increases of up to 45 per cent in living costs (see Kanji, 1994: 64). The second phase of the economic structural adjustment programme was eventually launched in 1997 under the title of the 'Zimbabwe Programme for Economic and Social Transformation' (EIU, 1996i: 13). Given the record of ESAP I, there is an understandably deep concern about the consequences for low- and middle-income people.

In the present economic and policy climate, it is perhaps no surprise that Zimbabwe's score on the HDI (0.539) places it towards the lower reaches of the UNDP's 'medium human development' category, and 121st out of an overall total of 174 countries (UNDP, 1995: Table 1). As of 1992, one of the major components of the HDI, adult life expectancy, averaged only 53.7 (and for women 55.1). Not only does this represent a rather marginal improvement on 1960 (when overall average life expectancy was 45.3 – UNDP, 1995: Table 4), but the fact that it is lower than the 1990 figure of 61 years (EIU, 1996i: 12) suggests that the squeeze on public expenditure linked with structural adjustment portends ominously for the nation's health and well-being (see Kanji et al., 1991). However, another factor contributing to falling life expectancy is HIV infection, which by the end of 1996 was estimated by Zimbabwe's National AIDS Coordination Programme (NACP) to affect 1.2 million people, constituting over one-tenth of the national population (EIU, 1996i: 12). The situation is now so critical that in August 1996 a bill was tabled in parliament to make knowingly passing on the HIV virus a criminal offence punishable by up to twenty years in prison (ibid.). As in other sub-Saharan African countries, deaths from AIDS tend to hit the economically active middle generation the hardest (Ferguson, 1997: Chapter 5).

In terms of the UNDP's GDI, which considers gender disparities in income, life expectancy, literacy, and school enrolment against overall achievements in human development, Zimbabwe was placed 82 out of 130 countries (about the same as its overall ranking within the HDI) (UNDP, 1995: Table 3.1). The adult literacy rate is now 83.4 per cent (UNDP, 1995: Table 2), a substantial improvement on 1970 when it was 55 per cent (ibid.: Table 4). Nevertheless, it is notable that adult women's literacy rate is lagging behind men's, at 77.9 per cent versus 89.1 per cent (ibid.). However, in respect of the GEM, which assesses women's share of income alongside their presence in administrative and managerial posts and professional and technical work, together with the proportion of seats they occupy in parliament, Zimbabwe ranks considerably higher, at 43rd out of 116 countries (UNDP, 1995: Table 3.5).

Zimbabwe's higher-ranking score on the GEM index is largely a result of women's political profile. In 1994, women held 12 per cent of parliamentary seats and were 3 per cent of ministers (UNDP, 1995: Tables 3.5 and A2.4). It is also reported that up to 30 per cent of posts on the central committee of ZANU (PF) are occupied by women (Karl, 1995: 66). Moreover, as one measure of the Zimbabwean government's pledge to raise women's status, an affirmative action policy in public services was introduced in 1991. This aimed to guarantee that 30 per cent of middle and senior management positions would be held by women (in accordance with women representing 30 per cent of recruits entering public service employment). As yet, however, these targets remain unmet (see Karl, 1995: 71), and this contributes to a more general picture of female disadvantage in the labour market. In 1994, women formed only 33 per cent of the overall workforce aged 15 or more (UNDP, 1995: Table 11), and in 1990, they were only 15.4 per cent of administrative and managerial workers (ibid.: Table A2.7). It is hardly surprising, therefore, that women's share of earned income (27.4 per cent) is lower than their share of employment (UNDP, 1995: Table 3.1).

Methodology

The interview survey was carried out by 45 students taking the course 'Women in African History' in the Department of History at the University of Zimbabwe during 1992. Given the preponderance of men in higher education, 70 per cent of the interviewers were male, and 30 per cent female. Most originated from rural areas of the country and held interviews with one woman from each generation in their own families or one of their peers' families. Substitutions of other families occurred where students wished to interview three generations of women who could be found in one place, and/or where peers' families had more education than their own. Greater education was perceived to make people more sympathetic to a university project, although it clearly skewed the sample towards a better-off segment of Zimbabwean society.

The students lacked experience in interviewing skills and tended to keep their sessions with respondents broad and quite open-ended, although the main foci were marriage and education. They later condensed their interview material into essays, which were reviewed by the project director and, in consultation with the students, amalgamated into a single report. Partly because they were translated from Shona or Ndebele into English, much of the 'raw narrative' of the original interviews has been lost. As such, this chapter is not able to draw on the same range of first-hand statements from informants as other discussions in the book. Notwithstanding this, and the fact that student essays varied in their content and interpretations, a general perception was that women's status had undergone a moderate amount of change during the twentieth century. In fact one student, Tatenda, claimed that: 'The position of women in Zimbabwean society has been metamorphosing from that of a kneeling submissive woman to a standing woman claiming her human rights.' At the same time, many students also emphasised that 'kneeling submission' was by no means a state that women in the older generations were happy with. In fact most were taken by surprise at the pent-up emotion and anger unleashed by their interviews. As one male student, Ishe, articulated:

I could not believe a lady of her time (born in 1925) had such ideas as the interview indicated. This personally showed me that many black African women are feminists at heart, but bow to social conventions for the sake of respectability.

The sense derived by the students of older women's resistance to gender subordination departed so much from prevailing stereotypes that when the results of the project were presented at the University in Harare at the end of 1994, black male historians in the audience alleged that students must have distorted their data. As it was, many students reported that their relatives had often withheld less prepossessing details of their family histories so as not to cast their kin in a bad light, and some of the male interviewers had felt moved to tone down the vehemence of their mothers' and grandmothers' testimonies. This suggests that history created with women's own voices can act to challenge male-biased assumptions that so often become conventional wisdoms within 'mainstream' historical interpretations.

Profile of informants Most informants, numbering 139 in total, originated from middle- or lower middle-class families from rural areas of Zimbabwe, and in the main were Shona- rather than Ndebele-speaking. The youngest generation had enjoyed a greater level of material privilege than their predecessors, and, being urban-based and better-educated, represent a rather small and selective group of Zimbabwe's contemporary population. This bias should be borne in mind when assessing changes in gender as perceived by respondents over the last hundred or so years.

All women from the oldest generation had been born in rural areas and the vast majority (94 per cent) had remained there all their lives. Collectively they had been born between 1880 and 1942, although the majority had reached their late teens and early twenties between 1925 and 1945. Although this period lies right at the core of the colonial era in Zimbabwe, many pre-colonial practices such as arranged marriages and polygamy persisted (see later).

The middle generation of women, the 'mothers', straddled the colonial and independence worlds during the central years of their adulthood. Most of them married during the 1950s and 1960s, and experienced, if not participated in, the war of liberation during their childbearing years.[6] Many felt that their chance to capitalise on new opportunities for women had already been forfeited by the time independence was won. Nevertheless, around one-fifth had obtained enough education to permit them to enter professions such as teaching and nursing and a greater number had moved to urban areas than their mothers.

The youngest generation, presently in their twenties, were for the most part single and still studying. Only one interviewee had not gone beyond primary school, and 83 per cent of those aged 20 or more had enrolled in and/or completed some form of tertiary education, 30 per cent at university level. Although the majority had not yet entered the labour force, their career options were widely perceived to have expanded compared with their forebears. This was construed as having reduced women's economic dependence upon men, and was almost universally regarded as a dramatic change for the better.

Gender roles and relations

Many authors have described contemporary Zimbabwe as a 'patriarchal society', in which women remain subordinate to men (see Feresu, 1996: 36; Ferguson, 1997). This does not, of course, preclude recognition that patriarchal influences vary in nature and intensity between different social and economic domains, across different groups of women and through space and time as well. Conceiving of time and space in an interrelated manner is particularly illuminating in Zimbabwe, where in many respects spatial locations (and dislocations) have been intimately bound up with shifts in symbolic and pragmatic aspects of gender. Historically, for example (at least during the twentieth century), rural areas have been associated with more traditional (pre-colonial) forms of gender subordination wedded to lineage considerations and the control of women by male kinsfolk. Urban areas have been linked, if not with the disappearance of gender subordination, then with the emergence of new or modified forms of gender inequalities.

For the oldest generation of women, the tendency to remain in rural areas for most (if not all) of their lives came through as significant in the ways in which they had experienced gender, especially during youth and middle age. Indeed, social and material constraints upon rural women in the first part of the twentieth century probably help to explain why most grandmothers did not speak of the direct impacts on their lives of colonial rule but emphasised the hardship they had experienced at the hands of individual male relatives, particularly fathers and husbands. Many reported having rarely openly questioned or criticised male authority, and one grandmother, Ruwa, declared that many women revered their husbands 'like a god'. On top of this, kin groups were held in such high esteem that the threat of causing offence to their ancestors if women 'ran away' from home acted as a powerful deterrent.

Women who did defect from their villages and move to towns were usually regarded as 'prostitutes'.[7] In some cases this was the only way they could make a living. It was also one of the most profitable, given the presence of not only a white male expatriate clientele but a large pool of lone black males who moved to waged work in towns and mining compounds for several months at a time (Jeater, 1993: Chapter 4). Common reasons for women's flight from the countryside were to avoid marriages their fathers had contracted for them, or to extricate themselves from marriages they were already in. Apart from the moral and symbolic ramifications for families and lineages, female desertion bore serious practical consequences for male kin. Fathers, for example, lost their prospective role in obtaining payment for their daughters on marriage (*lobola* or bridewealth) (see later). As Diana Jeater (1993: 174) notes:

> Non-payment by urban men of compensation or bridewealth payments indicated a disregard for those codes of practice which covered the spectrum of 'good behaviour' and upon which the power of the patriarchs depended. Refusing to allow women to go to work in town was a pragmatic and effective defence against this challenge to their power.

Women who married in town without lineage approval or transfer of bridewealth, and who became known as *mapoto* wives, could sometimes find themselves living with men who were already married by customary law to rural women. Although informal town marriages offended kinship norms, for women it was often a useful strategy to gain access to economic support, to secure male protection and to obtain a roof over their heads. Back in the countryside, however, distress over daughters who had absconded to urban areas was such that colonial court officials and native commissioners were sometimes called in to help mediate the grievances of affected parents. As for husbands, 'runaway wives' were problematic in so far as they could deprive men of their lineage-based entitlements in rural communities (Jeater, 1993: 116).

Although few grandmothers in the survey had actually gone so far as to flee their villages, some revealed that they had considered it, but backed out through fear of moral stigmatisation. There was also trepidation about how they might protect themselves cut off from their families and kin groups, especially given assumptions about the sexual availability of lone urban women (Jeater, 1993: 183).

Despite the fact that remaining in rural areas arguably implied even less autonomy for women, there were many covert ways in which informants had stood up to male authority. Strategies had included giving their children 'protest names',[8] expressing themselves through song, going behind their husbands' backs, sharing problems with other women, and urging their daughters to rebel against inequalities. The latter was undoubtedly an influence on the middle generation, who began to wrest themselves away from arranged marriages, who moved to towns in greater number, and who increasingly turned to the formal legal system for assistance, especially in the post-colonial period.

As for the youngest generation, the bulk of these respondents see themselves as considerably more empowered than their forebears. They have greater educational accomplishments, greater access to independent earnings, and more personal autonomy. One female interviewer, Chido, described young women as 'emerging from the muddy soil of political as well as cultural oppression'. Not all respondents shared this optimism, however, with Kuda, a university graduate, professing that her greatest goal in life was to 'destroy male chauvinism and to advocate for the liberation of women from the draconian dictates of traditional society'.

Indeed, despite changes in gender roles and relations in Zimbabwe, continuities are apparent in several domains. At the domestic level gendered divisions of labour remain quite marked, as indicated in relation to mining households by Chiwawa (1995: 103):

> The husband, being the head of the household, is seen as the provider of household cash income and the wife, seen as the helper, only provides supplementary income. Consequently, husbands, as the dominant decision-makers, have sought to specialise in 'productive' labour and confine their spouses to 'reproductive' labour.

In Chiwawa's view, men fear that women's involvement in productive labour will challenge their authority and decision-making power. Conversely, unless their wives are absent from home, men tend to eschew participation in reproductive labour (ibid.: 104–6). Such patterns are found in other segments of Zimbabwean society, who are closer to the characteristics of the respondents in the survey. For example, a study of male and female finalists at the University of Zimbabwe in Harare by Sibusisiwe Ncuba (1995: 156–7), revealed that domestic management (including the hiring and supervision of paid helpers) was regarded as primarily the wife's responsibility.

Beyond this, women are still less of a presence in urban areas than men. Although the sex ratio in urban areas has become less masculine in recent decades, falling from 1,412 men per 1,000 women in 1969 to 1,140 men per 1,000 women in 1982, in this latter year the national sex ratio was feminine (with only 960 men over 1,000 women). As such, the weighted average for 1982 is more marked than the crude figures suggest, working out at 1,188 men per 1,000 women (Gilbert and Gugler, 1992: Table 3.3). In short, women's spatial mobility is still more restricted than men's.

Parents, parenting and children Although the survey did not gather much specific information on parenting, it is clear that fathers and mothers have tended to occupy rather different roles in their daughters' lives throughout this century. Fathers have usually played a strong role in constraining women's freedom, especially in respect of marriage. This echoes a more general primacy of men in all aspects of household life (see Ncuba, 1995: 149).

Mothers, while unable to exercise power in such a visible way, seem to have consistently dedicated themselves to pushing their daughters forward in life, especially with regard to education. Chipo, a grandmother in her mid-seventies, was never given the chance to go to school herself, but made sure that her daughter, Tinashe, now a teacher, completed her primary education. The husband of Zuwa, a mother in her forties, was so adamant that their daughter, Kundai, did not need an education, that Zuwa secured financial assistance from her employers to put Kundai through school. Other mothers in the middle generation raised cash from their educated sons and other relatives, and/or sent their daughters to live with relatives in urban areas to ensure they received schooling. One 43-year-old woman, Thandiwe, even hired a tutor for her daughter, Zororo, and excused her from household chores so that she could study. Sacrifices made by mothers also extended to looking after their grandchildren when their daughters had married and given birth early on in life. Indeed, many women in the youngest generation attribute their privileged educational attainment (and prospective career mobility) not only to macro-level changes that have come about with independence, but to the sheer will and determination of their mothers, who, in turn, acknowledge a debt to the women who brought them into the world.

Sex and sexuality As indicated previously, sexuality has been an important factor underpinning attitudes towards rural–urban mobility among Zimbabwean women, especially for the oldest generation. While women in rural areas were heavily controlled by their kinsfolk, towns and cities proved to be arenas for the freer expression of sexual behaviour. As Diana Jeater (1993: 117) reports of the early twentieth century, 'cosmopolitan urban culture' provided a context where:

> the established system of regulating sexual behaviour through networks of close intimacy and surveillance began to break down. Whereas previously sexuality was constructed in terms of lineage membership, with both men and women regulating their sexual behaviour on the basis of lineage obligations and sanctions, now it was easier to think of sexual contact as taking place between individuals, not lineages.

Towns served as arenas not only for individually negotiated sexual relations, but for prostitution. Because women could sometimes earn enough from prostitution to live independently, they were able to eschew some of the shackles of patriarchal relations. At the same time, the commoditisation of women's bodies had less positive outcomes. The buying of sex became commonplace among black men (Jeater, 1993: 180), and in many ways can be seen as having exacerbated pre-colonial patterns of polygyny. These features may help to account for the persistence of 'sexual double standards' in Zimbabwe, where 'respectable' women sleep with one man only (preferably in the context of a formal marriage), but men are entitled to multiple sexual relations. In her work on rural Zimbabwe, for example, Clare Ferguson (1997: Chapter 5) found that while adultery on the part of women can lead men to demand divorce, it is considered normal for men to be unfaithful. Fear of losing men to other women also means that the sexual needs of wives are likely to take second place to those of husbands, whose 'natural promiscuity' is prone to lead them astray. As Ferguson further observes:

> Women are taught from an early age that they should meet the sexual demands of their husbands. Young girls are shown by their sisters how to stretch their labias, as this is thought to increase a man's sexual enjoyment. They are also taught about various herbal and chemical potions, such as toilet bleach, which are supposed to keep their vaginas 'dry and tight – like a virgin'. Most young women were keen to use these products as they believed that providing sexual pleasure was the key to retaining a husband (ibid.).

As for extra-conjugal sexuality, harassment by male teachers was noted as a problem by some young informants. Moreover, gay men and women are unlikely to be able to conduct relationships openly given that homosexuality remains illegal and, in the context of staunch anti-gay rhetoric and action on the part of the government, attacks on homosexuals have been rising in recent times (EIU, 1996i: 9).[9] In short, the dominance of heterosexism in Zimbabwe remains characterised by strong gender inequalities. For the majority of women, heterosexual interaction is channelled through marriage and monogamy. For men, heterosexuality may be expressed through multiple partners, and not only in the form of informal liaisons before and during wedlock, but with legal endorsement in the context of polygamous marriage, as discussed below.

Marriage, family and fertility

Courtship and marriage Women in Zimbabwe have traditionally had to marry in order to obtain the means of survival. This includes not only land and income, but a dwelling as well. As Ncuba (1995: 151) sums up: 'In traditional Zimbabwean culture, women [are] normally expected to marry into a house rather than buy one.' However, even if women with access to higher education are increasingly aspiring to obtain their own homes, or at least to joint ownership with a husband (ibid.), there are also strong social imperatives for women to marry because 'any woman who remains single but continues to have relationships with men is likely to be labelled as a prostitute' (Ferguson, 1997: Chapter 5). In other words, marriage remains women's major route to respectability and status (ibid.; see also Chiwawa, 1995: 104).

Marriage in Zimbabwe today may take one of three forms, which are not necessarily exclusive. One is Christian civil marriage endorsed by the Marriage Act of 1964, the second is registered customary marriage under the African Marriages Act of 1951, and the third is customary unregistered marriage, arranged through the payment of bridewealth (*lobola*) (Ferguson, 1997: Chapter 5). Prior to independence and the Legal Age of Majority Act (see earlier), a prospective son-in-law was expected to pay *lobola* to his father-in-law as a means of formalising the marriage. Although daughters were technically allowed to marry without the payment of *lobola* or even parental consent after 1982, the practice is still widely observed by all social classes (ibid.).

Among grandmothers in the survey, girls were often pledged as infants and had little choice in determining their husbands-to-be. Indeed, as many as 85 per cent of the oldest generation of respondents who were born after 1910 entered arranged marriages. This perpetuated a tradition stretching back into the pre-colonial period, with coercion into matrimony sometimes taking brutal forms. One grandmother, Rutendo, recalled that her own grandmother, Rudo, had been made to watch her mother having hot coals poured down her front. In such circumstances, Rudo had little option but to relent and marry the man of her father's choice.

During the colonial period itself, women were often married off to answer families' short-term survival crises. For example, the 1930 Land Apportionment Act, the drought of 1947 and the 1951 Animal Husbandry Act all triggered a precipitous downturn in the fortunes of peasant families. These events set off massive waves of marriages between young girls and wealthy male farmers ('Big Men') in return for immediate relief from food and cash shortages.

While arranged marriages 'worked' in some cases, in others, especially where women were 'passed on' to male relatives after their husbands' deaths, women's unhappiness could be such that they fled the marital home. Ruvimbo, who was born in 1917, was forced to marry her widowed uncle at the age of eight. Being a child bride and 'unable to understand the wishes of an older man', she rapidly became accustomed to regular beatings and reprimands. Her suffering extended throughout 20 years of marriage, although she stayed by her husband's side until his death in 1946. Ruvimbo's long-standing hopes of relief from servitude and sub-ordination were then dashed when she was 'inherited' by his younger brother, Munyaradzi. However, unwilling to suffer more of the same with a man who was equally brutal, Ruvimbo finally plucked up her courage to run away, even though she could survive only by selling her body.

Ruvimbo was not the only woman of her generation to defy social conventions. Although most women succumbed to their first arranged marriage, they were much more reluctant to conform with the custom of inheritance by their late husbands' brothers. Indeed, two women who had married their first partner out of choice rebelled, as widows, against the automatic 'passing on' to younger brothers-in-law. Anesu, now 70, was adamant in her refusal to be inherited and instead went to live with her own brother. Farai, a nonagenarian, sought help from her working sons in order to secure her independence as a widowed woman. In a few cases, however, widows or divorcées were able to choose their second husbands. Two grandmothers in this position, Fungai and Tendai, found the experience of being with men they had married out of love extremely positive after abusive first marriages, especially given that their second husbands accepted their children as their own.

Some of the women in the oldest generation, especially those who married older, richer men, were also subject to polygamy. One grandmother, Shingai, like many of her counterparts was very much against the practice, but was forced to concede to her husband, Tawanda, taking a second wife when he threatened to commit suicide. Although polygamy is still legally permissible under the African Marriages Act (Ferguson, 1997: Chapter 5), by the time the middle generation of women were growing up it was much rarer and women had more power over rejecting or accepting spouses. This was also the result of the struggle of their mothers, who in many cases were so committed to protecting their daughters from their own fate that they actively (if not visibly) collaborated in helping them leave home.

Nomathemba, who was born in 1921, had been forced into a loveless and violent marriage at a young age. Although Nomathemba tried to leave her husband, Garikai, and go back to her parents, their inability to repay the *lobola* meant that she was effectively trapped. As she began to bear children, she was adamant that her daughter, Sharai, would not have to contend with the same predicament, especially after Garikai pledged Sharai in marriage for a few bags of grain during the 1947 drought. Although Sharai was only five at the time, she 'ran away' to the safe haven of a mission station from where her father could not retrieve her. Under the tutelage of missionaries, Sharai was able to pursue a basic education and worked as a cook on mission stations throughout her life. Although Sharai ultimately divorced, she had enough independent income to put her own children through school and her daughter is now a university student. She has shown her gratitude to Nomathemba by building her a house in Harare.

Although daughters who had run away without their mothers' collusion were usually able to forge a reconciliation at a later stage, this was less likely with fathers. One middle-aged informant, Spiwe, has never been forgiven by her father, Thamsanqa, for having given birth to an out-of-wedlock child during her time as a domestic servant, even though she eventually married and became a successful businesswoman.

As for the youngest generation, the continued custom of bridewealth payments still gives fathers substantial control over their daughters' lives. As a result, one of the areas in which young women desire change is in lessening the amount of bridewealth requests. In order to circumvent paternal restrictions, some young women pay *lobola* to their parents out of their own money. Others even claim they want to postpone marriage indefinitely or to stay single. Elizabeth, who is currently in her teens, is set on becoming a nun; 25-year-old Marita wishes to continue working as an accountant until she feels she is established enough to take on the additional responsibility of marriage; Sarudzai, also in her mid-twenties, regards marriage as a hindrance to her plans to travel; and another of her peers, Chido, has already had two children in the context of a cohabiting relationship. However, such cases are comparatively rare, and Ann Schlyter's (1989: 180) work in Harare reminds us that, due to social conditioning or otherwise: 'Love and children within a happy marriage is central to the dreams of young girls.' Similarly, women usually work inordinately hard to keep their marriages intact and normally file for divorce only when husbands are violent or take second wives (ibid.: 181).

Reluctance or inability on the part of the parents to return bridewealth payments also seems to have been a major factor dissuading young women from leaving their husbands, not only across the generations, but in all classes. Kanji's work among low-income groups in Harare reveals that women often stay with husbands, no matter how difficult their marriages. Kanji attributes this not only to lack of alternatives (especially among older women who face most difficulties obtaining employment), but because men's rights over women are institutionalised through *lobola* payments. The latter gives rise to a situation in which women's labour is not only exploited, but they also have to accept 'inequalities and double standards in sexual behaviour, morality and leisure' (Kanji, 1994: 149–50; see also Chiwawa, 1995: 105–6).

Custodial arrangements for children also continue to present an important impediment to divorce in that women have traditionally stood to lose their children in the event of conjugal breakdown. Although, as a follow-up to the Matrimonial Causes Act of 1983, the Customary Law and Primary Courts Act of 1989 specifies that parental rights and duties shall be decided according to 'the best interest of the child', among peoples like the Ndau (part of the Shona population), the father's family tends to insist on keeping the children in the event of divorce or widowhood (Ferguson, 1997: Chapter 5).

Yet it should also be noted that shifts in legislation have given some women the courage and institutional support to change their lives. One mother, Sitheni, initiated divorce in the 1980s knowing that she could reasonably expect to retain custody of her children and a fair share of the conjugal home. Others have used post-independence laws to protect their rights following bereavement. For example, 40-year-old Tsatswani has used the new legislation to retrieve property that her late husband's relatives had taken away from her. However, the scope of legislative frameworks is often curtailed by socio-cultural constraints on women's power and autonomy. Indeed, most women who end up alone do not enter this state voluntarily (Schlyter, 1989: 180). This is significant given the large percentage of households in contemporary Zimbabwe that are headed by women.

Family formation and family structure As of 1990, 32.6 per cent of households in Zimbabwe were female-headed (UNDP, 1995: Table A2.5). As in other Southern African countries, women-headed households are more of a rural than an urban phenomenon, with the level of female household headship in Harare being only around half the national average (Schlyter, 1989: 27). Greater rates of female headship in rural areas result from male out-migration, and rural units are more likely to be *de facto* than *de jure* female-headed – *de jure* female headship referring to cases where women are separated, divorced or widowed, and *de facto* household headship describing those households that are only temporarily headed by women due to male labour migration.

Alhough numbers of women-headed households have been rising in Zimbabwe in recent decades (Moghadam, 1996: 34), they have a long history, especially in rural areas. For example, *de facto* female headship was common in the colonial period due to the movement of men to towns and mining compounds (Kanji, 1994). Temporary female headship was not necessarily negative for women in that male absence gave them scope for greater independence and more say in farming decisions. For some women in the oldest generation in the survey, this provided an opportunity to make extra cash by selling off their 'women's crops' of groundnuts and vegetables. The proceeds were often invested in their daughters' schooling. At the same time, some elderly female respondents felt that male out-migration merely added to their labour burdens and had unhappy recollections of their forced dependence on remittances. Among the middle generation, male absences occurred not only as a result of labour migration, but because of the liberation war.

Regardless of such fragmentary influences and the weakening of lineage-based identity male household headship remains a normative ideal. Reflecting the legacy of patriarchal kinship obligations, extended households are also quite common. For example, among the Ndau, the 'ideal household' consists of a male head, his wife, sons, unmarried daughters, and daughters-in-law (Ferguson, 1997: Chapter 5). Young brides moving into their husbands' homes tend to have low status and some still follow the custom of kneeling in front of their in-laws. Although mothers-in-law are a significant presence in the lives of young brides (especially where husbands are away), it is the sisters of the husband, as the more direct blood relatives, who are often more important. For example, when young wives have a problem with marital or household matters they usually first consult their sisters-in-law for advice, even when the latter are younger and have less experience of life (ibid.).

While some tendency to household nuclearisation has been observed in urban areas, increased poverty in recent years may be reversing this process. Even though poverty has compelled some households to shed relatives who become a major economic burden, Kanji's work in a low-income community in Harare in 1991 and 1992, during the early stages of ESAP I, revealed that extended households increased from 32 per cent to 42 per cent of her sample population in that time (Kanji, 1994: 117–18).

Fertility and childbearing While household extension may be on the increase in Zimbabwe, fertility is on the decline. Since 1992, population growth rates have dropped to 2.3 per cent per annum, compared with an average annual rate of 3.2 per cent in the 30 years preceding (UNDP, 1995: Table 16). With nearly half the population (43 per cent) now using contraception (ibid.), the total fertility rate in Zimbabwe as of 1994 was 4, compared with 6.8 in 1980 (World Bank, 1996: Table 6).

While female informants in the survey were not asked specifically about fertility, it was clear that in the past, and particularly among the oldest generation, children were an immense source of pride among women. This was especially the case where they managed to see them into adult-hood with at least a basic education. Over time, however, as schooling (and its costs) have expanded and educational demands among employers have risen, limiting births has been one way of ensuring that daughters will get a better chance of completing their education. This is not to suggest, however, that decisions on fertility are in women's hands, as these are still widely subject to the final say from men, as heads of household and family breadwinners (Feresu, 1996: 37). Moreover, since infertility can prove to be grounds for conjugal instability (ibid.: 41), women may find it unwise to resist their husbands' demands regarding when and how many children to have.

One crucial factor responsible for declining fertility, however, is that Zimbabwe has one of the most extensive family planning programmes in the whole of sub-Saharan Africa (Ferguson, 1996: 1). Contraception is provided through Ministry of Health clinics and hospitals, or through the services of the Zimbabwe National Family Planning Council (ZNFPC). The latter provides contraception through state clinics and 'community-based distributors' (CBDs). Most women use the pill, although condom use has been on the increase in the last few years as a result of the AIDS crisis.

Declining birth rates are also influenced by infant mortality, which has virtually halved in the last three decades. The rate of infant mortality is presently 67 per 1,000 live births compared with 110 per 1,000 in 1960 (UNDP, 1995: Table 4). However, the fact that it was as low as 49 per 1,000 in 1990 indicates a recent reversal in achievements (EIU, 1996i: 12). Indeed, clinic and hospital maternity fees, which were increased in January 1992, have excluded many women, especially from among the poor, from giving birth under medical supervision. As Valentine Moghadam (1996: 34) sums up: 'a combination of drought, ESAP, and AIDS has resulted in a rise in the rate of maternal mortality and in the number of babies born before arrival in hospitals' (see also Kanji, 1994: 66). Another significant feature is a marked disparity between urban and rural areas. In the 1980s, for example, both infant and child mortality rates were around twice the level in rural as in urban areas (Gilbert and Gugler, 1992: Table 3.2).

Education and work

Education Access by informants to education has risen dramatically over the course of the twentieth century. For example, 73 per cent of the grandmothers had no formal education or less than one year of schooling. The only women who grew up in the 1920s and 1930s who were likely to obtain some kind of education were those from families that had converted to Christianity. Christian households frequently lived on mission stations where instruction was provided at little or no cost. Given the perception that receipt of a Western education, and its role in transmitting Western values, culture and religious beliefs, was an important means of surviving in the colonial era, many fathers encouraged their daughters to attend mission schools for as long as possible. Tsitsi, who was born into a Christian family in 1923 and whose father was a priest, ended up completing her primary education and stood out as unique among her female peers. However, it is also the case (and most notably among poorer families) that sons continued to be given preference in education right up until the 1960s. Although all the women in the middle generation of informants had at least received some primary education, only half proceeded to secondary school and no woman in this group had received the same education as her brothers. Having said this, around 20 per cent of the women managed to obtain tertiary education, usually oriented to the nursing and teaching professions, and often through their own efforts. Eunice, born in 1948, found her route to educational attainment blocked when her father took a second wife who stopped all spending on the children's education. Eunice was able to continue her education only once she had married and began studying for her 'O' levels by correspondence. She is now a highly qualified nurse. In addition to following correspondence courses after marriage, some of the mothers took advantage of further education schemes offered after independence such as adult literacy classes. This, however, could exact a high price, with one woman, Stella, being divorced by her husband, Tinei, for so doing.

Although, on the basis of 1990 data, rates of primary school enrolment among boys and girls of the relevant age group (6–11) are broadly equal, at secondary level (corresponding to the 12–17 age group), there are only 95 women per 100 men, and at tertiary level (18–23), the gap remains marked, at 39 women per 100 men (UNDP, 1995: Table A2.1). It must also be borne in mind that (as of 1993), only 6 per cent of the relevant age group were enrolled in institutions of tertiary education (World Bank, 1996: Table 7).

Quite apart from the fact that keeping children in school can deprive households of potential earnings, schooling also costs. Under ESAP I, fees for primary schools were introduced in addition to individual school levies. Although fees already charged in rural secondary schools were maintained at the same level, for their counterparts in urban 'high-density suburbs'[10] the costs to parents rose by 40 per cent, and in low-density communities by as much as 200 per cent (Kanji, 1994: 65). Since only very poor households are exempt from fees, and parents are usually extremely concerned to protect their children's education, most have had to cut back on consumption items and take extra jobs (ibid.: 99). However, resources can only stretch so far, and the increase in primary and secondary school fees under structural adjustment is particularly likely to hit girls, especially those wishing to enter higher education and/or who live in rural areas (ibid.; Ferguson, 1997: Chapter 5; Moghadam, 1996: 34).

On top of this, many school leavers cannot find jobs and are forced into dependence on their families (EIU, 1996i: 18). This, amongst other things, is likely to reduce the resources available for the education of younger siblings. As Kanji and Jazdowska (1995: 134–5) sum up: ' ... youth and high levels of education are two important characteristics of the unemployed, these being shared by many other African countries.'

Work and economic livelihood   Agriculture continues to employ well over two-thirds of the labour force in Zimbabwe (71 per cent in 1990–92). While services now occupy 21 per cent of the workforce (compared with 13 per cent in 1965), the proportion employed in industry has remained constant (at 8 per cent) over the last 30 years (UNDP, 1995: Table 11).

In rural areas access to land remains a serious problem, especially among women. Land is classified into four main types: small-scale commercial farms, large-scale commercial farms, resettlement areas and communal lands (Ferguson, 1997: Chapter 5). These latter areas, also known as 'communal areas' (CAs), cover 49 per cent of Zimbabwe's agricultural territory and were created out of former tribal reserve lands.[11] Despite providing the homes and livelihood of up to two-thirds of Zimbabwe's population, these lands are increasingly overcrowded as urban dwellers drift back to the countryside in the wake of job lay-offs (EIU, 1996i: 18). Government pledges to redistribute more land to rural people have not yet materialised to any great degree. This is serious given that peasants were promised land reform in return for their staunch support during the independence campaign, and when it is considered that 75 per cent of CA land is in low rainfall areas which, along with the environmental degradation caused by heavy population pressure, means that soils are progressively less productive (McDonald, 1996: 2).

Among the survey respondents, access to land seemed to have been particularly problematic for women in the oldest generation, who could obtain use rights only through their husbands. Although women were theoretically entitled to their own small plots, generally dedicated to subsistence cultivation, they spent the bulk of their time working their husbands' land, often alongside co-wives. There were few other sources of employment available in rural areas, and, given the social sanctions on women's migration to towns, most remained in the countryside. Moreover, those who did have jobs – for example as mission school secretaries, domestic servants and teachers – usually gave these up when they first had families.

Training for employment was very limited for women of the oldest generation and most tended to pick up skills informally from other women. In rural areas, mission stations and white farms gave additional opportunities to acquire experience in sewing, cooking and cleaning, which could often prove invaluable in the event of divorce or widowhood. Indeed, while the mission stations were primarily concerned with instilling obedience, submission and domesticity into girls, they also provided them with tools for upward social mobility and self-reliance.

As for the middle generation, rural women were sometimes able to supplement their income from farm produce by selling pottery, brewing beer or making doilies. Many women who were employed as nurses or teachers, however, found themselves out of work as the liberation struggle forced closure of schools and clinics in the countryside. Although the resultant move of many women to Harare for security reasons obviously disrupted their employment, they were often able to get new jobs in the capital, and in some cases urban migration brought the chance to upgrade skills and qualifications. One middle-aged nurse, Makhanani, became a State Registered Nurse after moving to the capital.

After independence, opportunities tended to open up for black Zimbabweans in the formal sector, yet women were disadvantaged by lack of education. As a result, women tended to continue with small-scale informal activities such as knitting, sewing and retailing, especially the sale of vegetables (Nachudwa, 1995: 138). This has persisted into the 1990s, with women estimated to make up two-thirds of workers in small-scale enterprises and in the informal sector (Zhou, 1995: 163). In the formal sector, alternatively, women form only 34.2 per cent of sales and clerical workers, 29.6 per cent of service workers, and 15.4 per cent of administrative and managerial workers (UNDP, 1995: Table A2.7). In industry, women's share of employment is even lower, being a mere 7 per cent of paid employees in Zimbabwean industry during the 1980s (Gilbert and Gugler, 1992: Table 4.2).

Although women's rising levels of education embody prospects for offsetting their disadvantage in the labour market (especially among the better-educated survey respondents), other factors that are important in relegating women to what might be termed 'secondary' livelihood activities include men's normative position as family breadwinners. Even in the 1990s, the idea that women should supplant men's primacy in the labour market is such that many men are rather hostile to 'successful business women' (Zhou, 1995). Another important influence in perpetuating, if not exacerbating, the tendency for women's preponderance in informal employment is exerted by structural adjustment and its associated retrenchments. In turn, because more women are being pushed into the informal sector through lack of alternatives, the result has been increased competition, fewer new opportunities, and lower profit margins (Kanji et al., 1991: 90). Although labour law stipulates equal pay for women, entitlement to maternity leave, and guarantees of non-discrimination in matters of recruitment, promotion and so on, the small proportion of women em-ployed in the formal workforce means that these provisions go largely unobserved (Kanji and Jazdowska, 1995: 135).

One recent development, however, is the incorporation of women into chromite, tin and tantalite production (Chiwawa, 1995). This has occurred steadily since the mid-1980s as mining companies have been forced to cut production costs and have sub-contracted most of their expensive, thin-seam chromite operations to mining cooperatives.[12] Women's involvement in mining is argued to have been forced by the desperate need of house-holds to generate more income in the wake of structural adjustment, although it has not radically 'de-gendered' this traditional male preserve. Over four-fifths (87 per cent) of women are employed in tin and tantalite mining, which is a surface operation, yet only a small minority (13 per cent) are in chromite mining, which entails underground as well as surface operations (ibid.: 101). In addition, the majority of female cooperative members (63 per cent) are heads of household and it is much rarer for married women to work in the mines due to husbands' reluctance to let their wives work (ibid.: 104–5). In the mines themselves, women tend to occupy the less skilled jobs as a result of men's historical advantage in mining operations and the perception that, due to their physical strength, men are better workers (ibid.: 113).

While women clearly have a long way to go before their status in the labour market equals that of men, it cannot be denied that men too suffer unemployment, meagre wages and poor working conditions, and, as Kanji (1994: 190) argues, greater equality between classes in Zimbabwe forms an essential component of the struggle for gender equality.

Conclusion

Bearing in mind that this chapter has concentrated almost exclusively upon women and that the project informants are urban-based and enjoy higher social status than most other groups in contemporary Zimbabwe, it is clear that many of women's needs and interests remain to be addressed. This is not to undervalue the substantial achievements that have been made in some spheres. The expansion of educational provision has played a crucial part in helping to emancipate women in the survey families from some of the more inequitable constraints of colonial (and post-colonial) culture. Another welcome development is the progressive relaxation of family control on the rights of women to choose their marriage partners and their greater autonomy after divorce and widowhood. Here various pieces of legislation passed since independence have contributed to changes for the better. Nevertheless, apart from sexual harassment from male teachers, the greatest problems identified by young women were their fathers' continued demands for large sums of bridewealth, and male dominance in women's personal lives. In other words, the argument that legislation has not really tackled some of the root problems of gender inequalities in Zimbabwe has resonance within the context of young women in the project. This signposts a critical route that might be taken by the Zimbabwean government at the end of a century in which three generations of women have battled hard against gendered boundaries in the interests of a fairer future for their daughters, and their daughters' daughters.

Recommendations

In line with the grievances expressed by the respondents, the following might prove useful foundations for future policy initiatives.

- The affirmative action policy in public service employment should be enforced to ensure 30 per cent female representation in middle and senior management posts. Where possible, consideration might be given to raising entry and promotion targets to a level where women and men have roughly equal representation in all tiers of the state sector.
- Action to extend social development assistance to ensure that structural adjustment does not impact unduly on women's health and education. While some households could be exempted from fees altogether, it might be worth exploring the possibilities of offering fee-waiving to poor women *within* households.
- Outlawing of bridewealth (and the effective enforcement of prohibitive legislation) to increase women's independent decision-making capacity regarding marriage.
- The repeal of legislation making homosexuality a criminal offence.
- Encouragement of more equitable roles and relations within households through the introduction of consciousness-raising programmes in schools and communities and the provision of services for the resolution of conjugal and family conflict.
- Guarantees of the upholding of court decisions in child custody cases and where possible, an even balance of male and female judges in family courts.

Notes

1. Compiled from a report prepared by Dr Julia Wells, Department of History, Rhodes University, Grahamstown, Eastern Cape, South Africa.

2. Zimbabwe's former name, Rhodesia, was taken from the Englishman Cecil Rhodes, who, having exploited mineral resources in South Africa, was attracted to gold deposits in the area. During the 1890s, Rhodes abused the Ndebele King Lobenguela's grant to mining rights and sent his newly formed British South Africa Company to invade the surrounding territory. The Ndebele waged war on the company, first in 1893, and then again in 1896–97, when they were joined by Shona forces from the north. Defeat of the indigenous population led to the formation of Southern Rhodesia as a formal British colony, federated with Northern Rhodesia (now Zambia) and Nyasaland (now Malawi) (see Kanji, 1994: 68n). During Ian Smith's period in office, the country was known simply as Rhodesia.

3. Zimbabwe's first president was Canaan Banana, a Methodist preacher and theologian (see also note 9).

4. Smaller political parties in Zimbabwe include the Zimbabwe Unity Movement (ZUM) and its breakaway party, the Democratic Party, the Forum Party of Zimbabwe (FPZ), United Parties (UP), and the Front for Popular Democracy (EIU, 1996i: 4).

5. For example, the German Embassy in Harare has recently reassessed its appraisal of Harare as a 'safe tourist destination' (EIU, 1996i: 22).

6. Although most women had limited their participation to the provision of support to male guerrillas, some were active combatants.

7. This is also reported for other African countries such as Ghana (Brydon, 1987, 1992) and Kenya (Nelson, 1992).

8. The symbolic use of names as a means of protest and recrimination is discussed by Richard Werbner (1991: 65–7) in his research on Ndebele families in the early part of this century. Meanings of names conferred by co-wives on their children included 'Despised', 'You should be polite', 'You rejected us', 'You provoke fights' , 'You are bad', 'You make us vomit', 'The hamlet is mine', and 'I am a wasted gourd' (kicked around).

9. In his campaign against homosexuals, President Mugabe described them as 'lower than dogs and pigs', and has routinely had gay activists placed under surveillance. In this light it is no surprise that recent allegations of homosexual activity on the part of former Zimbabwe president, Canaan Banana, have met with extreme shock in the country (see Angus Shaw, 'Banana "forced officer to have sex"', *Guardian*, 25 February 1997).

10. 'High-density suburbs' have evolved out of townships built in the colonial period for black workers. Although not all the inhabitants of present-day high-density suburbs are poor, unlike low-density neighbourhoods, they remain exclusively black (Kanji, 1994: 41n).

11. The policy of granting poorer lands to Africans while reserving the best areas for the whites was established throughout most of Southern Africa by the second half of the nineteenth century but came later in Zimbabwe due to Southern Rhodesia's relatively delayed conversion to the status of formal colony (see Dickenson et al., 1996: 42; Kanji, 1994: 52).

12. Mining cooperatives owe their origins to lay-offs from large-scale mines and their reorganisation into cooperatives by the parastatal Zimbabwe Mining Development Corporation (Chiwawa, 1995: 97).

BIBLIOGRAPHY

Anderson, P. (1986) 'Conclusion: women in the Caribbean', *Social and Economic Studies*, 35:2, 292–324.

Asia Partnership for Human Development (APHD) (1985) *Awake: Asian Women and their Struggle for Justice* (Sydney: APHD).

Beall, J. (1996) 'Social security and social networks among the urban poor in Pakistan', *Habitat International*, 19:4, 427–45.

— (1997) 'Households, livelihood and the urban environment: social development perspectives on solid waste disposal in Faisalabad City, Pakistan', PhD thesis in preparation, Department of Geography, London School of Economics.

Bedford, R. D. and L. D. B. Heenan (1987) 'The people of New Zealand: reflections on a revolution', in P. G. Holland and W. B. Johnston (eds), *Southern Approaches: Geography in New Zealand* (Christchurch: New Zealand Geographical Society), 133–77.

Besson, J. (1993) 'Reputation and respectability reconsidered: a new perspective on Afro-Caribbean peasant women', in J. H. Momsen (ed.), *Women and Change in the Caribbean: A Pan-Caribbean Perspective* (London: James Currey), 15–37.

Bhutto, B. (1995) 'Pakistan: women judges appointed to the Superior Courts for the first time', in UNDP, *Human Development Report 1995* (New York: Oxford University Press), 112.

Bradnock, R. (1992) 'The changing geography of the states of the South Asian periphery', in G. Chapman and K. Baker (eds), *The Changing Geography of Asia* (London: Routledge), 44–73.

Brydon, L. (1987) 'Who moves? Women and migration in West Africa in the 1980s', in J. Eades (ed.), *Migrants, Workers and the Social Order* (London: Tavistock, Association of Social Anthropologists Monograph No. 26), 165–80.

— (1992) 'Ghanaian women in the migration process', in S. Chant (ed.), *Gender and Migration in Developing Countries* (London: Belhaven), 91–108.

— and S. Chant (1993) *Women in the Third World: Gender Issues in Rural and Urban Areas* (reprinted edn) (Aldershot: Edward Elgar).

Buang, A. (1993) 'Development and factory women: negative perceptions from a Malaysian source area', in J. H. Momsen and V. Kinnaird (eds), *Different Places, Different Voices: Gender and Development in Africa, Asia and Latin America* (London: Routledge), 197–210.

Buvinic, M. (1995) *Investing in Women* (Washington, DC: International Center for Research on Women, Policy Series).

Chant, S. (1991a) *Women and Survival in Mexican Cities: Perspectives on Gender, Labour Markets and Low-income Households* (Manchester: Manchester University Press).

— (1991b) 'Gender, households and seasonal migration in Guanacaste, Costa Rica', *European Review of Latin American and Caribbean Studies*, 50, 51–85.

— (1995) 'Gender and development in the 1990s', *Third World Planning Review*, 17:2, 111–16.

— (1997) *Women-headed Households: Diversity and Dynamics in the Developing World* (London: Macmillan).

— and McIlwaine, Cathy (1995a) *Women of a Lesser Cost: Female Labour, Foreign Exchange and Philippine Development* (London: Pluto).

— (1995b) 'Gender and export manufacturing in the Philippines: continuity or change in female employment? The case of the Mactan export processing zone', *Gender, Place and Culture*, 2:2, 149–78.

Chiwawa, H. (1995) 'Women in co-operative mines in Zimbabwe', in S. Sithole-Fundire, A. Zhou, A. Larsson and A. Schlyter (eds), *Gender Research on Urbanisation, Planning, Housing and Everyday Life, GRUPHEL, Phase One* (Harare: Zimbabwe Women's Resource Centre and Network), 92–114.

Commonwealth Secretariat (1995a) *The 1995 Commonwealth Plan of Action on Gender and Development* (London: Commonwealth Secretariat).

— (1995b) *Working Towards Gender Equality* (London: Commonwealth Secretariat).

Dickenson, J., B. Gould, C. Clarke, S. Mather, M. Prothero, D. Siddle, C. Smith and E. Thomas-Hope (1996) *Geography of the Third World*, 2nd edn (London: Routledge).

Duncan, S. (1995) 'Theorising European gender systems', *Journal of European Social Policy*, 5:4, 263–83.

Economist Intelligence Unit (EIU) (1996a) *Trinidad and Tobago, Guyana, Suriname, Netherlands Antilles, Aruba, Windward and Leeward Islands, Country Report, 2nd quarter 1996* (London: EIU)

— (1996b) *Jamaica, Belize, Bahamas, Bermuda, Barbados, Country Report, 2nd quarter, 1996* (London: EIU).

— (1996c) *Malaysia, Brunei, Country Report, 2nd quarter, 1996* (London: EIU).

— (1996d) *Pacific Islands: Papua New Guinea, Fiji, Solomon Islands, Western Samoa, Vanuatu, Tonga, 2nd quarter, 1996* (London: EIU).

— (1996e) *Pakistan, Afghanistan, Country Report, 4th quarter, 1996* (London: EIU).

— (1996f) *Cyprus, Country Report, 3rd quarter, 1996* (London: EIU).

— (1996g) *New Zealand, Country Report, 2nd quarter, 1996* (London: EIU).

— (1996h) *Canada, Country Report, 2nd quarter, 1996* (London: EIU).

— (1996i) *Zimbabwe, Country Report, 4th quarter, 1996* (London: EIU).

— (1997) *Pakistan, Afghanistan, Country Report, 1st quarter, 1997* (London: EIU).

Ellis, P. (1986) 'Introduction: an overview of women in Caribbean society', in P. Ellis (ed.), *Women of the Caribbean* (London: Zed), 1–24.

Feresu, S. (1996) 'Reproductive health: how can it be studied? Results from the Zimbabwe study', in Institute for Development Research Amsterdam and Medical Anthropology Institute, University of Amsterdam and Health Action Information Network, the Philippines (eds), *Gender, Reproductive Health and Population Policies: Proceedings from the Zimbabwe Networking Workshop, 14–18 June 1995* (Amsterdam: University of Amsterdam), 35–44.

Ferguson, C. (1996) 'Reproductive rights in Zimbabwe', paper presented at the OXFAM/LSE seminar 'Reproductive rights and citizenship: services in the post-Cairo era', Gender Institute, London School of Economics, 29 November.

— (1997) 'Reproductive rights and citizenship in Zimbabwe', PhD thesis in preparation, Gender Institute, London School of Economics.

Fleras, A. and J. L. Elliot (1992) *Multiculturalism in Canada: The Challenge of Diversity* (Scarborough, Ontario: Nelson Canada).

Gearing, J. (1995) 'Fear and loving in the West Indies: research from the heart (as well as the head)', in D. Kulick and M. Willson (eds), *Taboo: Sex, Identity and Erotic Subjectivity in Anthropological Fieldwork* (London: Routledge), 186–218.

Gilbert, A. and J. Gugler (1992) *Cities, Poverty and Development: Urbanisation in the Third World*, 2nd edn (Oxford: Oxford University Press).

González de la Rocha, M. (1994) *The Resources of Poverty: Women and Survival in a Mexican City* (Oxford: Blackwell).

— (1997) 'Hogares de jefatura femenina en México: patrones y formas de vida', paper presented at the session 'Pobreza, género y desigualdad: jefatura femenina en hogares urbanos Latinoamericanos', XX International Congress of the Latin American Studies Association, Guadalajara, Mexico, 17–19 April.

Griffin Cohen, M. (1994) 'The implications of economic restructuring for women: the Canadian situation', in I. Bakker (ed.), *The Strategic Silence: Gender and Economic Policy* (London: Zed), 103–16.

Harris, I. (1995) *Messages Men Hear: Constructing Masculinities* (London: Taylor and Francis).

Harrison, K. (1994) *New Zealand Women in the Twentieth Century* (London: Macmillan).

Harriss, B. and E. Watson (1987) 'The sex ratio in South Asia', in J. Momsen and J. Townsend (eds), *Geography of Gender in the Third World* (London: Hutchinson), 85–115.

Humm, M. (1995) *The Dictionary of Feminist Geography*, 2nd edn (New York/London: Prentice Hall/Harvester Wheatsheaf).

IDS Bulletin (Sussex) 26:3 (1995) 'Getting institutions right for women in development'.

Ingrams, D. (1983) *The Awakened: Women in Iraq* (London: Third World Centre for Research and Publishing).

Jahan, R. (1995) *The Elusive Agenda: Mainstreaming Women in Development* (London: Zed).

Jeater, D. (1993) *Marriage, Perversion and Power: The Construction of Moral Discourse in Southern Rhodesia, 1894–1930* (Oxford: Clarendon Press).

Jeffery, P. (1979) *Frogs in a Well: Indian Women in Purdah* (London: Zed).

Jud, G. D. (1974) 'Tourism and economic growth in Mexico since 1950', *Inter-American Economic Affairs*, 19–43.

Kabeer, N. (1994) *Reversed Realities: Gender Hierarchies in Development Thought* (London: Verso).

Kanji, N. (1994) 'Gender and structural adjustment: a case study of Harare, Zimbabwe', unpublished PhD thesis, Department of Geography, London School of Economics.

— and N. Jazdowska (1995) 'Gender, structural adjustment and employment in urban Zimbabwe', *Third World Planning Review*, 17:2, 133–54.

Kanji, N., N. Kanji and F. Manji (1991) 'From development to sustained crisis: structural adjustment, equity and health', *Social Science and Medicine*, 33:9, 985–93.

Karim, W. J. (1992) *Women and Culture: Between Malay Adat and Islam* (Boulder, CO: Westview).

— (1995) 'Bilateralism and gender in Southeast Asia', in W. J. Karim (ed.), *'Male' and 'Female' in Developing Southeast Asia* (Oxford: Berg), 35–74.

Karl, M. (1995) *Women and Empowerment: Participation and Decision Making* (London: Zed).

Katz, C. and J. Monk (1993) 'Making connections: space, place and the life course', in C. Katz and J. Monk (eds), *Full Circles: Geographies of Women Over the Life Course* (London: Routledge).

— (eds) (1993) *Full Circles: Geographies of Women over the Life Course* (London, Routledge).

Kawar, M. (1997) 'Gender, employment and the life course: the case of working daughters in Amman, Jordan', unpublished PhD thesis, Department of Geography, London School of Economics.

Lapchick, R. and S. Urdang (1982) *Oppression and Resistance: The Struggle of Women in Southern Africa* (London: Greenwood Press).

Levy, C. (1992) 'Gender and the environment: the challenge of cross-cutting issues in development policy and planning', *Environment and Urbanisation*, 4:1, 134–49.

Longhurst, R. (1996) 'Refocusing groups: pregnant women's geographical experiences of Hamilton, New Zealand/Aotearoa', *Area*, 28:2, 143–9.

McCann, L. D. (1982) 'Heartland and hinterland: a framework for regional analysis', in L. D. McCann (ed), *Heartland and Hinterland: A Geography of Canada* (Scarborough, Ontario: Prentice Hall), 3–35.

McDonald, B. (1996) *The Tea Factor: Smallholder Tea Production in a Zimbabwean Communal Area* (London: Catholic Institute of International Relations, International Cooperation for Development).

MacDonald, M. (ed.) (1994) *Gender Planning in Development Agencies: Meeting the Challenge* (Oxford: Oxfam).

McIlwaine, C. (1993) 'Gender, ethnicity and the local labour market in Limón, Costa Rica', unpublished PhD thesis, Department of Geography, London School of Economics.

— (1995) 'Gender, race and ethnicity: concepts, realities and policy implications', *Third World Planning Review*, 17:2, 237–43.

— (1996) 'The negotiation of space among sex workers in Cebu City, the Philippines', *Singapore Journal of Tropical Geography*, 17:2, 150–64.

McKee, D. (1988) *Growth Development and the Service Economy in the Third World* (New York: Praeger).

McKenzie, H. (1986) 'The educational experiences of Caribbean women', *Social and Economic Studies*, 35:3, 65–105.

Masini, E. B. and S. Stratigos (eds) (1991) *Women, Households and Change* (Tokyo: United Nations University Press).

Massey, D. (1996) 'A global sense of place', in S. Daniels and R. Lee (eds), *Exploring Human Geography: A Reader* (London: Edward Arnold), 237–45.

Massiah, J. (1986) 'Work in the lives of Caribbean women', *Social and Economic Studies*, 35:2, 177–239.

Maynard, M. (1994) 'Methods, practice and epistemology: the debate about feminism and research', in M. Maynard and J. Purvis (eds), *Researching Women's Lives from a Feminist Perspective* (London: Taylor and Francis), 10–26.

— and J. Purvis (1994) 'Doing feminist research', in M. Maynard and J. Purvis (eds), *Researching Women's Lives from a Feminist Perspective* (London: Taylor and Francis), 1–9.

Mernissi, F. (1996) *Women's Rebellion and Islamic Memory* (London: Zed).

Moghadam, V. (1995) 'The Fourth World Conference on Women: dissension and consensus', mimeo, United Nations University, World Instititute for Development Economic Research, Helsinki.

— 1996) 'The feminisation of poverty: notes on a concept and trends', report prepared for UNDP, *Human Development Report*, September.

Momsen, J. H. (1993) 'Development and gender divisions of labour in the rural eastern Caribbean', in J. H. Momsen (ed.), *Women and Change in the Caribbean: A Pan-Caribbean Perspective* (London: James Currey), 232–46.

Monk, J. and Katz, C. (1993) 'When in the world are women?', in C. Katz and J. Monk (eds), *Full Circles: Geographies of Women Over the Life Course* (London: Routledge), 1–26.

Moser, C. (1993) *Gender Planning and Development: Theory, Practice and Training* (London: Routledge).

Murton, B. (1987) 'Maori territory', in P. G. Holland and W. B. Johnston (eds), *Southern Approaches: Geography in New Zealand* (Christchurch: New Zealand Geographical Society), 91–115.

Nachudwa, D. (1995) 'Women in micro-enterprises: the case of Mbare, Zimbabwe', in S. Sithole-Fundire, A. Zhou, A. Larsson and A. Schlyter (eds), *Gender Research on Urbanisation, Planning, Housing and Everyday Life, GRUPHEL, Phase One* (Harare: Zimbabwe Women's Resources Centre Centre and Network), 145–62.

Nagata, J. (1995) 'Modern Malay women and the message of the "veil"', in W. J. Karim (ed.), *'Male' and 'Female' in Developing Southeast Asia* (Oxford: Berg), 101–20.

Ncuba, S. (1995) 'Ideologies on everyday life: finalists at the University of Zimbabwe', in S. Sithole-Fundire, A. Zhou, A. Larsson and A. Schlyter (eds), *Gender Research on Urbanisation, Planning, Housing and Everyday Life, GRUPHEL, Phase One* (Harare: Zimbabwe Women's Resources Centre Centre and Network), 135–44.

Nelson, N. (1992) 'The women who left and those who have stayed behind: rural–urban migration in central and western Kenya', in S. Chant (ed.), *Gender and Migration in Developing Countries* (London: Belhaven), 109–38.

Ng, C. (1991) 'Malay women and rice production in west Malaysia', in H. Afshar (ed.), *Women, Development and Survival in the Third World* (London: Routledge), 188–210.

O'Connell, H. (1994) *Women and the Family* (London: Zed).

Olssen, E. (1980) *Women, Work and Family in New Zealand* (London: George Allen and Unwin).

Ong, A. (1987) *Spirits of Resistance and Capitalist Discipline: Factory Women in Malaysia* (New York: State University of New York Press).

Page, H. J., R. J. Lesthaeghe and I. H. Shah (1982) *Illustrative Analysis: Breastfeeding in Pakistan* (Voorburg, Netherlands: International Statistical Institute, Scientific Report No. 37).

Pantelidou, A. (1992) *History of Cyprus: Medieval and Contemporary* (Nicosia: Ministry of Education).

Parnwell, M. (1993) *Population Movements and the Third World* (London: Routledge).

Parpart, J. (1993) 'Who is the "other"?: A postmodern feminist critique of women and development theory and practice', *Development and Change*, 24, 439–64.

— and M. Marchand (1995) 'Exploding the canon: an introduction/conclusion', in

M. Marchand and J. Parpart (eds), *Feminism/Postmodernism/Development* (London: Routledge), 1–22.

Pearson, D. and D. Thorns (1983) *Women and Inequality, in Eclipse of Equality* (London: George Allen and Unwin).

Phoenix, A. (1994) 'Practising feminist research: the intersection of gender and "race" in the research process', in M. Maynard and J. Purvis (eds), *Researching Women's Lives from a Feminist Perspective* (London: Taylor and Francis), 49–71.

Pictilä, H. and J. Vickers (1994) *Making Women Matter: The Role of the United Nations*, revised and expanded edn (London: Zed)

Potter, R. (1983) 'Tourism and development: the case of Barbados, West Indies', *Geography*, 68, 46–50.

Powell, D. (1984) 'The role of women in the Caribbean', *Social and Economic Studies*, 33:2, 97–121.

— (1986) 'Caribbean women and their responses to familial experiences', *Social and Economic Studies*, 35:2, 83–130.

Pulsipher, L. M. (1993a) '"He won't let she stretch she foot": gender relations in traditional West Indian houseyards', in C. Katz and J. Monk (eds), *Full Circles: Geographies of Women Over the Life Course* (London: Routledge), 107–21.

— (1993b) 'Changing roles in the life cycles of women in traditional West Indian houseyards', in J. H. Momsen (ed.), *Women and Change in the Caribbean: A Pan-Caribbean Perspective* (London: James Currey), 50–64.

Rahat, N.-I. (1986) 'Meharabad, a Punjabi village: male out-migration and women's changing roles', in F. Selier and M. Karim (eds), *Migration in Pakistan: Themes and Facts* (Lahore: Vanguard), 139–60.

Rathgeber, E. (1995) 'Gender and development in action', in M. Marchand and J. Parpart (eds), *Feminism/Postmodernism/Development* (London: Routledge), 204–20.

Rigg, J. (1994) *Southeast Asia: A Region in Transition*, reprinted edn (London: Routledge).

Robinson, J. L. (1989) *Concepts and Themes in the Regional Geography of Canada* (Vancouver: Talonbooks).

Rosario, V. O. del (1995) 'Mainstreaming gender concerns: aspects of compliance, resistance and negotiation', *IDS Bulletin* 26:3 (Sussex), 102–9.

Rubenstein, H. (1991) 'Household structure and class stratification in St Vincent: a critical reply to Young', *Social and Economic Studies*, 40:3, 187–97.

Rudie, I. (1995) 'The significance of "eating": cooperation, support, and reputation in Kelantan Malay households', in W. J. Karim (ed.), *'Male' and 'Female' in Developing Southeast Asia* (Oxford: Berg), 227–46.

Saadawi, N. El (1980) *The Hidden Face of Eve: Women in the Arab World* (London: Zed).

Schlyter, A. (1989) *Women Householders and Housing Strategies: The Case of Harare, Zimbabwe* (Gävle: National Swedish Institute for Building Research).

Sen, Kasturi (1994) *Ageing: Debates on Demographic Transition and Social Policy* (London: Zed).

Shorey-Bryan, N. (1986) 'The making of male–female relationships in the Caribbean', in P. Ellis (ed.), *Women of the Caribbean* (London: Zed), 69–73.

Smyke, P. (1991) *Women and Health* (London: Zed).

South Pacific Commission (1994) *Pacific Island Populations* (Auckland: Stredder Print).

Summers, L. (1992) *Investing in All the People* (Washington, DC: World Bank, Policy Research Working Paper No. 905).

Tacoli, C. (1996) 'Gender, life course and international migration: the case of Filipino labour migrants in Rome', unpublished PhD thesis, Department of Geography, London School of Economics.

Thompson, L. (1992) 'Feminist methodology for family studies', *Journal of Marriage and the Family*, 54, 3–18.

Tomasevski, K. (1993) *Women and Human Rights* (London: Zed).

Truelove, M. (1996) 'Minding the baby in Canada', in K. England (ed.), *Who Will Mind the Baby? Geographies of Childcare and Working Mothers* (London: Routledge), 36–45.

United Nations Development Programme (UNDP) (1995) *Human Development Report 1995* (New York and Oxford: Oxford University Press).

— (1996) *Human Development Report 1996* (New York and Oxford: Oxford University Press).

Werbner, R. (1991) *Tears of the Dead: The Social Biography of an African Family* (Edinburgh: Edinburgh University Press for the International African Institute, London).

World Bank (1995) *World Development Report 1995* (New York and Oxford: Oxford University Press).

Young, V. H. (1990) 'Household structure in a West Indian society', *Social and Economic Studies*, 39:3, 147–79.

Zhou, A. (1995) 'Women's access to trading space at growth points in Zimbabwe: a case study of Mataga', in S. Sithole-Fundire, A. Zhou, A. Larsson and A. Schlyter (eds), *Gender Research on Urbanisation, Planning, Housing and Everyday Life, GRUPHEL, Phase One* (Harare: Zimbabwe Women's Resources Centre and Network), 164–84.

INDEX

women, 15, 45, 63; provision of
recreational facilities, 42
United Nations (UN), 18; Fourth
Women's Conference, Beijing 1995,
3, 18
UN Convention on the Elimination of
All Forms of Discrimination
Against Women (CEDAW), 18, 88,
109
UN Decade for Women, 18
UN Development Programme
(UNDP), 6, 7, 15, 17, 18, 45; five-
point strategy, 19
United States Agency for International
Development, 18
universities: Calgary, 181; Carleton, 181;
Cyprus, 138, 153; Laval, 181; Malaya,
71; Ottawa, 181; Punjab, 113; St
Mary's, Halifax, 181; Victoria, 160,
181; West Indies, 44, 47 (Women
and Development Unit (WAND),
24); Winnipeg, 181; Zimbabwe, 207
urbanisation, 8, 85, 86, 89, 90, 99, 107,
149, 153, 157, 161, 162

village disputes, increase in, 101
violence, 11, 26, 38, 40, 42, 136, 205;
against women, 16, 19, 41, 42,
140–1, 160, 191, 214, 216 see also
physical punishment of children
virginity, female, 12, 145, 146, 147, 166,
213
Voluntary Service Overseas, 18
voting rights of women, 17

waged work of women, 10, 11, 15,
37–40, 46, 51, 53, 56, 88, 106, 112,
128–9, 131, 137, 140, 153, 154, 160,
171, 173, 188, 197–8, 207; home-
based, 112; in administration and
management, 137, 181, 207, 224; in
factories, 81; in informal sector, 222
wages of women, 23, 46, 126, 129, 137,
154, 160, 173, 174, 181, 198, 200,
207
water, access to, 23
welfare state, erosion of, 159, 161, 173,
180
widows, 215, 222, 224; 'passing on' of,
214–15
women: as bus drivers, 52; as cheaper
labour, 15, 38; as housewives, 26;
education of, 14, 82, 125, 131, 152,
172, 196, 222, 224; emotional
expression of, 50; in liberation wars,
203; in waged work see waged work
of women; independence of, 40, 44,
56, 184; rights of, 67, 109; wages see
wages of women; work outside
home, 39, 48, 53; young,
representation of, 47
women's affairs ministries, 16, 160, 203
working day, reduction of, 153
World Bank, 18
World Trade Organization, 22

Zia, General, 113, 120
Zimbabwe, 3, 4, 6, 8, 9, 11, 13, 14, 15,
16, 202–25; country profile, 202–7

ZED TITLES IN WOMEN'S STUDIES

A Diplomacy of the Oppressed: New directions in international feminism
Edited by Georgina Ashworth

A Place in the Sun? Women writers in 20th century Cuba
Catherine Davies

A World of Widows
Margaret Owen

African Women and Development: A history
Margaret C. Snyder and Mary Tadesse

Arguing with the Crocodile: Gender and class in Bangladesh
Sarah White

Between Monsters, Goddesses and Cyborgs: Feminist confrontations with
  science, medicine and cyberspace
Edited by Nina Lykke and Rosi Braidotti

Biopolitics: A feminist and ecological reader
Edited by Vandana Shiva and Ingunn Moser

Capital Accumulation and Women's Labour in Asian Economies
Peter Custers

Changing Identites of Chinese Women: Rhetoric, experience and self-
  perception in twentieth-century China
Elisabeth Croll

Color, Class and Country: Experiences of gender
Edited by Gay Young and Bette J. Dickerson

Ecofeminism
Maria Mies and Vandana Shiva

Ecofeminism as Politics: Nature, Marx and the postmodern
Ariel Salleh

Embodied Violence: Communalising female sexuality in South Asia
Edited by Kumari Jayawardena and Malathi de Alwis

Empowerment and Women's Health: Theory, methods, and practice
Jane Stein

Feminism and Nationalism in the Third World
Kumari Jayawardena

Feminist Perspectives on Sustainable Development
Edited by Wendy Harcourt

Gender and National Identity: Women and politics in Muslim societies
Edited by Valentine M Moghadam

Gender and Catastrophe
Edited by Ronit Lentin

Gender and Development in the Arab World: Women's economic
participation: patterns and policies
Edited by Nabil F Khoury and Valentine M Moghadam

Gender and Slum Culture in Urban Asia
Susanne Thorbek

Gender and Tribe: Women, Land and Forests
Govind Kelkar and Dev Nathan

Gender in Popular Education: Methods for Empowerment
Shirley Walters and Linzi Manicom

Gender, Education and Development
Edited by Christine Heward and Sheila Bunwaree

Getting Institutions Right for Women in Development
Edited by Anne-Marie Goetz

Injustice Systems: Women's access to the law
Edited by Margaret Owen and Georgina Ashworth

Islam and Gender Hierarchy in Turkey
Julie Marcus

Knives and Angels: Women writers in Latin America
Edited by Susan Bassnett

Making Women Matter: The role of the United Nations
Hilkka Pietilä and Jeanne Vickers

Male Daughters/Female Husbands: Gender and sex in an African society
Ifi Amadiume

Monitoring Family Planning and Reproductive Rights: A manual for empowerment
Anita Hardon, Ann Mutua, Sandra Kabir and Elly Engelkes

Mortgaging Women's Lives: Feminist critiques of structural adjustment
Edited by Pamela Sparr

Negotiating Reproductive Rights: Women's perspectives across countries and cultures
Edited by Rosalind P Petchesky and Karen Judd/IRRRAG

Of Woman Caste: The experience of gender in rural India
Anjali Bagwe

Ours by Right: Women's rights as human rights
Edited by Joanna Kerr

Palestinian Women: Identity and experience
Edited by Ebba Augustin

Patriarchy and Accumulation on a World Scale: Women in the international division of labour
Maria Mies

Paying the Price: Women and the politics of international economic strategy
Mariarosa Dalla Costa and Giovanna F Dalla Costa

Population and Reproductive Rights: Feminist Perspectives from the South
Sonia Correa

Power, Reproduction and Gender: The intergenerational transfer of knowledge
Edited by Wendy Harcourt

Promoting Gender Equality at Work: Turning vision into reality for the 21st century
Edited by Eugenia Date-Bah

Purity and Communal Boundaries: Women and social change in a Bangladeshi village
Santi Rozario

Radically Speaking: Feminism reclaimed
Edited by Diane Bell and Renate Klein

Re-Inventing Africa: Matriarchy, religion and culture
Ifi Amadiume

Refugee Women
Prepared by Susan Forbes Martin Women

Reproductive Rights in Practice: A feminist report on the quality of care
Edited by Anita Hardon and Elizabeth Hayes

Rewriting Gender: Reading contemporary Chinese women
Ravni Rai Thakur

Space, Culture and Power: New identities in globalizing cities
Edited by Ayşe Öncü and Petra Weyland

States of Conflict: Gender, violence and resistance
Edited by Susie Jacobs, Ruth Jacobson and Jennifer Marchbank

Staying Alive: Women, ecology and development
Vandana Shiva

Subversive Women: Women's movements in Africa, Asia, Latin America
and the Caribbean
Edited by Saskia Wieringa

The Blue Room: Trauma and testimony among refugee women
Inger Agger

The Circumcision of Women: A strategy for eradication
Olayinka Koso-Thomas

The Daughters of Development: Women in a changing environment
Sinith Sittirak

The Elusive Agenda: Mainstreaming women in development
Rounaq Jahan

The Hidden Face of Eve: Women in the Arab World
Nawal El Saadawi

The Nawal El Saadawi Reader
Nawal El Saadawi

The Power to Change: Women in the third world redefine their environment
Women's Feature Service

The Space Beween Us: Negotiating gender and national identites in conflict
Cynthia Cockburn

The Strategic Silence: Gender and economic policy
Edited by Isabella Bakker

The Trade in Domestic Workers: Causes, mechanisms and consequences of international migration
Edited by Noeleen Heyzer, Geertje Lycklama à Nijeholt and Nedra Weerakoon

The Traffic in Women: Human realities of the international sex trade
Siriporn Skrobanek, Nataya Boonpakdee and Chutima Jantateero

The Women, Gender and Development Reader
Edited by Nalini Visvanathan with Lynn Duggan, Laurie Nisonoff and Nan Wiegersma

Third World Second Sex
Edited by Miranda Davies

Vaccination Against Pregnancy: Miracle or menace?
Judith Richter

What Women Do in Wartime: Gender and conflict in Africa
Edited by Meredeth Turshen and Clotilde Twagiramariya

Where Women are Leaders: The SEWA movement in India
Kalima Rose

Women's Rebellion and Islamic Memory
Fatima Mernissi

Women and Human Rights
Prepared by Katarina Tomasevski

Women and Chinese Patriarchy: Submission, servitude and escape
Edited by Maria Jaschok and Suzanne Miers

Women and Disability
Prepared by Esther Boylan

Women and Empowerment: Participation and decision-making
  Prepared by Marilee Karl

Women and Health
  Prepared by Patricia Smyke

Women and Literacy
  Prepared by Marcela Ballara

Women and Right Wing Movements: Indian experiences
  Edited by Tanika Sarkar and Urvashi Butalia

Women and the Environment
  Prepared by Annabel Rodda

Women and the Family
  Prepared by Helen O'Connell

Women and the New World Economy
  Gita Sen

Women and the World Economic Crisis
  Prepared by Jeanne Vickers

Women and Violence: Realities and responses worldwide
  Edited by Miranda Davies

Women and War
  Jeanne Vickers

Women and Work
  Prepared by Susan Bullock

Women in Modern Turkish Society
  Sirin Tekeli

Women of Asia: Envisioning a new Asia for the 21st century
  Yayori Matsui

Women's Studies and Culture: A feminist introduction
  Edited by Rosemarie Buikema and Anneke Smelik

Women, Citizenship and Difference
  Edited by Pnina Werbner and Nira Yuval-Davis

Women, Population and Global Crisis: A political-economic analysis
Asoka Bandarage

Women, the Environment and Sustainable Development: Towards a theoretical synthesis
Rosi Braidotti, Ewa Charkiewicz, Sabine Häusler and Saskia Wieringa

Women@Internet: Creating new cultures in cyberspace
Edited by Wendy Harcourt

Writing African Women: Gender, popular culture and literature in West Africa
Edited by Stephanie Newell

These books should be available from all good bookshops. In case of difficulty, please contact us:

Zed Books Ltd, 7 Cynthia St, London N1 9JF, UK.
Tel +44 (0)171 837 4014; Fax +44 (0)171 833 3960
e-mail: sales@zedbooks.demon.co.uk